Hellenic Studies 49

CHRISTIANITY AND HELLENISM
IN THE FIFTH-CENTURY GREEK EAST

Recent Titles in the Hellenic Studies Series

http://chs.harvard.edu/chs/publications

CHRISTIANITY AND HELLENISM IN THE FIFTH-CENTURY GREEK EAST

THEODORET'S APOLOGETICS AGAINST THE GREEKS IN CONTEXT

YANNIS PAPADOGIANNAKIS

CENTER FOR HELLENIC STUDIES
Trustees for Harvard University
Washington, D.C.
Distributed by Harvard University Press
Cambridge, Massachusetts, and London, England
2012

Christianity and Hellenism in the Fifth-Century Greek East
   by Yannis Papadogiannakis
Copyright © 2012 Center for Hellenic Studies, Trustees for Harvard University
All Rights Reserved.
Published by Center for Hellenic Studies, Trustees for Harvard University, Washington, D.C.
Distributed by Harvard University Press, Cambridge, Massachusetts, and London, England
Production: Nancy Wolfe Kotary
Cover design and illustration: Joni Godlove
Printed by Edwards Brothers, Inc., Ann Arbor, MI

LIBRARY OF CONGRESS CATALOGING-IN-PUBLICATION DATA

Papadogiannakis, Yannis.
  Christianity and Hellenism in the fifth-century Greek east : Theodoret's apologetics
  against the Greeks in context / by Yannis Papadogiannakis.
     pages. cm. -- (Hellenic studies ; 49)
  ISBN 978-0-674-06067-8 (alk. paper)
  1. Theodoret, Bishop of Cyrrhus--Criticism and interpretation. 2. Christian literature,
  Early--History and criticism. 3. Apologetics--History--Early church, ca. 30-600. I.
  Title. II. Series: Hellenic studies ; 49.

BR65.T756P37 2012
239'.3--dc23

                                                                    2012024439

To Anastasia, Lampros, and Sofia-Melanthia

Contents

Acknowledgments

IT IS MY PLEASANT DUTY to acknowledge the help of a number of people whose support and encouragement sustained me throughout the time during which this project, first as a thesis and now as a book, took shape. My gratitude goes to my former supervisor Professor Peter Brown and to Professors John Gager and Kathleen McVey. I have also profited immensely over the years from discussions with a number of scholars who have generously read and commented on parts of the book: Glen Bowersock, Averil Cameron, Jean Noël Guinot, Elaine Pagels, Fergus Millar, Susanna Elm, Neil McLynn, Philip Rousseau, Heinrich von Staden, Anthony Grafton, Robin Darling Young, Michael Frede, Christoph Riedweg, Paul C. Finney, Michael B. Trapp, Claudia Rapp, Caroline Bynum, Richard Goulet, Fritz Graf, Ruth Webb. I would like to thank them all for their willingness to do so and their helpful comments and suggestions. None of them is responsible, of course, for the way their advice has been applied. Any remaining shortcomings are entirely the fault of my obstinacy. During a year spent at the Institute for Advanced Study at Princeton in 2005–2006, I was able to make initial revisions and enjoy the intellectual vibrancy of an extraordinary research institution. It was an unforgettable experience that transformed my research horizons and ideas, for which I am deeply grateful to Professor Patricia Crone.

I thank Professor Thomas Halton for sharing his draft translation of the *Therapeutikê*, which is forthcoming from Paulist Press. I also wish to thank the staff of Firestone Library, Princeton University, and Speer Library, Princeton Theological Seminary, for their enormous help. I am greatly indebted to Dr. Stephen Crocco for allowing me to make an expanded use of the Speer Library resources, and to Dimitri Gondicas and the Hellenic Studies Program for their help and support, as well as to Jane Baun, Chris Lee, Andromache Karanika, George Karakostas, Emmanuel Papoutsakis, Harry Platanakis, Michalis Dafermos, Nina Papavasiliou, and Joseph Munitiz for their friendship. I am no less grateful to my teachers from my undergraduate years and especially to Lampros Siasos, Panayotis Pachis, and Andreas Nanakes for their unfailing support throughout both my undergraduate and graduate studies.

Acknowledgments

My colleagues at Oxford, Dr. Mark Edwards, Dr. Johannes Zachhuber, Professor Angelos Chaniotis, Professor Averil Cameron, and Professor Fergus Millar, have been a source of inspiration and support.

For the long-term nurture of this book I owe an exceptional debt of gratitude to the financial support of the AG Leventis Foundation, and Mr. A. Leventis in particular, for their generosity, love, warmth, and sustained and unswerving support of Humanities in times that their intrinsic value is called into question.

I would also like to thank the editors and publications team at the Center for Hellenic Studies for their enthusiasm for this project and for including it in the Hellenic Studies Series. I am particularly grateful to Jill Curry Robbins and Scott Johnson for warmly embracing the project and seeing the manuscript to publication with unsurpassed professionalism. Their encouragement, patience, and assistance went a long way toward overcoming several problems. Also, Noel Spencer has been a masterful copy-editor and an absolute delight to work with. Special thanks are also due to the Wolfson College librarian Fiona Wilkes for her help with various texts.

I dedicate this book to my parents Λάμπρο and Μελανθία, to whom I owe both τὸ ζῆν καὶ τὸ εὖ ζῆν, and to my wife Anastasia for her loving support.

Oxford
March 2012

Preface: An Introduction
to Theodoret's Life and Writings

Εἰς τοὺς ἁγίους πατέρας ἱστορημένους,
ἐν οἷς ἦν καὶ ὁ Θεοδώρητος.

Ἀνιστορήσας τοὺς σοφοὺς διδασκάλους
καὶ τὸν Θεοδώρητον αὐτοῖς συγγράφω
ὡς ἄνδρα θεῖον, ὡς διδάσκαλον μέγαν,
ὡς ἀκράδαντον ὀρθοδοξίας στύλον.
εἰ δ' ἐκλονήθη μικρὸν ἔκ τινος τύχης,
ἄνθρωπος ἦν. ἄνθρωπε, μὴ κατακρίνης·
οὐ γὰρ τοσοῦτον δυσσεβὴς ἦν ὁ κλόνος,
ὅσον μετεῖχε τῆς ἐριστικῆς βίας.
τί γὰρ Κύριλλον πανταχοῦ νικᾶν ἔδει,
καὶ δογματιστὴν ὄντα καὶ λογογράφον;
ὅμως δὲ τοῦτο καὶ διώρθωται πάλιν.
τὰ δ' ἄλλα πάντα τῶν μεγίστων ποιμένων
βλέπων τὸν ἄνδρα μηδενὸς λελειμμένον
ἐνταῦθα τούτοις εἰκότως συνεγγράφω.[1]

Life

IN AD 393 THE MATRON of a wealthy family in Antioch,[2] having asked for the intercessory prayer of an ascetic whom she often visited, a Syrian by the name of Macedonius, "conceived and bore a burden in her womb." Shortly thereafter "she went to the holy man to show the sheaves of the seeds of his blessing."[3] Macedonius, in his response to her, said that "it would be fitting to give the child

---

[1] Ioannes Mauropous, Metropolite of Euchaita, Epigram 49, from de Lagarde 1979:27. On Theodoret's reception in Byzantium, see below, p. 9.

[2] See Bardy 1946:299–325; Guinot 2001:250–254. For the most recent treatment, see Pásztori-Kupán 2006.

[3] *Religious History* 13.18, trans. Price 1985:106. See also Horn 2007:439–462.

back to the one who gave it [*viz.* God]." [4] The child's very name would serve as a constant reminder of this: Theodoret 'given as a gift from God'.

When Theodoret's mother, in the fifth month of her pregnancy, was at risk of miscarriage, Macedonius, who had received a vision to that effect, arrived to help her. He comforted her by saying, "Have confidence and do not fear; for the giver will not rescind the gift, unless you transgress the agreements made. You promised to give back what will be given to you and to consecrate it to God's service." [5] Then he gave her consecrated water to drink and "the danger of a miscarriage vanished." [6] In frequent visits as a child to Syrian ascetics with his mother, Theodoret was reminded by Macedonius of his vocation thus:

> ... you were born, my child, with much toil: I spent many nights begging this alone of God, that your parents should earn the name they received after your birth. So live a life worthy of this toil. Before you were born, you were offered up in promise. Offerings to God are revered by all, and are not to be touched by the multitude: so it is fitting that you do not admit the base impulses of the soul, but perform, speak, and desire those things alone that serve God, the giver of the laws of the virtue. [7]

Elsewhere Theodoret provides us with occasional glimpses of his childhood. While he was sitting at the feet of holy men "Daniel used to say 'That boy will be a bishop.' But old Peter would not agree with him, knowing how much my parents doted on me. Often he used to put me on his knees and feed me grapes and bread." [8]

Growing up in an environment suffused with Christian devotion contributed to a heightened sense of Theodoret's vocation, poised as he was between the world of Christian charismatics and the need to live up to what was expected of him. While little is known about his education, Theodoret was almost certainly educated in Antioch, which at the time boasted not only one of the highest concentrations of grammarians in the empire but also some of the greatest rhetors, among them Libanius[9] and John Chrysostom.

At the age of 23 Theodoret became a monk in the monastery of Nicerte near the city of Apameia, southeast of Antioch. By 423 he had been consecrated bishop of Cyrrhus, a town about two days away from Antioch. His correspondence, of

---

[4] *Religious History* 13.16, trans. Price 1985:106.
[5] *Religious History* 13.17, trans. Price 1985:106.
[6] *Religious History* 13.17, trans. Price 1985:106.
[7] *Religious History* 13.18, trans. Price 1985:107.
[8] *Religious History* 9.4, trans. Price 1985:83.
[9] Cribiore 2007.

which only half survives,[10] reveals a bishop willing to confront the social and fiscal strains suffered by his flock by petitioning the emperor and governors,[11] but also keen to help refugees from Carthage and students in search of good Greek education.[12]

Increasingly embroiled in the Christological controversy at growing cost to his official status, Theodoret emerged as one of the chief exponents of Antiochene Christology.[13] Deposed, without trial, by the second council of Ephesus (known as the Robber Council) as a supporter of Nestorius in 449, Theodoret was reinstated by the council of Chalcedon in 451 only after being forced to anathematize Nestorius. Wearied by years of bitter controversy, he retired to his monastic refuge. In the absence of any writings from that period Theodoret slips from view. The exact date of his death remains uncertain, but it may have been as late as 466.[14]

Not long after Theodoret's death, the subsequent theological divisions between Nestorians and Monophysites led the Monophysite Severus, patriarch of Antioch, not only to denounce Theodoret publicly in a homily delivered in Antioch on 29 December 514,[15] but also to have his name struck from the diptychs of his bishopric in Cyrrhus. In 518 the Monophysite Philoxenus followed Severus's example. However, Sergius II restored Theodoret's name to the diptychs.[16]

The council of Constantinople in 553 would affect Theodoret's reputation and cast a long and lingering shadow on his life and his contribution to theology. In this council, which was summoned by Justinian in order to assuage the Monophysites, some of Theodoret's writings (Refutation of Cyril's Anathemas, Pentalogos,[17] now lost, Defence for Diodore and Theodore), along with those of Theodore of Mopsuestia and Diodore of Tarsus, were condemned summarily.[18] This was not enough, however, to diminish the admiration of later Byzantine authors, who drew extensively on what Theodoret had originally been respected for, his Biblical scholarship and his erudition.[19]

---

[10] Allen 2006:3–21.

[11] Tompkins 1993; Bellini 1977:227–236; Di Paola 2006:155–176.

[12] Theodoret's epistolary and patronage network is fully analyzed by Schor 2011:133–179.

[13] For a recent but not unproblematic assessment of his Christology, see Clayton 2007. Fairbairn 2007:100–133.

[14] So Honigmann 1953:174–184. Azéma 1984:137–155 argues for the earlier date of 460.

[15] Allen and Hayward 2004:17.

[16] Pásztori-Kupán 2006:27.

[17] For a recently discovered fragment of this work, see Guinot 2007:117–129.

[18] For further details, see Price 2007:17–37.

[19] For the reception of Theodoret in Byzantium and beyond, see below, p. 9.

Writings

Theodoret was an exceedingly prolific author and a consummate stylist. Marked by the challenge to develop a more solid Christian literature by building upon and adapting preexisting Greek literary culture, his wide range of writings is matched only by the breadth of his vision. A large part of these writings, from apologetic works against paganism to Biblical commentaries and Christological treatises, are his response to the debates and controversies outlined above.

The majority of Theodoret's work has been preserved. The *Therapeutikê* and the *Ten Discourses on the Divine Providence* are considered among his earliest works, written between 427 and 437 and 435 and 437, respectively.[20] But Theodoret's defense of Christianity and concern with paganism extended well beyond the time of the composition of these two works. In fact, it lasted throughout his life. In the 440s, motivated as much by theological concerns as by the need to situate Syrian ascetics in a spiritual context, Theodoret wrote the *Religious History* (or *History of the Monks of Syria*), a series of portraits of Syrian ascetics.[21] This work was the first effort to present Syrian ascetics and their wayward practices in terms recognizable to Christian and non-Christian intellectuals.

In the *Ecclesiastical History*, written in 450s and covering the period between the death of Constantine, the beginning of the Arian controversy (ca. 325), and the death of Theodore of Mopsuestia (428)[22]—roughly thirty years after the *Therapeutikê*—Theodoret revisits a number of issues with unremitting fervor. Instead of dwelling on the prosperity of the empire and the relative stability that it enjoyed (as Sozomen and Socrates do),[23] Theodoret emphasizes in a compact, episodic narrative the continued struggle of the church against its enemies.[24] Among other events, he chronicles the Arian controversy, Julian's reign and death, the destruction of pagan temples and the demise of Chrysostom, the translation of his relics, and the destruction of the Serapeum in Alexandria, as well as the persecutions of the Christians in Persia that took place during his lifetime.[25] Each of these episodes would become emblematic of his world and his times.[26]

---

[20] Richard 1935:83–106.
[21] Canivet 1977-1979; Canivet 1977; Urbainczyk 2002.
[22] Theodoret, Kirchengeschichte, ed. Parmentier 1998. See also *Histoire ecclésiastique* / Théodoret de Cyr, ed. Parmentier and Hansen 2006(I).
[23] Van Nuffelen 2004.
[24] See Chapter Five.
[25] Leppin 1996a.
[26] See more recently Martin 2005:135–147.

An enormous amount of theological learning informed Theodoret's careful choice of literary forms. His ability to articulate within these different forms would not have been an easy task, given that, at the time, Christian literature as such was still in the making. Many authors were still grappling with such issues as how to accommodate the emperor in historical accounts and how to write in praise of asceticism, monastic and other. Theodoret's work acts as a response to such (literary) challenges. His literary endeavors display remarkable independence and versatility.[27] That he accomplished the task so seemingly effortlessly must not lead us to underestimate the enormous amount of effort and difficulty involved.

Alongside such compendia as the *Therapeutikê*, Theodoret put together in 452 or 453 the heresiological tract *Compendium of Heretical Falsehoods*,[28] the second half of which has been called a "Christian *de principiis*."[29] During his involvement in the Christological controversies, Theodoret employed the dialogue, in the *Eranistês*, to discuss his ideas and provide proof-texts for debate.[30]

His Biblical commentaries, much admired and relied upon by the Byzantines for their concision and clarity of exposition, constitute a large part of his literary output. These commentaries cover topics ranging from the 14 Pauline epistles,[31] the Song of Songs, the Psalms, the major and minor prophets, Baruch, and Jeremiah to the books of Isaiah and Daniel,[32] in addition to a famous collection of questions and answers on disputed passages in the first eight books of the Old Testament.[33]

The Text and Content of the *Therapeutikê*

Composed in the 420s, the *Therapeutikê* is considered one of Theodoret's earliest literary works. Most likely, it was written in the monastery of Nicerte, southeast of Antioch, which, tellingly, was two to three miles from Apameia, birthplace of the Neoplatonic philosopher Iamblichus and well-known center of Neoplatonic philosophy. Epitomizing as it does Theodoret's apologetic program, the *Therapeutikê* forms the core of the book that follows. It comprises 12 lectures

---

[27] On the literary merits of Theodoret and his approach to writing, see Krueger 1997:393–419 and 707–719. Both are included in Krueger 2004.

[28] See Cope 1990 and Sillett 2000:261–273.

[29] Young 1983:288.

[30] *Eranistês*, ed. Ettlinger 1975.

[31] *Commentary on the Letters of St. Paul*, Hill 2001.

[32] *Theodoret of Cyrus: Commentary on Daniel*, Hill 2006.

[33] *The Questions on the Octateuch*, ed. Petruccione 2007. Guinot (forthcoming); Petruccione (forthcoming).

(*dialexeis*). A list of the titles will give an idea of the overall plan and the subject matter of the work:

> *Dialexis* I. On Faith
>
> *Dialexis* II. On the First Principle
>
> *Dialexis* III. On Angels, Gods, and Demons
>
> *Dialexis* IV. On Matter and Cosmos
>
> *Dialexis* V. On Human Nature
>
> *Dialexis* VI. On Providence
>
> *Dialexis* VII. On Sacrifices
>
> *Dialexis* VIII. On the Cult of the Martyrs
>
> *Dialexis* IX. On Laws
>
> *Dialexis* X. On True and False Oracles
>
> *Dialexis* XI. On the End and (Final) Judgment
>
> *Dialexis* XII. On Practical Virtue

Theodoret appears to be sensitive to the limitations of his chosen format, as well as to the way that it affects the presentation of his thought. He prefaces the set of lectures with an introduction that lays out the structure of the work and expounds the rationale behind it. The *Therapeutikê* is arranged in such a way as to enable contemporary readers to explore progressively a number of important issues that were resonating throughout the empire. As will be shown in Chapter Five of this book, by adopting the flexible and versatile *dialexis*, and by adapting it to suit his needs, Theodoret is able not only to address and refute pagan criticisms, but also to instruct through a careful selection of philosophical set-pieces.

Each of the *dialexeis* focuses on a carefully delimited topic, as indicated by title, but Theodoret also takes care to convey his rationale. He eases into each topic with a general statement, a quotation from a Greek author, a reflection on a specific issue, or an image. Depending on the subject matter (e.g. *Dialexis* IV. On Matter and Cosmos) he gives a doxographic account interlaced with his approval or disapproval (qualified or unqualified). As a general pattern (but see exceptions; e.g. *Dialexis* XII. On Practical Virtue) the first half of each *dialexis* deals with the critical examination of *doxai* and the second half with the discussion of their compatibility with the Bible (which is the ultimate criterion except when there are no Biblical precedents to support a Christian practice; e.g. the cult of relics). For the latter, Theodoret tends to provide abundant proof texts from the

Bible to buttress his claims. At a number of points in the *Therapeutikê*, he stops to look back, restate, summarize, or anticipate an argument, and thereby to render explicit certain conceptual links. On top of this cross-referencing, at the end of each *dialexis* he makes sure to restate the main argument and to contextualize it within the overall direction of the work. Thus Theodoret makes sure that the *dialexeis* cohere.[34] This cohesiveness, combined with his "relaxed" style,[35] accords well with Theodoret's overarching concern, accessibility.[36]

As will become clear, while Theodoret is selectively responding to Julian's critique in the *Therapeutikê*, he refrains from doing so on a point-by-point basis. Instead, he is equally concerned with untangling several knotty and contested issues in the order and with the priority that he, and not Julian, deems important for clarifying, simplifying, and reducing a mass of material into well-articulated positions. More importantly, in each *dialexis* Theodoret makes sure to give a careful presentation of central beliefs, and he accounts for those beliefs with ample proofs from the Bible.

The main bulk of quotations aside, the *Therapeutikê* resembles, in many respects, another set of lectures, the *Ten Orations on the Divine Providence*, which Theodoret most likely delivered in Antioch.[37] Both are organized thematically and demonstrate Theodoret's homiletic skills. These affinities leave open the (intriguing) possibility that in the case of the *Therapeutikê* we may be dealing with a redacted form of lectures possibly originally delivered in Antioch.

In its current version, however, the *Therapeutikê* was meant to address a much broader audience that extended well beyond Antioch. Thus in assessing Theodoret's *Therapeutikê* we must look beyond the immediate conditions that might have led to its writing. For, just as Cyril sought to circulate his *Against Julian* along with other works across the empire,[38] so too did Theodoret envision an audience far beyond the geographical confines of Antioch or Syria. His was a bid for recognition of literary merit, not only from his colleagues, but ultimately from posterity.

---

[34] In comparison with the *Against Julian*, begun by Theodoret's contemporary Cyril of Alexandria perhaps in 420s but completed around 439–441, Theodoret's *Therapeutikê* is more wide-ranging in its scope. When he wrote the *Therapeutikê*, he was aware of Cyril's *Against Julian*, as shown by his letter 83, in which he congratulates Cyril on his achievement.

[35] *Therapeutikê*, prologue 3: "τὸν ἀνειμένον δὲ χαρακτῆρα τοῖς λόγοις ἐντέθεικα· τῇ διδασκαλίᾳ γὰρ εἶναι τοῦτον ὑπείληφα πρόσφορον."

[36] See Chapter Five.

[37] Halton 1988:3.

[38] For Cyril's literary ambitions and his efforts to have his works circulate across the empire, see Russell 2000:222n151.

Previous Scholarship on Theodoret's Apologetics

As important as this apology is, and as often as it has been cited by scholars to illustrate fifth-century Christian attitudes and debates (seldom on the basis of a thorough acquaintance with the text itself),[39] the text is almost unknown except to specialists in the field.

The first two-volume monograph on Theodoret, by Nikolai Glubokovskii, is *Blazhennîi Feodorit episkop Kirrskii* (Moscow, 1890), which includes a discussion of Theodoret's apologetic writings and more specifically the *Therapeutikê*. Karl Joseph Schulte's monograph *Theodoret von Cyrus als Apologet. Ein Beitrag zur Geschichte der Apologetik* (Vienna, 1904) represents the first serious and more widely available attempt to ascertain and quantify Theodoret's sources, to examine the origin of the criticisms that Theodoret seeks to refute, and to assess the value of the apology.

The first critical edition of the *Therapeutikê*, by Raeder, follows Schulte in 1908, and a French edition with translation—the only one in any modern European language—is not published until the middle of the twentieth century, in 1958. An English translation is still missing. Pierre Canivet's *Histoire d'une entreprise apologétique au Ve siècle* (Paris, 1957) goes a long way toward providing a historical, literary, and archaeological context for the *Therapeutikê*.

Schulte's and Canivet's works are of great industry and lasting value. However, many of the points made in them are due for revision in light of advances that have been made in recent scholarship. The narrowly defined analysis as to whether or not Theodoret knew firsthand the authors he cites (an important issue in itself) overlooks other aspects of his apologetics that are just as interesting. Furthermore, their approach leaves a series of important issues unaddressed. It does not sufficiently account for the use of medical and philosophical lore, which on closer investigation, as I will argue, can yield important results that will ultimately lead to a new and better understanding of both Theodoret's methods and his achievement.

Since the publication of the studies mentioned above, thinking about Theodoret entirely or almost entirely in terms of the attributes he shares with his predecessors and contemporaries has been characteristic of a large part of twentieth-century (and especially English-speaking) scholarship on Theodoret's apologetics. A more detailed analysis has been long overdue.

The dissertation upon which the current monograph is based, *Christian Therapeia and Politeia: The Apologetics of Theodoret of Cyrrhus against the Greeks* (Princeton University, 2004), picks up where these studies leave off and seeks

---

[39] Runia 1997:106; Kaldellis 2008:138; Kahlos 2007. Schott 2008:170 speaks of the ossification of apologetics in the case of Theodoret, Cyril, and Augustine.

to fill in the gaps that remain. Another recent study of Theodoret's apologetics, Siniossoglou's *Plato And Theodoret: The Christian Appropriation of Platonic Philosophy and The Hellenic Intellectual Resistance* (Cambridge, 2008), focuses on Theodoret's interpretation and use of Plato. Siniossoglou's narrow focus often overlaps with the work of Eduard des Places, who analyzes Theodoret's quotations of Plato in detail. His study certainly does not represent the full range of Theodoret's concerns, nor does it encapsulate the extent of his thinking on the relationship between Hellenism and Christianity, for there are important aspects of his apologetics left unaddressed.

This book, then, is the first study in English of the *Therapeutikê for Hellenic Maladies* (hereafter *Therapeutikê*) in its religious, literary, and cultural contexts, including original translations of some of the most important passages. Combining close textual readings with larger theological, historical, and cultural issues, the book analyzes in detail Theodoret's argumentation against Greek religion, philosophy, and culture. While the focus is on the *Therapeutikê*, the study draws on the other works of Theodoret, as well as on a wide range of late antique Greek literature, in order to give a sense of the wider religious and intellectual context that gave weight to many of the themes with which Theodoret grappled.

Theodoret's Reception

Not long after its composition, the *Therapeutikê* became a resource, not only for Christian authors engaged in debate with pagans, but also—in the long run—for Byzantine intellectuals for whom Theodoret became a highly respected authority. Citations and active use of the *Therapeutikê* continued into the Byzantine period, past the fifteenth century, and beyond.

Zacharias of Mytilênê draws on Theodoret's *Therapeutikê* in his dialogue *Ammonius*,[40] written in the early sixth century to refute pagan beliefs in the eternity of the world. Passages from the *Therapeutikê* were later added in the extremely popular seventh-century collection of *erôtapokriseis* by Anastasius of Sinai,[41] in the martyrdom of Trophimus.[42] There are many other indications that the *Therapeutikê* and other works by Theodoret were circulating as resources, not least among the Slavs in translated compilations,[43] throughout the Byzantine

---

[40] Especially the first four books of the *Therapeutikê* and perhaps the *Ten Discourses on the Divine Providence*. See Zacharias of Mytilênê *Ammonius*, ed. Minniti Colonna 1973:45, 47, 51.

[41] PG 89:397–400 (Q. 8), 481–484 (Q. 16), 691 (Q. 46), 624 (Q. 57); Canivet 2000–2001(II):467. These questions, however, do not belong to the original collection as edited by Richard and Munitiz 2006.

[42] Mercati 1901:207–226, esp. 218; Canivet 2000-2001(II):468.

[43] Thomson (forthcoming).

period. Another example can be found in the work of Peter of Argos, a bishop writing in the Peloponnese in the second half of the ninth century. In his *Funeral Oration on Athanasius of Methonê*, he draws from *Therapeutikê* IX. On the Laws[44] to extol Athanasius' teachings over those of the ancient lawgivers Zalmoxis, Anacharsis, Lykourgos, and Solon, among others.[45]

From the same period comes evidence that the emperor Leo VI, the "Wise" or the "Philosopher," received a copy of the *Therapeutikê* as a gift.[46] Also in the ninth century, George the Monk's *Chronicle* relies heavily on the *Therapeutikê* for its polemical presentation of Hellenic paganism; in it Theodoret is presented as an authority on par with Athanasius and John Chrysostom.[47] The *Therapeutikê* at that time was one of the works that constituted "the philosophical collection" that circulated among Constantinopolitan intellectuals.[48]

The high status later accorded to Theodoret, however, is best summed up in the attitude of the eleventh-century bishop of Euchaita, and teacher of Michael Psellos, Ioannes Mauropous, who himself established the feast of the three hierarchs, which is celebrated to this day in the Greek Orthodox Church.[49] In an epigram, Ioannes praises Theodoret's erudition, proclaiming him a Doctor of the Church and praying to God for his salvation.[50] Such was his esteem for Theodoret that Ioannes even commissioned an icon of the three hierarchs that also included Theodoret.[51]

In the twelfth century, the Byzantine polymath Michael Glykas adapts material from Theodoret's *Therapeutikê* for his *Annales* and his collection of *Kephalaia* (or *erôtapokriseis*).[52] In the same century Ioannes Tzetzes, another Byzantine polymath, cites Theodoret and the *Therapeutikê* as one of the many authorities in his miscellany,[53] as to a greater extent does the author of the anonymous miscellany from the late fifteenth century.[54] Theodoret's views on the ensouling of the embryo, presented in *Dialexis* V. On the Human Nature,[55] would become very influential in patristic discussions and informed Byzantine legal thinking,

---

[44] *Therapeutikê* 9.11–13.
[45] Kyriakopoulos 1976: "Πέτρου Ἄργους, Ἐις τὸν Ἀθανάσιον ἐπίσκοπον Μεθώνης'" (54); see Kyriakopoulos 1976:37–67; 214–223; 275–316.
[46] Schamp 2004:537, esp. n5. Also Westerink 1990:105–123.
[47] Karpozêlos 1997–2002(II):243–249; Canivet 2000–2001(II):467–468.
[48] Cavallo 2007:155–165.
[49] Gazê 2004:140–141.
[50] Epigram 49, ed. de Lagarde 1979:27.
[51] Karpozêlos 1982:104.
[52] *Eis tas aporias tes Theias Graphes Kephalaia*, ed. Eustratiades 1906(I):241 (Q. 20); idem, *Annales*, ed. Bekker 1836:151, 201. See also Papadogiannakis 2009:130–142, at 134.
[53] Ioannis Tzetzae *Book of Histories* 9.861–863, ed. Leone 1968:379–380.
[54] Nyström 2009:68, 97, 134, 152–155, 162, 212–213.
[55] Crego 1996:19–37.

as illustrated by its appearance in the discussions of the patriarch Gennadius Scholarius in the fifteenth century.[56]

During the Renaissance, manuscripts containing the works of Theodoret became highly sought after.[57] The sustained interest in his works, and in the *Therapeutikê* in particular, elevated him to the status of a Christian classic. Collections soon followed that combined Theodoret with such authors as Basil, John Chrysostom, and Gregory Nazianzen.[58] The famous Florentine humanist Zanobi Acciaiuoli translated the *Therapeutikê* into Latin, thus making it available to a much wider audience.[59] An edition of Theodoret's collected works prepared by Eugenios Voulgarês in Halle between 1768 and 1775 and the frequent use of Theodoret as an authority by the Greek polymath Georgios Koressios (1570ci.– 1659/60)[60] point to continued interest in the value of Theodoret's contribution.[61]

[56] Troianos 1999:179–184.

[57] Petitmengin 2002:3–31.

[58] For further details, see Bossina 2006:231–291, esp. 257.

[59] Zanobi Acciaiuoli (1461–1519) and Friedrich Sylburg (1536–1596), *Theodorētou episkopou Kyrou Hellēnikōn pathēmatōn therapeutikē* (Heidelberg: Ex typographeio H. Commelini, 1592). On Acciaiuoli's use of Theodoret, see Nardi 1991:9–63. Guerra Morisi 1991:89–108. See Vicario 2000:119–158.

[60] Stoupakês 2000:273, 309, 466, 472, 518.

[61] Jacques Sirmond (1559–1651) and Johann Ludwig Schulze (1734–1799), *Tou Makariou Theodoretou Episkopou Kyrou Hapanta* = *B. Theodoreti Episcopi Cyri, opera omnia* (Halae: Typis et Impensis Bibliopolii Orphanotrophii, 1769–1774).

Introduction:
Theodoret and the Fifth Century

*Earth and sea are freed from their ancient ignorance; the error of idols
is no longer to be seen; the darkness of ignorance has been dispersed, and the
light of knowledge fills with its rays the whole inhabited world. Greeks, Romans,
and Barbarians recognize the divinity of the crucified and venerate the sign of
the cross. The Trinity is worshipped in place of a multitude of false gods.[1]*

Therapeutikê 6.87

THEODORET CHOSE TO DESCRIBE his times in terms that expressed more
his aspirations than contemporary reality. However, the defining features
of fifth-century society under the Byzantine Empire were transition and transformation. While the bulk of this book will focus on specific topics, the stage
needs to be set with the discussion of a range of contextual issues: the state
of Christianity at the time, the state of paganism, and the issues surrounding
Hellenic culture's most exalted good, *paideia*, and its relationship with late
Roman elites.

By Theodoret's time Christianity had made considerable headway toward
social and intellectual acceptance. In the process of negotiating its position
with regard to the imperial administrative apparatus, the church had developed its own administrative structures. A series of imperial edicts starting with
Constantine and continuing with Theodosius had progressively—at least in
theory—banned animal sacrifices, religious festivals, and divination.[2] The liturgical calendar was filled with commemorations of the saints. Sunday was being
celebrated as the day of the Lord.[3] The structures of conciliar Christianity had
been developed. Art and iconography were developing.[4] Asceticism had spread
in all levels of the society. Monastic communities and ascetics had multiplied in
the East during the fourth century.

---

[1] Translations of Theodoret's *Therapeutikê* are from a draft translation by Thomas Halton, often
with my own adaptations.
[2] For the full dossier, see Trombley 1993–1994(I):1–97.
[3] Rordorf 1962.
[4] Elsner 1998.

As a result of these developments, the late antique landscape was dotted with monasteries, particularly in Egypt, Syria, and Palestine. Literary works advertising the pious lives of Christian ascetics were circulating throughout the empire.[5] The spread of the cult of the martyrs led to the erection and multiplication of *martyria* and such forms of piety as pilgrimage.[6] Ambitious and elaborate building programs were transforming the outlook of the Holy Land and the new capital of the empire, Constantinople.

But if Christianity had evolved by Theodoret's time so had Greek pagan beliefs.[7] Contrary to a deep-seated tendency to view paganism as moribund, there remained considerable vitality in the religious traditions of Hellenism, but also in other forms of Semitic paganism.

Neoplatonism

As a result of symbiosis, confrontation, and competition with Christians, pagan intellectuals such as Sallustius, Iamblichus, and Proclus attempted to synthesize strands of different traditions and thus create a systematic theology that brought together Platonic, Stoic, Pythagorean, Orphic, and Chaldean elements.[8] This combination of religion and philosophy became known as Neoplatonism.

Neoplatonists invested Platonic texts and their exegesis with sacral awe.[9] Plotinus, the founding figure of Neoplatonism, provided the first synthesis toward the elaboration of Platonic doctrine in the third century.[10] It was left to his disciple Porphyry to make available these teachings, which he did in an edition entitled the *Enneads*. A consummate logician himself, Porphyry sought among other things to protect, by means of allegory, the most venerable texts of Hellenism, Homer's *Odyssey* and *Iliad*,[11] while attacking Christians in one of the most formidable anti-Christian treatises of late antiquity.[12]

---

[5] On asceticism and the developments that took place, see Brown 1998:601–634 and Rousseau 1998:745–780.

[6] Caseau 1999:21–59; Bitton-Ashkelony 2005; Elsner and Rutherford 2005.

[7] Leppin 2004:59–81; Caseau 2011:111–134. By using the term paganism I am aware of the fact that the term lumps into one category an array of practices and beliefs of various religious systems. I am not assuming, however, a unitary category or understanding of paganism. Despite its pejorative connotations the term has recognizability and is still useful if employed with an awareness of its shortcomings. See the most recent discussion by North 2005:125–143 and Van Nuffelen 2011:89–109; for a defense of the term, see Cameron 2011:14–32. For arguments for the use of the term 'polytheism' instead, see Fowden 2005:521–522.

[8] Saffrey 1992:35–50.

[9] Hadot 1987:13–34.

[10] Edwards 2006.

[11] Buffière 1956:392–558; Brisson 2004.

[12] Morlet 2011b; Levieils 2007.

Among intellectuals Platonic texts formed the basis of study and, in combination with a collection of oracles (the Chaldean Oracles, supposedly from Julian, the second-century theurgist), breathed new life into old and venerable traditions. As early as the third century AD, Sallustius' *On the Nature of Gods*, a compendium of pagan belief,[13] sought to present a unitary understanding of Hellenic paganism. Iamblichus, a contemporary of Sallustius, attempted to synthesize different religious traditions in his *On the Mysteries*, a "summa of polytheist belief."[14] On a broader level, however, more than conscious of Christianity but deprived of its civic outlook and function, paganism receded into a state of mind.[15] And yet in the fifth century, there remained considerable vitality in the religious traditions of Hellenism, both in its rural and its philosophical form, but also in other forms of paganism (e.g. Semitic).

All this systematizing of late pagan philosophical and religious thought "produced a doctrine and an identity and it is their [pagan] response that justifies the use of the word 'pagan-ism'."[16] This did not result in a coherent or consistent attitude toward the Christians or in an organized oppositional front against Christianity, as scholars have until very recently posited.[17] Instead, reactions to Christianity ranged from covert polemical allusions to *damnatio* by exclusion from narratives. These attitudes went hand in hand with debates and

---

[13] Sallustius *Concerning the Gods and the Universe*, ed. Nock 1926. Melsbach 2007.

[14] Fowden 1999:82–106 at 86.

[15] Fowden 1998: "there were long-term resistances offered by educated elites concerned with the preservation of something less tangible, a tradition of thought and personal conduct as well as of cult" (555). Caseau 2004:105–144, esp. 137: "The issue of pagan *temples* and of pagan *practices* should not be confused." On the destruction of temples, see Hahn 2011, Lavan 2011:15–65. and Saradi 2011:263–309.

[16] North 2005:137. North continues by rightly observing that "[t]he conception of the history of pagan-ism . . . is that the crucial factor is not some internal change or transformation, still less an evolution according to some pre-determined process, but rather the necessary effects of confrontation and co-existence with the new types of religious groups, Jewish, Christian, and others, with which pagans in all the cities of the empire had to deal from the first century onwards. The effect was to create a self-consciousness about their own position and a need to define and justify themselves, which had simply not existed before, when there were no alternative systems against which they had to measure themselves. It is in this context that they themselves have to produce a doctrine and an identity, and it is their response that justifies the use of the word 'pagan-ism'. It is not necessary for this view that there should have been much, if any, violent conflict between pagans and others; what we have to believe is that there was a steady drift of pagans away from their traditional attachments and a great deal of peaceful co-existence and discussion; but that the survival of pagan practice depended on their success in retaining numbers, generation by generation. It remains, of course, a serious question why pagans did so drift away from traditional attachments." See also Van Nuffelen 2011:89–109.

[17] Some examples of these approaches are De Labriolle 1934, Momigliano 1963, and recently Siniossoglou 2008 and Schäfer 2008. For a critique of the "conflict" model, see Lizzi Testa 2009 and Brown 2009:277–285. Cameron 2011 has delivered the *coup de grâce*.

disagreements between Neoplatonists themselves about the role of ritual and religious practice in their conception of Neoplatonism.[18]

Challenges . . .

Challenges to Christianity in the fifth century were not new. In the third century Porphyry had written a devastating critique of Christianity, of which only fragments survive.[19] Eusebius, Apollinaris, Macarius Magnes, Philostorgius, Philip of Side, Methodius, and Jerome had all sought to refute it, and two emperors, Constantine and Theodosius II, had even commissioned its destruction. [20] Then, an emperor—Julian, no less—wrote a damaging treatise entitled *Against the Galileans*,[21] which attacked the fundamental tenets of Christianity. Written by a lapsed Christian[22] with a thorough knowledge of the Bible and of Greek philosophy, the work caused great alarm to many Christians. Alongside his overt polemic against the Christians, and building on Iamblichus' reworking of different religious traditions, Julian sought to define Hellenism more narrowly, emphasizing the religious character of the classical literature and placing a hitherto unprecedented emphasis on the religious affiliation of those who were to profit from it.[23]

By Theodoret's time the continued resonance of Porphyry's and Julian's anti-Christian polemic had trickled down to broader circles of intellectuals, providing philosophically inclined pagans with ready arguments against Christianity. Writing in the 420s, Cyril of Alexandria justifies his decision to refute Julian's *Against the Galileans* by referring to pagans who, "when they meet Christians, they upbraid them with the taunt that 'none of our teachers is capable of rebutting or refuting his works'."[24] Macarius of Magnesia's apology *Monogenes (Apokritikos)*, from the late fourth (or early fifth) century, reinforces this fact.[25] In the same period the church historian Philostorgios reputedly wrote

---

[18] Saffrey 2008:489–511.

[19] The nature and extent of the work have been the subject of prolonged and intense debate among scholars. Its very existence as an independent work has been doubted by Beatrice 1994:221–235, but forcefully argued by Goulet 2004:61–109. For several attempts to reconstruct the work by collecting (and discussing) the fragments, see Berchman 2005, Ramos Jurado et al. 2006, and Muscolino 2009. For a recent discussion of the nature of the work, see Edwards 2007a:111–126 and Morlet 2011b:11–49.

[20] Sarefield 2006:287–296; Herrin 2008:205–222.

[21] *Against the Galileans*, ed. Masaracchia 1990.

[22] Bouffartigue 2007:25–38.

[23] On this see Chapter Five. See also Elm 2003:493–515.

[24] Wilken 2000:70–84, esp. 81.

[25] *Macarios de Magnésie. Monogénès*, ed. Goulet 2003.

a treatise against Julian. Philip of Side too wrote a treatise against Julian, though it is now lost. Thus Theodoret, like many other contemporary Christian authors, was still contending with aggressive pagan criticism that echoed the polemics of Porphyry and Julian, whose impact reverberated long after their deaths.

Similar challenges to Christianity are registered in other fifth-century sources, confirming Christian concerns and offering us insights into the tensions that existed in Theodoret's time. These include, not only Ps.-Justin's *Quaestiones et responsiones ad orthodoxos* and the correspondence of Isidore of Peluse[26] and Nilus of Ancyra, but also the *Life of Severus* by Zacharias of Mytilênê.[27] The corpus of Isidore's and Nilus' letters reveals an array of *scholastikoi*, grammarians, imperial officials, sophists, and soldiers raising issues similar to the ones with which Theodoret is dealing: the appeal of Christianity to the uneducated masses, skepticism and repugnance toward the cult of the relics, and the role of divine providence, among others.[28] The fact that the names of these correspondents are known to us, then, is enough to maintain that their existence need not be argued simply from silence.

How much distance Christianity had still to travel in the fifth century can also be seen in the world of education, as vividly conjured in the *Life of Severus* by Zacharias of Mytilênê from the 480s.[29] His account offers glimpses of students in Alexandria and Beirut, eagerly devoted to Hellenic paganism.[30] It has been called a "vigorous agitated academic world that was cut off neither from the provinces

---

[26] Isidore *Lettres*, ed. Evieux 1997. Isidore, in a letter to Olympiodorus, conjures up pagan reactions thus: "θαυμάζω, ὅπως οὐ μόνον οἱ παιδεύσεως ἄμοιροι τῶν Ἑλλήνων ἐπαγγελόμενοι, καὶ οἱ ἐπὶ εὐγλωττίᾳ ἐναβρυνόμενοι, ἐπὶ διαλεκτικῇ τε αὐχοῦντες, καὶ συλλογισμοῖς ἐπερειδόμενοι, καὶ τὰς μὲν ἐναντιώσεις τῶν λογισμῶν ὁρῶντες, τὰς δὲ τῶν πραγμάτων μὴ καθορῶντες, οὐκ αἰσθάνονται, δι'ὧν τὸ κήρυγμα τὸ θεῖον κατατοξεύουσι, διὰ τούτων μᾶλλον ἑαυτοὺς καταισχύνοντες. Φέρει γάρ τινα φιλοτιμίαν τοῖς κεκρατημένοις, ἡ τῶν κεκρατηκότων ὑπεροχή, Αὐτοὶ δὲ φάσκουσι νεκρὸν τὸν Ἰησοῦν, ἵνα νεκροῦ ἀποφανθῇ τῶν παρ'αὐτοῖς θεῶν ὁ δῆμος ἀδρανέστερος. Κωμῳδοῦσι τὸν σταυρὸν, ἵνα κωμῳδηθῶσι σφοδρότερον, ἀτίμως πεπορθημένοι καὶ νενικημένοι σταυρῷ. Σκώπτουσι τὴν τῶν ἀποστόλων ἀμαθίαν, ἵνα λαμπρότερον οἱ θρυλλούμενοι παρ'αὐτῶν στηλιτευθῶσι σοφοί, ἰδιωτῶν ἀνδρῶν διδασκαλίᾳ ἡττηθέντες. Τὸν τοῦ Χριστοῦ προσκυνούμενον χλευάζουσι τάφον, ἵν' οἱ παρ'αὐτοῖς περιφανεῖς ναοί, γέλωτα ὀφλείωσι μείζονα, χλευαζομένῳ παραχωρήσαντες τάφῳ. Παντὸς ἐπιλαμβάνονται ὡς εὐτελοῦς τοῦ κηρύγματος, ἵνα τὰ παρ'αὐτοῖς περιφανῆ πλέον ὀφθῇ καταγελαστότερα, τῇ τῶν εὐτελῶν ὑποκύψαντα φύσει" (Ep. 27, PG 78:1080). See also the study by Evieux 1995.

[27] Zacharias of Mytilênê *Life of Severus*, ed. Kugener 1907; rev. edition, Turnhout 1971:207–264. The Greek text has been lost but is preserved in Syriac and has been translated into French and, partially, into English by Young 1990:312–328. For a full more recent translation, see now Zacharias Bishop of Mytilênê *The Life of Severus*, ed. Ambjörn 2008.

[28] For the caution with which Nilus' correspondence (still not available in a critical edition) should be approached, see Cameron 1976:181–196.

[29] Probably retouched by Zacharias in Constantinople in the years between 510 and 520 according to Watts 2005:437–464, esp. 439.

[30] Discussed by Chuvin 1991:108–117, Trombley 1993–1994(II):1–51, Hall 2004:192–217, and Watts 2005:437–464.

from which its members originated, nor from the major cities that received them."[31] In the midst of such a climate of religious antagonism and debate, Zacharias' protagonist Severus is presented in his preparation for becoming a Christian as feeling the lure of pagan literature. He is therefore counseled "to set the orations of Basil and Gregory, the illustrious bishops, in opposition to the orations of Libanius the Sophist, by whom, with the ancient rhetoricians, he was dazzled."[32] While the reader is left with no doubt as to who finally wins Severus' heart, his biographer later mentions that Severus "still needed to read even more of the orations of the rhetoricians and philosophers, because the pagans even now excessively consider themselves superior and glorify themselves in these studies, and they should be freely debated from these writings."[33] Describing the readings of Christian students on Sundays, Zacharias writes:

> [They] began with the treatises that different ecclesiastical authors have written against the pagans. After this we read the *Hexaemeron* of Basil, then various of his works and letters, after that the treatise addressed to Amphilochius refuting Eunomius, and finally the *Address to Young Men* in which he informs them how to profit from the writings of Hellenic authors.[34]

This is a priceless glimpse into the reading habits of Christian students. Their search for refutations of paganism went hand in hand with the search for a way in which they could still profit from their reading of the classical authors while also pursuing instruction in their faith. The list of authors whose refutations were consulted includes Athanasius, Gregory Nazianzen, and John Chrysostom. Theodoret's *Therapeutikê*, conspicuously absent from the list, was almost certainly read, though, as Trombley notes, it was likely not mentioned due to Theodoret's role in the continuing Christological controversies. Zacharias, however, included materials from the *Therapeutikê* in his anti-pagan dialogue *Ammonius*, in which he refuted pagan arguments against the eternity of the world.[35]

---

[31] Chuvin 1991:105; Nesselrath 2006:179–192; Poggi 1986:57–71; Watts 2010:123–154 For the activities of sophists, grammarians, and teachers and a prosopography, see Szabat 2007:177–345. For a more skeptical approach to the claims of these texts and an emphasis on the caution with which these accounts must be read, see now Chuvin 2004:15–31.

[32] Zacharias of Mytilênê *Life of Severus* 317.

[33] Zacharias of Mytilênê *Life of Severus* 319.

[34] Trombley 1993–1994(II):32.

[35] See the section on Theodoret's reception, Zacharias *Ammonius*, ed. Minniti Colonna 1973:112n34.

The *Life of Severus* offers us another scene of Christians debating with pagans as an illustration of the need for contemporary Christians to respond to pagan eagerness for debate:

> After reading many treatises of the church fathers who had opposed the Hellenes, [Stephen] received grace from God to defeat them utterly in his debates with them . . . He refuted the sophistic objections made by the Hellenes against Christians. Then he retorted against the offenses of the pagans to Paralios: the infamous mysteries of their gods, the dream-oracles of polytheism, the obscure and embarrassed responses of these gods, their ignorance of the future, and other frauds of those same daimones. Stephen persuaded Paralios to submit his doubts to Horapollon, Heraiskos, Asklepiodotos, Ammonius, Isidore, and the other philosophers close to them, giving just weight to what each side [of the controversy] said. Paralios engaged in conversations with the pagans many days thereafter. He found their responses weak and without foundation.[36]

Not only do these glimpses corroborate the urgency of Theodoret's task, but they also complement our picture of the range of issues that were debated in the fifth century, casting into sharper relief at least part of his intended audience as well as the use to which texts such as the *Therapeutikê* might have been put. The latter is an issue to which we will return.[37]

Thus the confidence that the empire had finally become Christian went hand in hand with the uncertainty of how Christian late Roman society had become. For "a post-pagan world was not, by any means, necessarily a Christian world."[38] Attachment to paganism remained strong precisely in the areas that Theodoret was most concerned with, in the circles of intellectuals, grammarians, and students, but also in rural settings.[39]

Although Theodoret is perhaps deliberately vague about the precise identity of those whose reactions he describes, conjuring up imagined opponents allows him to engage his audience on various fronts. His real targets, however, may have lain closer to him. In the aftermath of Constantine's conversion, the large number of converts who became Christian were motivated by different factors. It is estimated that during the fourth century, "an age of spectacular mass-baptisms . . . a thousand persons might be initiated every year at Easter in

---

[36] Passage in Trombley 1993–1994(II):5.
[37] This will be discussed more fully in Chapter Five.
[38] Brown 2003:46.
[39] Lizzi Testa 2010:77–113.

any large city."[40] This growth exerted pressure on the church and affected the process of Christianization in many ways, as Harold Drake articulates:

> The combination of a constant infusion of converts—who necessarily brought with them a wide range of experiences and preconceptions about everything from the proper ordering of society to the role of divinity in human affairs—and the small number during this same period who were able to discern and articulate the unique demands of the Christian message shows us a movement that was exceptionally fragile, as well as one that necessarily had to engage in constant dialogue, both with other Christians and with the larger world from which new Christians came.[41]

Alongside those who genuinely believed in the superior spiritual value of Christianity, some acted from expediency, and religious coercion undeniably played its role.[42] The renowned rhetor Libanius in an address to the emperor Theodosius sums up this latter problem in the fourth century thus:

> But if they tell you that others have been converted by these [coercive] acts and are now of the same religious opinion as themselves, do not let it elude you that they are speaking of *seeming* converts, and of factual ones. For they put off nothing of their [belief], but only *say* they have. This is not to say that they honor one set of cults instead of others, but that the [Christian authorities] have been fooled. For they go with the crowds through the other places where they go for the sake of appearances, but when they assume the mien of men praying, they either call upon no one or else the gods, it not being proper to call upon them from such a place, but they do it all the same.[43]

As for those who truly espoused Christianity, the question of "how much of the old life could be carried into the new" loomed large with an inescapable urgency;[44] for "we must beware of supposing that what it meant to be a

---

[40] Brown 1998a:617.
[41] Drake 2005:4. Fowden 1998 writes: "in communities but recently thrown into disarray by attacks on their sanctuaries, and in individuals too, conversion might be a purely external conformity, an either more or less self-conscious cryptopolytheism from which stress easily provoked return to old, well-tried gods" (557). On the problem of apostasy from Christianity, see now Schöllgen 2004:58–80.
[42] On coercion and conflict, see Brown 1998a:632–664 and Gaddis 2005.
[43] Libanius *Orations* 30.28, trans. A. F. Norman. For a discussion of the context, see Trombley 1993–1994(II):134–204.
[44] Markus 1990:32.

Christian was a matter of unanimity within the community as a whole."[45] Contrary to the previous understanding of conversion as a dramatic one-time event, recent scholarship has emphasized the complexity of this transition and the slow transformation that followed from the act.[46] These considerations raise questions about the nature and terms of conversion as well as the quality of the converts' instruction in the Christian faith.[47] Conversion to Christianity left many with a host of questions in need of answers. Thus Christianity came to be challenged not only externally by impenitent pagans but also internally by searching new Christians.

Erôtapokriseis: Ps.-Justin's *Quaestiones et responsiones ad orthodoxos*

Nowhere is this searching more apparent than in a collection of inquiries that were posed to an anonymous Christian teacher probably during the fifth century,[48] Ps.-Justin's *Quaestiones et responsiones ad orthodoxos*[49] (hereafter QRO). The QRO provides a particularly useful demonstration of the topics that came up for discussion and debate as well as the challenges that both Christian authors such as Theodoret and, on a broader level, fifth-century Christianity in general faced. This collection of 161 inquiries from an Antiochene perspective establishes a world full of tensions with a directness not easily discernible in other sources.

By following the seemingly random compilation of the QRO, we can trace the preoccupations of a society still debating a number of unresolved contemporary problems.[50] The QRO highlights focal points in these debates, revealing a fluidity in the beliefs held by Christians at the time while underscoring the challenges

---

[45] Scourfield 2007:4; Sandwell 2010:523–542. For a questioning of the pagan vs. Christian divide and a nuanced model of assessing pagan and Christian investment in religion, see Cameron 2011:175–177.

[46] For a nuanced discussion, see Brown 2004:103–117. For a recent reappraisal of conversion, see Mills and Grafton 2003.

[47] Soler 2010:281–291.

[48] While the issue of its dating is not settled yet and while, as a compilation, the QRO may contain materials from both an earlier and a later period, what is not in doubt is that the central core of the collection is from the fifth century.

[49] On the authorship, see Harnack 1901:33–44; Funk 1907(III):323–350. Recently, Riedweg 1998:848–873, esp. 868–869. For the purposes of this study I use the edition of Papadopoulos-Kerameus 1895, reprinted 1976, Leipzig. All translations of the QRO are my own.

[50] Dagron 1981: "Le ps.-Justin des Quaestiones ad orthodoxos, qui est peut-être Théodoret de Cyr lui même, en toute cas l'un des ses contemporains; Il nous place, comme les vies du Ve siècle, au carrefour de deux mondes, entre un paganisme qui n' est plus un rival, mais une composante culturelle encore mal assimilée, et une fois nouvelle qui explore un autre coprus de textes et a découvert la voie parallèle d' une histoire vétérotestamentaire" (144).

that this fluidity posed to the formation of a Christian identity.[51] Because the range of issues the *QRO* is meant to address overlaps so markedly not only with Theodoret's concerns but also with those of many Christian apologists of the time, it is particularly relevant for assessing the state of Christianization in the fifth century and beyond.[52]

Seen in this light, Theodoret and the anonymous author of the *QRO* are attempting to respond to the pressing concerns of contemporary late antique society. The literature of *erôtapokriseis* to which the *QRO* belongs began growing significantly in the fifth century not only as a response to debates but also as a way to address the deeply-felt need that converts had for instruction.[53] For, contrary to the tendency to see catechesis as restricted only to the preparation for admission to the liturgical life of the church, we must regard religious instruction as a longer process, one encompassing all aspects of the life of the Christian.

Other challenges facing Theodoret were the internal divisions of Christianity and Judaism. Theological divisions, to which Theodoret devotes considerable attention in his *Ecclesiastical History*, had beset the eastern empire and Antioch in particular in John Chrysostom's time but were still causing controversy in the fifth century. The situation was further compounded by the continued vitality of Judaism in Syria, as well as in other parts of the eastern empire.[54] As the closest alternative to Christianity, Judaism continued to be a challenging presence capable of attracting Christians. A generation earlier, Chrysostom had gone to great lengths to divert his congregation in Antioch from Jewish practices.[55] Debate and polemic against Judaism continued to inform Theodoret's work in varying degrees, most predominantly with respect to his exegesis.[56] At the same time, the lingering problem of heretics and Manichaeans[57] and the menacing presence of Persia—with its sporadic persecution of Christians toward the end of the reign of Yazdgard I (399–421)—contributed to a climate of worrisome uncertainty.[58]

---

[51] On the problem and challenge, see Piepenbrink 2005 and Sandwell 2007; Gemeinhardt 2008:453–476.

[52] See for further details Papadoyannakis 2008:115–127.

[53] Papadoyannakis 2006:91–105.

[54] Millar 2004:1–24, esp. 15–16.

[55] Wilken 1983; Soler 2006; Sandwell 2007.

[56] On this, see Guinot 1997:153–178; McCollough 1984 and 1989(II):157–174.

[57] See Ep. 81, ed. Azema, where Theodoret refers to eight villages of Marcionites, one village of Eunomians, and one village of Arians. Also Hutter 2002:287–294. For Marcionites, see Tardieu 1997–1998:596–605.

[58] See Chapter Five. See also Dignas 2007:223–255.

Hellenism = Paganism?

As further analysis will demonstrate,[59] Theodoret's *therapeutic* approach is based on a model deeply rooted in the traditions of Greek medicine and philosophy. According to this model, to have the wrong religious beliefs is tantamount to a failure of cognition, which must be remedied by means of discourse. Nevertheless, the rejection of Hellenic religion did not imply a wholesale rejection of Hellenic culture. Recent scholarship has shown how Hellenism had been variously defined, and it remained a fluid concept even among its non-Christian adherents.[60] As such, 'Hellenism' designated, among other things, attachment to pagan beliefs/ancient ideas about religious practice, ritual, and even good command of classical Greek language and literature.[61] It conjured up an entire culture of enormous sophistication. The multivalence of the term 'Hellenism' rendered it inherently ambiguous and therefore subject to competing conceptualizations. The line between its religious and non-religious elements was very hard to negotiate. Not only was the 'pagan' element of Hellenism not uniformly defined or understood, it was also often left to the eye of the Christian beholder to determine its content and contours. Different Christian authors chose to draw the line at different points.[62]

If Theodoret inveighs against this religious aspect of Hellenism (viz. paganism) in his work, he nevertheless considered other aspects too important to be rejected. By exploiting what common ground existed (as well as what ground *could be seen* to exist) between Hellenic literary culture and philosophy and Christianity, he sought to redefine the way his readers related to a corpus of classical texts and ideas. To accomplish this—and to help his readers across what was made to look like a firm divide—Theodoret incorporated a broad array of Greek texts in a manner integral to his apologetics. In the same vein he elucidated the title of the work *Therapeutikê of Hellenic Maladies* by adding: "Proof-recognition (*epignôsis*) of the Gospel from Greek philosophy." These strategies reiterate an idea found in earlier apologists that paganism may have been based on misguided thinking. In the process of refuting this thinking, apologists could

---

[59] See Chapter Three.

[60] Whitmarsh 2001: "Greek cultural identity, at least in the highly energized world of elite literary production, was manipulated strategically in order to serve the interests of the speaker or the writer. Each literary articulation of Greekness, then, needs to be interpreted in context, in the light of the aims and ambitions of the actor in question, and not simply taken for granted as an expression of ethnic unrest" (305). See also Konstan and Saïd 2006; Johnson 2011:165–181.

[61] Bowersock 1990; Rapp 2008:127–147. Recently, Kaldellis 2007:120–187, though there is a tendency to overstate the conflict and overlook significant points of convergence.

[62] Johnson 2006:55–93; Kahlos 2007:1–112; McLynn 2009:572–587; Cameron 2007:21–46; Bagnall 2008:23–41.

highlight intimations of Christian truth, which helped to confirm the correctness of their theology. Theodoret's entire apologetic enterprise, then, could be regarded by readers, not only as a refutation of paganism, but as both a justification and a guideline for the Christian use of classical texts.

Theodoret's time saw the culmination of Christianity's grappling with Hellenism, which was embedded in a wider and longer running pattern of opposition to and integration of Hellenism, along with Christianity, into the Roman elite culture. The challenge for Theodoret was to continue the tradition, established by Clement of Alexandria, Basil, Gregory Nazianzen, and Gregory of Nyssa, of harmonizing scripture and Hellenic philosophy and culture.[63] Christians were contending with a host of challenges: the accommodation of the emperor in the narrative of Christianization, the accounting for and defense of the cult of martyrs that played an increasingly important role, the assimilation of asceticism into the new reality of the Christian Empire, the justification of Christianity's success. These challenges called out for a sustained engagement with Hellenism, and Greek *paideia* provided a precious resource.

There were other areas too, where the appeal of Hellenic paganism found expression, particularly biography and historiography. Biography ensured that models of pagan piety remained highly visible and that the bearers of the true Hellenic *paideia* were properly praised. Biographies of the time abounded in miracles, signs, and oracles and such practices as fasting, sexual abstinence, miraculous healing, and divinatory practices,[64] but also in covert polemic against Christianity.[65] In line with predecessors Porphyry (*Life of Plotinus*, *Life of Pythagoras*) and Iamblichus (*Life of Pythagoras*), Eunapius, composing portraits of holy men in the later fourth century, advertised the spiritual values of a community threatened by the rise of Christianity;[66] Marinus (*Life of Proclus*) in the fifth century and Damascius (*Life of Isidore*) in the sixth century continued this tradition. Philosophers were presented as accomplished religious figures who, having progressed in a graded system of virtues through their discipline and piety, had achieved a divine status. The underlying values of these philosophers were oriented toward a union with God. Collectively, the real heroes of these biographies were Hellenic education and religion. Despite the bleak view these authors took of the fate of the ideals they propounded, their texts also carried a very potent message: divine power still abides in the people who choose to adhere to the time-honored religious traditions of Hellenism and to the ideals that it fosters. At the same time, the histories of Eunapius and Zosimus (the

---

[63] Breitenbach 2003.
[64] See Goulet 1981:161–208 and 1998:217–265; Edwards 2000.
[65] Clerc 1994:294–313; Saffrey 1975:553–563 and 1992b:421–431.
[66] Penella 1990.

former only partially preserved in the latter) were motivated by the view that the abandonment of time-honored religious practices and traditions would bring about the decline of the Empire.[67]

Hellenism and Christianity

Even a cursory look into Theodoret's writings suffices to show that his engagement with Hellenism—understood as both a set of religious traditions and cultural and literary expressions—lasted throughout his life. Seen as a set of religious traditions, Hellenism was incompatible with Christianity, and Theodoret argued vigorously against it. But as a set of literary and cultural expressions Hellenism was not only a defining component of the world he described; it was essential to its survival. Writing almost two generations after Julian's attempt to define Hellenism more narrowly, Theodoret was aware of the fact that, to a significant degree in the East, Greek literature and culture had a crucial part to play in the continuing development of the eastern Roman Empire (Byzantium) in particular. Greek literary culture was an index of Roman identity.[68]

The focus, then, on the relationship between Hellenism and Christianity—both terms appear in the sources of the period, often as conventional opposites[69]—raises many issues for Theodoret, at once a bishop faced with the task of Christianizing late Roman society and a Hellenized Syrian staking his claim to full participation in that society to Greco-Roman identity.[70] Philip Rousseau has summed up well the challenge facing bishops like Theodoret:

> Christianization was not a matter merely of defeating 'paganism': it meant implanting more securely the system of belief that the population had already in theory embraced—converting the converted. Nor could a bishop rest content with the force of law or secular authority no matter how friendly he might be with those who wielded it. He was faced with more than criminal intransigence and had to deploy other traditional forms of role and status—those of the orator, the scholar, the man of virtue—in order to bring to bear in this new cause the established techniques of instruction and persuasion.[71]

---

[67] Leven 1988:177–197; Green 1974. For the historiography of this period, see Winkelmann 1998:123–159. But see recently the critique and qualifications offered by Cameron 2011:644–654, 668–678.

[68] See Millar 2006.

[69] See *QRO* Q. 16, Q. 34, Q. 55, Q. 86.

[70] See Chapter Five. Millar 2007:105–125.

[71] Rousseau 2008:36–37.

The complex interplay between these two traditions in the work of Theodoret was inevitable given his family background, education, his vocation. Theodoret realized, as did many a classically educated bishop, that he could neither fully concede the elite's belief in *paideia* as the locus of highest worth nor entirely shake free of it.

Admittedly, many of the above challenges were not new. Tensions went back to Clement of Alexandria and were addressed by Origen, Basil, Gregory Nazianzen, Gregory of Nyssa, and John Chrysostom, among others.[72] However, the issue had by no means lost its immediacy and relevance in Theodoret's time. In fact, as Christians sought to envisage a Christian future, the question of how to deal with Hellenic *paideia* remained all the more pressing; for the cultivated audience of the time, Christian and non-Christian alike, did not simply require the refutation of pagan criticisms. Rather, they sought a view of where and how Christianity fitted with the literary culture they had been brought up to admire.[73] Accordingly, Christian authors themselves had to continue to worry about how to accomplish such a synthesis. How was the relationship between Christianity and Hellenism to be defined? What were the implications for Christian identity and for *paideia*?

Paideia and the Formation of Elites

Following the efforts of numerous Christian authors in the preceding generations, the fourth and fifth centuries saw Christianity consolidating its position

---

[72] Sandnes 2007:124–195.

[73] Julian summed up this supreme confidence in the intrinsic value of Greek *paideia* by taunting Christians thus: "But you yourselves know, it seems to me, the very different effect of your writings as compared with ours; and that from studying yours no man could attain to excellence or even to ordinary goodness, whereas from studying ours everyone would become better than before, even though he were altogether without natural fitness. But when a person is well endowed, and moreover receives the education of our literature, he becomes actually a gift of the gods to humankind, either by kindling the light of knowledge, or by founding some kind of political constitution, or by routing numbers of his country's foes, or even by traveling far over the earth and far by the sea, and thus proving himself a person of heroic mold. Now this would be a clear proof: choose out children from among you all and train and educate them in your scriptures, and if when they come to manhood they prove they have nobler qualities than slaves, then you may believe that I am talking nonsense and am suffering from spleen. Yet you are so misguided and foolish that you regard those chronicles of yours as divinely inspired, though by their help no man could ever become wiser or braver or better than he was before; while, on the other hand, writings by whose aid men can acquire courage, wisdom and justice, these you ascribe to Satan and to those who serve Satan!" (*Against the Galileans* fr. 55, trans. Wright LCL). While Julian's attitude cannot be taken as representative of all those classically educated non-Christians, it certainly had considerable resonance among the literati and highlighted the challenge that Christians had to be prepared to meet on the role of classical education in a Christian empire.

as a pervasive element in Roman elite culture. This period was thus crucial for the formation and maintenance of Christian elites.[74] Theodoret's focus on the formation of a Christian *paideia* bears directly upon this process, as Christian elites sought to maintain and redefine their place within late Roman society and its traditions.[75] Classical *paideia* was tied to social esteem, and it conferred status on its holders. In the absence of a Christian educational system, young men had to acquire an education through the study of Homer and other pagan authors. This meant that they had to immerse themselves in pagan literary and religious values, as Robert Kaster explains:

> If in theory the man of traditional education could be presumed to be the '*right sort*', in practice the presumption provided entry into the networks of personal relationships and patronage by which local and imperial governments were managed and through which the rewards were distributed. The man thus prized and rewarded for his culture was a figure of continuity in the empire from its beginning until its end, whatever changes the life and structure of the empire experienced. In the wake of such changes it was a function of the traditional education to continue its old job of sorting out and identifying the elite, of providing reassurance that nothing basic had shifted, that the right, honorable men were still conspicuously present and in control. Tenacious in its maintenance of a familiar order, this culture of language and texts continued to perform its job as long as the structures of the imperial government remained standing in the Latin west, and still longer in the Greek east.[76]

Thus Hellenism, bound up with *paideia* as it was, became essential. The capacity of Greek literature to induce a sense of cultural (and religious) identity made it a field of contestation *par excellence*. Furthermore, increasing bureaucratization made education, and hence the study of classical authors, a highly desirable path for advancement. As Christianity had not yet developed its own curriculum and relied instead on the traditional educational system, Christian authors were concerned with the fact that the study of the classics involved encountering literature steeped in Hellenic religious ideas and beliefs.[77] Their challenge was to affect the way with which the elites related to this corpus of texts and ideas

---

[74] See the contributions in Rapp and Salzman 2000; also Salzman 2002.

[75] Cameron 2004:91–107.

[76] Kaster 1999:421–423, at 423. On *paideia* and education in late antiquity, see Watts 2006.

[77] Sandnes 2009; on the varying ways in which Christians dealt with Greek myths, see recent contributions in Von Haehling 2005.

while at the same time precluding adherence to the 'pagan' religious element of classical *paideia*.[78] Brown sums up the problem thus:

> Culture was not a surrogate for religion. For many the classical liter-
> ature and art and the sense of history and language were central to
> culture, inherited from the deep past of Rome, *were*, in effect, the reli-
> gion. It was a religion in which all members of the ruling class could
> share. It spoke with a heavier voice and elicited a thrill of numinous
> awe that often resonated more deeply and more widely among its
> devotees than did the novel tingle of sectarian loyalties.[79]

On a broader level, reverence for the classical *paideia* went hand in hand with the need to create a more polished Christian literature intended to cater to the literati.[80] Theodoret's time was one of literary vigor, actively supported by the patronage of Theodosius II, which led to the writing of hagiography as well as the recasting of Biblical narratives in classisizing poetry.[81] The confidence that this move was meant to convey should not be underestimated: to Christian and non-Christian eyes, it was important that Christianity be seen as able to present its protagonists on the "brightly-lit stage of Late Roman opinion."[82] Because they would be recognizable to readers schooled in Greek rhetoric, Christian Syrian ascetics would begin to enter the literary mainstream and become known throughout the empire. Without excluding other potential motives behind the writing of the *Religious History*, this one has received the least attention.[83]

Theodoret was not alone in deliberately fusing classical literary ideals with Christian ones. The obvious parallel that comes to mind from this same period is Eudocia. As consort of emperor Theodosius II, Eudocia was heavily invested in promoting a Christian Hellenism that sought to integrate Hellenic and Christian literary ideals. Perhaps unsurprisingly, Theodoret's texts, among others, were precisely what Eudocia was reading.[84]

As the evidence suggests, the Christianization of the empire during Theodoret's time was still very much in progress. In the context of continuous fluidity, there remained a continual need for new syntheses and responses. As

---

[78] McLynn 2009:585 argues similarly.
[79] Brown 2011:69.
[80] Bevegni 2006:389–405.
[81] On this literary phenomenon, see Whitby 2007:195–231, Nesselrath 2005–2006:43–53, Johnson 2006, and Nazzaro 1998:69–106.
[82] Brown 1998:656.
[83] *Pace* Leppin 1996b:212–230.
[84] Cameron 1982:217–289 at 280.

the rest of this study will illustrate, the methods Theodoret uses to articulate his apologetic enterprise have yet to be fully understood in light of the above considerations. While an exhaustive study is too large in scope to address here, the subsequent chapters will highlight cumulatively the following interlocking key themes.

Chapter One surveys the notion of *therapeia* and its role in the apology. Drawing on a number of texts it will show how medical/philosophical notions are employed in the refutation of pagan polemic and how Greco-Roman theories of the role of the emotions provide a framework for persuading Theodoret's readers.

Chapter Two considers the polemic against the conceptualization of Greek gods and other intermediaries (angels, heroes, daemons) and how Theodoret replaces them with angels. A major part of Theodoret's polemical intent is to cast pagan Gods and intermediaries into the category of demons. The role of demons in divination and sacrifice requires Theodoret to engage both aspects of Greek religion.

Chapter Three focuses on the cult of martyrs. It examines the criticisms underlying Theodoret's defense of the cult and how this is played against the background of the hero cult.

Chapter Four examines the presentation of Christianity as a practical universal philosophy. It shows how Greek philosophy is used to articulate a contrast between Christianity and paganism. This contrast also informs the opposition of local versus universal and that of Greek philosophers and the true philosophers, the Christian ascetics.

Finally, Chapter Five is a study of Theodoret's rhetoric, style, and argumentation and their integral role in the articulation of his apologetic program. Particular attention is given to the literary form of *dialexis* and its significance for the format of the *Therapeutikê*. In light of the surrounding literary activity, this chapter also advances a new suggestion for the intended role of the work.

The following analyses will enable us to see Theodoret as a creative apologist—not just adding a new inflection to old themes but creating his own unique perspective—by closely examining the polemical literary context that shaped his views and the emergence of ideas born from his experience contending with pagan criticism.

1

The Notion of *Therapeia* in Theodoret: The Apologetic Use and Role of Greek Medicine and Philosophy against the Greeks

A S DEMONSTRATED BOTH IN particular comments scattered throughout his corpus of writings and more generally in the *Therapeutikê*,[1] Theodoret displays a thorough knowledge of Greek medicine.[2] While the use of insights from Greek medicine and philosophy is not unique to Theodoret—the practice goes back at least as far as the Gospels and the apostolic fathers[3]—it takes on a greater degree of complexity in the framework of Theodoret's apologetics because of his focus on curing/persuading his audience to recognize Christianity's superiority. Nowhere does this become more apparent than in the *Therapeutikê*, where the notion of *therapeia* is applied as a major theme for his enterprise.

Therapy, an important concept in ancient Greek philosophy, is just one example demonstrating the intimate connection between Greek philosophy and medicine. Medical concepts and analogies were used at a very early stage by Greek philosophers and poets for a variety of purposes.[4] Plato was one of the first philosophers to employ systematically analogies, metaphors, and imagery in order to argue various points or convey ideas to his readers. Aristotle, the Stoics, and Epicurus developed the figurative use of medical language further.[5]

---

[1] Through medical imagery, analogies, and the episodes describing healing that punctuate his narratives, especially the *Religious History* and the *Ecclesiastical History*, the image of the doctor is never allowed to slip from view. Borelli 2007:467–477; Guinot 2002:131–151. Canivet has very competently discussed Theodoret's medical knowledge and sources but has failed to pursue their implications for Theodoret's literary and apologetic aims.

[2] Canivet 1957:307; Adnès and Canivet 1967:53–82 and 1967:149–179.

[3] Leven 1987; Ferngren 2009.

[4] See Cordes 1994, Leschhorn 1985, Ruess 1957 and 1967:95–103, Kornexl 1970, Wells 1998, and Wilfried 1978. See Rolke 1975, esp. for the Stoic use of medical imagery.

[5] Recent work in ancient Greek philosophy has forcefully brought out the importance of passion and the function of emotions and has generated a complex discussion. See Nussbaum 1986:31–74 and 1994, Sorabji 2000, Konstan 2006, Graver 2007, and Tsouna 2009:249–265.

In the prologue (προθεωρία) to the *Therapeutikê*, Theodoret programmatically states his aim and the approach he will take to accomplish it. He justifies the 12 treatises both as the therapy (θεραπεία) for those diseased (νοσούντων) and as assistance for those of sound mind in religious opinion. After this brief prologue Theodoret proceeds to elaborate on the notion of *therapeia*. He employs the medical analogy of health and disease, transposing this scheme to the soul:

Ἰατρικὴ θεραπεία ἔστι μέν που καὶ σώματος, ἔστι δ' ἄρα καὶ ψυχῆς· καὶ γὰρ δὴ καὶ ταύτῃ κἀκείνῳ συχνὰ προσγίνεται πάθη, ἀλλὰ τῷ μὲν ἀκούσια, τῇ δέ, ὡς ἐπίπαν, αὐθαίρετα. Τοῦτο οὖν εὖ εἰδώς, οἷα δὴ πάνσοφος ὁ Θεὸς καὶ ψυχῶν καὶ σωμάτων καὶ τῶν ὅλων δημιουργός, ἑκατέρᾳ φύσει προσένειμεν ἁρμόδια φάρμακα, καὶ μέντοι καὶ ἰατροὺς ἐπέστησε, τοὺς μὲν ταύτην, τοὺς δὲ ἐκείνην ἐκπαιδεύσας τὴν ἐπιστήμην, καὶ στρατηγεῖν καὶ ἀριστεύειν κατὰ τῶν νοσημάτων ἐκέλευσεν. Ἀλλ' οἱ μὲν τὸ σῶμα οὐκ εὖ διακείμενοι καὶ τὴν νόσον δυσχεραίνουσι καὶ ὑγείας ἱμείρονται καὶ τοῖς ἰατροῖς εἴκουσιν, οὐ μόνον ἤπια προσφέρουσι φάρμακα, ἀλλὰ κἂν τέμνωσι, κἂν καίωσι, κἂν λιμώττειν κελεύωσι, κἂν πικρῶν τινων καὶ ἀηδῶν μεστὰς προσφέρωσι κύλικας· καὶ διὰ τοιαύτης ἀνιαρᾶς ἐπιμελείας τὴν ὑγείαν καρπούμενοι, μισθὸν τοῖς οὕτως ἀκουμένοις ὀρέγουσι, καὶ τὴν θεραπείαν δεχόμενοι τὴν τῶν φαρμάκων οὐ περιεργάζονται σκευασίαν· τὴν γάρ τοι σωτηρίαν ποθοῦσιν, οὐ τὸν ταύτης τρόπον ἀνερευνῶσιν. Οἱ δὲ τῆς ἀπιστίας τὴν λώβην εἰσδεδεγμένοι οὐ μόνον ἀγνοοῦσι τὴν παγχάλεπον νόσον, ἀλλὰ καὶ τῆς ἄκρας εὐκληρίας ἀπολαύειν ὑπολαμβάνουσιν· ἢν δέ τις τῶν ταῦτα θεραπεύειν ἐπισταμένων ἀλεξίκακον φάρμακον τῷ πάθει προσενεγκεῖν ἐθελήσῃ, ἀποπηδῶσιν αὐτίκα, καθάπερ οἱ φρενίτιδι κατεχόμενοι νόσῳ καὶ τὴν σφίσι προσφερομένην ἀποσείονται θεραπείαν καὶ τὴν ἰατρείαν ὡς ἀρρωστίαν ἀποδιδράσκουσιν. Χρὴ μέντοι τοὺς ταύτην μετιόντας τὴν ἐπιστήμην καὶ χαλεπαίνοντας φέρειν καὶ λοιδορουμένων ἀνέχεσθαι, κἂν πὺξ παίωσι, κἂν λακτίζωσι, τοιαῦτα γὰρ δὴ ἄττα πλημμελοῦσιν οἱ παραπαίοντες· καὶ οὐ δυσχεραίνουσι τούτων γινομένων οἱ ἰατροί, ἀλλὰ καὶ δεσμὰ προσφέρουσι καὶ καταιονῶσι βίᾳ τὰς κεφαλὰς καὶ πᾶσαν μηχανὴν ἐπινοοῦσιν, ὥστε τὸ πάθος ἐξελάσαι καὶ τὴν προτέραν τῶν μορίων ἁρμονίαν ἀποδοῦναι τῷ ὅλῳ. <u>Τοῦτο δὴ καὶ ἡμῖν ποιητέον, καὶ τῶν οὕτω διακειμένων ἐπιμελητέον εἰς δύναμιν.</u> Εἰ γὰρ καὶ ὀλίγοι λίαν εἰσὶν οἱ τῷ πάθει δεδουλωμένοι καὶ ἐοίκασιν ὑποστάθμῃ τινὶ παχείᾳ τῶν τοῦ διυλιστῆρος οὐ διϊκνουμένη πόρων διὰ παχύτητα, ἀλλ' οὖν οὐκ ἀμελητέον αὐτῶν οὐδὲ παροπτέον φθειρομένους ὑπὸ τοῦ πάθους, ἀλλὰ πάντα πόρον ἐξευρητέον, ὥστε τὴν ἐπικειμένην αὐτοῖς ὁμίχλην ἀποσκεδάσαι καὶ τοῦ νοεροῦ φωτὸς ἐπιδεῖξαι τὴν αἴγλην. Οὐδεὶς γὰρ φιλόπονος γεωργὸς τὰς μὲν πολλὰς ἀκάνθας ἐκτέμνει, τὰς δὲ ὀλίγας ἐᾷ, ἀλλὰ κἂν δύο εὕρῃ, κἂν μίαν, πρόρριζον ἀνασπᾷ καὶ καθαρὸν ἀποφαίνει τὸ λήϊον. Πολλῷ δὴ οὖν μᾶλλον τοῦτο ποιητέον ἡμῖν· οὐ γὰρ ἐκτέμνειν, ἀλλὰ μεταβάλλειν τὰς ἀκάνθας ὁ τῆς ἡμετέρας γεωργίας παρακελεύεται νόμος. Φέρε τοίνυν καὶ ὡς ἀκάνθαις τὴν γεωργικὴν προσενέγκωμεν δίκελλαν καὶ τῇ μακέλλῃ τοῦ λόγου τὰς τῶν ἀκοῶν ἀνευρύνωμεν αὔλακας, ἵνα μηδὲν τῶν ἐν μέσῳ κειμένων κωλυμάτων ἐπίσχῃ τῆς ἀρδείας τὸ ῥεῖθρον· καὶ μὲν δὴ καὶ ὡς ἀρρωστοῦντας καταιονήσωμεν καὶ τὰ σωτήρια καὶ παιώνια προσενέγκωμεν φάρμακα.

Therapeutikê 1.1–2

There is a healing treatment for the body. There is also one for the soul. For while it is true that frequent ailments beset both body and soul, bodily ailments are for the most part involuntary, while spiritual ailments are voluntary. Well aware of this, God, the supremely wise creator alike of body and soul and all things, provided appropriate remedies for each part. He put physicians in charge. Some He taught the art of healing bodies, others the art of healing souls. The former He ordered to leaders and champions in the war against disease.

Those who are sick in body bear the illness badly and desire health. They entrust themselves to the care of physicians who not only prescribe gentle drugs but also cut, cauterize, order diets and offer portions of bitter and ill-tasting medicines. Through such unpleasant treatments they reap good health and hand a fee to those who treated them. As long as they receive treatment they are not concerned about the preparation of the remedies. They long for good health; how it is achieved they do not inquire into. Those who have contracted the stain [λώβην] of unbelief not only do not perceive the seriousness of the illness but suppose they are enjoying the peak of health. If one with skill in healing wishes to offer a therapeutic drug for the disease, they immediately back away like those afflicted with delirium, and they shrug off the proffered remedy and run from the cure as they run from sickness. Those of this profession must put up with ill-tempered patients and endure abuse, when the sick strike with the fists and kick. The delirious do such mistaken things. Doctors are not upset by such demonstrations. They confine them in restraining garments, and anoint their heads forcefully, and devise every means to drive out the sickness and restore the former harmony of the parts of the whole body.

This is what we must do. We must, to the best of our ability, look after the spiritually sick. Even if there are but a few afflicted with this illness and resemble a thick sediment which does not pass through the holes of the strainer on account of its coarseness, still they must not be neglected and overlooked and allowed to waste away their illness. Every means must be sought so as to dissipate the mist that has settled upon them and to show the radiance of the spiritual light. No industrious farmer cuts away the majority of thorns and leaves a few, but if he finds two, or even one, he hacks them out by the roots and leaves the meadow clean. Much more should we act in a similar fashion. For the law of our husbandry dictates that the thorns should be not eradicated, but transformed.

Come now, and just as we apply the hoe in agriculture to the thorns, so with the mattock of the word let us widen the furrow of their ears so that nothing will impede the irrigation of their senses. Similarly, just as in the case of those who are ill, let us apply saving and healing medicines.

It is this powerful analogy that establishes Theodoret's approach.[6] The symptoms of unbelief (ἀπιστία, literally lack of *pistis*) are paralleled with those of madness. Just as insanity involves fundamental changes in perception and the physical state, so lack of *pistis*—construed as a psychosomatic phenomenon—affects deeply those who suffer from it.[7]

The medicalization of religious deviance was pervasive in the literature of the time.[8] Porphyry and Julian had attacked Christians on multiple occasions, accusing Christianity of being a disease and Christians of being sick.[9] In his portrayal of pagan madness, Theodoret draws on images from the treatment of madness by contemporary doctors.[10] Literary madness is tied closely to the

---

6   The same analogy is employed in *On Providence*: "Let us imitate the best doctors who seeing their patients refusing to take nourishment and nauseated by the food set before them, outwit by medical tricks and break down their refusal to eat. By mixing pleasant seasonings with the rather dry and bitter fare they manage to make the ill-tasting victuals more palatable to the sick. Our adversaries, like the sick criticize all they see and all that happens. Illness befalls the sick against their will, and in excruciating pain they refuse to take food. Though they would like to partake, they are prevented by the illness. But voluntary and self-aroused passions war against our adversaries and their nausea is caused not by foods and delicacies but by all the wise and just arrangements of Providence" (PG 83:668c, trans. Halton).

7   See Grant 2006:369–404.

8   For the way it informed the late Roman legal system, see Zuccotti 1992.

9   E.g. Porphyry *Against the Christians* fr. 27, ed. Muscolino 2009:224–225; Julian *Epistles* 36d: "Though indeed it might be proper to cure these, even against their will, [ἄκοντας ἰᾶσθαι] as one cures the insane, [φρενιτίζοντας] except that we concede indulgence to all for this sort of disease [νόσου]. For we ought, I thought, to teach, but not punish, the demented" (trans. Wright LCL).

10   But what is also interesting is that, by using the image of "a thick sediment which does not pass through the holes of the strainer on account of its coarseness," he is perhaps alluding to the idea

physical condition, described in Greek medical literature with an eye ultimately to the spiritual implications of the disease.[11] The other important feature of the metaphor is its ability to "restore the former harmony of the parts of the whole body,"[12] stressing the holistic nature of the offered therapy. By implication disease is construed as a disruption of the harmony of the whole. *Logos* is the means by which Theodoret seeks to restore the mental health of those who suffer from the disease. Another point should be stressed: by using this elaborate analogy in the beginning of the *Therapeutikê*, Theodoret is aiming at making himself—he is, after all, the person administering this treatment— ethically respectable by assuming the implied role of the physician. And, as any good physician who must show the dramatic workings of a disease to patients who ignore or are reluctant to accept it, Theodoret uses the arresting and thoroughgoing analogy to illustrate the effects of the disease and the urgency with which its cure must be applied.[13] Further, in the same way that the physician's authority is based on medical knowledge and the mastery of medical skill, Theodoret must show his knowledge of Greek philosophy and culture in order to

---

found in medical literature that madness results from some blockage in the veins and a kind of asphyxia.

[11] On madness as a psychosomatic disease in the ancient world, cf. Moss 1967:709–722. For a fuller treatment, cf. Pigeaud 1987; Stok 1996:2282–2409.

[12] *Therapeutikê* 1.5: "τὴν προτέραν τῶν μορίων ἁρμονίαν ἀποδοῦναι τῷ ὅλῳ."

[13] A strikingly similar analogy, with supporting rationale, is found in Stobaeus' *Anthology* in a summary of a book by the Academic Skeptic Philon of Larissa (110/9–86 BC): "Philo was a Larissan by birth, an academic philosopher, a student of Clitomachus, and someone who made reasonable progress [in his works]. Philo showed acuity in his other writings as well as his division of philosophical doctrine, which I append [since it is relevant to my work]. He says that the philosopher is like a doctor. *Just as it is the function of the doctor, then first to persuade the sick person to accept his therapy, and secondly to undermine the arguments of those urging him against treatment, so it is also for the philosopher.* Each of these, however, is found in what is called the *protreptic* discourse [since a protreptic discourse is one which exhorts to virtue]. Of this, one part displays the great utility of virtue, while the other refutes those arguing against or attacking, or otherwise slandering philosophy. The discourse after this, the second, has the second place in the analogy with medicine. Just as it is the function of the doctor, after persuading the patient to accept it, to introduce therapy—part of which consists in eradicating the causes productive of disease, and part in inserting causes conducive to health—so it is also with the science of philosophy. For after protreptic, the philosopher tries to introduce *therapeutic*, for which he uses stimulants of two kinds. *One kind introduces the discourse which is destructive of falsely begotten beliefs (through which the critical faculties of the soul are diseased); the other the discourse which inserts beliefs in a healthy state.* Thus the second subject is that concerning the protreptic was introduced. The third subject will again correspond to the third medical function. For as in medicine every effort concerns the end, i.e. health, so in philosophy it concerns happiness. But the discourse concerning lives is conjoined to the discourse on ends. For it is not sufficient in medicine to create health, but there is also a need to provide rules about health by attending to which patients will safeguard the good condition of the body; so also there is a need in life for certain theorems which will bring about the safeguarding of the end" (Stobaeus 2.2.2, 1–51, trans. Brittain 2001:255–256 [emphasis mine]). Theodoret seems to be following most of the steps in the order described in this synopsis. The method is almost identical! On this passage, see Schofield 2002:91–109.

establish himself as an authoritative figure entitled to administer the necessary cure. He proceeds to define one of the passions/symptoms that he will attempt to cure, namely *oiêsis*.[14] The term means self-conceit, but it is used in a complex way.[15] On the face of it, *oiêsis* denotes the deep-seated feeling of intellectual and cultural superiority that Greek ideals and education could inculcate in people who—on account of their history—were thoroughly imbued in them. *Oiêsis* is not only a disease of the soul (*pathos*), it is an *emotion* with cognitive content greater than other emotions, if only because of its association with a nexus of judgments. In other words, it is a complex cognitive disposition.[16] Furthermore, it is a cultural attitude that prompts some (on Theodoret's admission) to resist the new way of life that Christianity enjoins.

[14] In a similar manner a dogmatist's *oiêsis* needs to be cured by the skeptic: "Because of his love of humanity the skeptic wishes to cure by argument [ἰᾶσθαι λόγῳ], so far as he can, the conceit and precipitancy of the dogmatists. Accordingly, just as the doctors who treat physical symptoms [σωματικῶν παθῶν] have remedies that differ in strength and prescribe the severe ones for people with severe symptoms and milder ones for those mildly affected, so too the skeptic sets forth arguments differing in strength. And in the case of those who are severely afflicted with precipitancy he employs arguments that are weighty and capable of vigorously disposing of the dogmatists' symptom of conceit [τὸ τῆς οἰήσεως τῶν δογματικῶν πάθος], but in the case of those who have this symptom in a superficial and easily curable way, and are capable of being restored to health by milder persuasion, he uses milder arguments. Hence the person motivated by skepticism does not hesitate to advance at one time arguments that are weighty in persuasiveness and at another time such as even appear weak—he does this purposely, on the assumption that many times the latter suffice for accomplishing his task" (Sextus Empiricus *Outlines of Pyrrhonism* 3.279, trans. Mates 1996).

[15] Instead of discussing the *pathê* one by one Theodoret also employs such terms as *alazoneia*, *tûphos*, *agnoia*, *lobê*, *nosos*, and he is far from consistent in his use of these terms. However, these emotions are interconnected, especially *alazoneia* and *tûphos*, and they form a complex system. For the use of these terms by the church fathers, see Adnès 1982:907–933 and Prokopé and Kehl 1989:795–858. *Tûphos* is a medical term used to describe a kind of fever accompanied by stupor (LSJ). On its use by various Greek and Christian authors, see Courcelle 1975:245–288 and Decleva Caizzi 1980:53–66.

[16] *Oiêsis* is cognate with the verb *oiomai* 'to think, to have an opinion that could be potentially false or wrong'. *Oiêsis* is employed with an eye to the subjective and potentially illusory knowledge that people affected by it can possess. A few lines below in the same passage, Theodoret provides an excerpt from Timon of Phlius (320–230 BCE) that supports precisely this reading: "Οὐ μόνον ἄρα ἡμεῖς τὸ τῆς οἰήσεως ἐπιπροσθεῖν ὑμῖν εἰρήκαμεν πάθος· πάλαι γὰρ καὶ πρόπαλαι ταύτην ὁ Τίμων τῶν ὑμετέρων φιλοσόφων τὴν κατηγορίαν πεποίηται. Ἄλλο δέ ἐστιν εἰδέναι, καὶ ἄλλο τὸ οἴεσθαι εἰδέναι, μηδὲν ἐπιστάμενον. Πολλῷ γάρ τινι διαφέρουσιν, ὦ φιλότης, ἀλλήλοιν ἀλήθεια καὶ στοχασμὸς ἀληθείας· ὁ μὲν γὰρ στοχασμὸς καὶ διαμαρτίας ἔχει πολλάς, ἡ δὲ ἀλήθεια ἐκπαιδεύειν οὐδὲν ἐναντίον ἀνέχεται. Τοιγαροῦν ἄλλως τις ἀληθείας πέρι τεκμαιρόμενος λέγει, καὶ ἄλλως αὐτὴ ἑαυτὴν ἑρμηνεύει·" ("We are not the only ones who said that self-conceit is the malady which has blinded you, since long, long ago Timon has made the same complaint against your philosophers: To know is one thing; but to think that you know when you know nothing is another. There is a great difference, my friend, between truth and mere conjecture. For conjecture admits of many errors, but truth does not tolerate any contradictory teaching. That is why the language of the person making conjectures about truth is one thing, while the appearance under which truth is interpreted is something else." *Therapeutikê* 2.21–22).

But how exactly does *oiêsis affect* people? In *Therapeutikê* 2.4–5 Theodoret gives a description of the symptoms:

Τίς ἀπολογίας ὑπολείπεται λόγος τοῖς νῦν μεσημβρίᾳ τυφλώττουσι καὶ τοὺς ὀφθαλμοὺς μύουσιν, ἵνα μὴ τοῦ φωτὸς ἀπολαύσωσιν;οὐκ ἐᾷ δὲ αὐτοὺς τὴν ἀχλὺν ἀποσκεδάσαι τῶν ὀφθαλμῶν τὸ τῆς οἰήσεως πάθος. Πάντων γὰρ ἄμεινον εἰδέναι νομίζουσι τὴν ἀλήθειαν, ἐπειδὴ τοῖς τῶν ἐλλογίμων ἀνδρῶν μαθήμασιν ἐνετράφησαν . . . Οὐδὲ μὴν ἐκεῖνο ξυνορῶσιν, ὡς τῆς ἀληθείας οὐ πάντως ἡ εὐγλωττία διδάσκαλος.

Therapeutikê 2.5

What defense, he says, remains for these people who at midday are still blind and press their eyes shut in order not to take advantage of the light? The disease of self-conceit [τὸ τῆς οἰήσεως πάθος] will not let them remove the mist [ἀχλὺν ἀποσκεδάσαι] from their eyes. They think they knew the truth better than all men since they were nurtured in the learning of their famous men . . . Neither do they understand that beauty of language is not the perfect teacher of truth.

And in a passage in *On Providence* he uses a similar analogy to describe the resistance of the pagans to the truth of Christianity:

Καὶ οὗτοι δὲ ὁμοίως ἐκείνοις , πᾶσι τοῖς ὁρωμένοις καὶ γινομένοις ἐπιμέμφονται. Ἀλλ᾽ ἐκείνοις μὲν ἡ νόσος παρὰ γνώμην συμβαίνει, καὶ ἀλγυνόμενοι λίαν τῶν σιτίων ἀπέχονται, καὶ μεταλαβεῖν ποθοῦντες ὑπὸ τῆς νόσου κωλύονται· τούτοις δὲ ἑκούσια καὶ αὐθαίρετα πολεμεῖ τὰ πάθη, καὶ τὸ δυσάρεστον ἔχουσιν, οὐ περὶ σιτία καὶ ὄψα, ἀλλὰ περὶ πάντα τὰ σοφῶς καὶ δικαίως ὑπὸ τῆς θείας προμηθείας οἰκονομούμενα.

PG 83:668

Those who blame everything they see and experience resemble them [i.e. sick men]. The sick, however, are smitten by disease against their will and they refuse food because of grievous pain: they desire to eat, but are hindered by illness. The others are preyed on by sufferings [πάθη] that are voluntary and self-chosen; they are difficult, not in matters of food and drink, but in everything that is arranged by the wisdom and justice of the divine providence.[17]

---

[17] Trans. Halton 1988.

37

These descriptions stress an important feature that inheres in Theodoret's depiction of the pagan reaction to Christianity. Pagan beliefs are presented as a psycho-somatic disease that has a direct impact on the people whom it afflicts. The use of the image of the mist in particular is employed to highlight the symptoms of the disease.[18] The emphasis on the physicality of what is presented as a moral and intellectual failing is foundational in Theodoret's apologetics against pagans.

Some passages present this disease as an outright mental crippling (ἀναπηρία). The language of disease then allows Theodoret to illustrate vividly how deeply pagan preconceptions (προλήψεις)[19] affect human nature and, consequently, how deep the intended therapy is meant to reach. In a passage in *On Providence* he addresses his audience in these words:

Οἱ μὲν εὖ μάλα πως τὸ σῶμα διακείμενοι, τῆς ἀπὸ τῶν ἰατρῶν θεραπείας οὐ δέονται· ἀκραιφνὴς γὰρ ὑγεία τῆς τῶν φαρμάκων ἐπικουρίας οὐκ ἐνδεής· οἱ δ' ὑπὸ νόσου πολεμούμενοι, καλεῖν εἰώθασι τοὺς ἰατροὺς εἰς βοήθειαν, καὶ τοῖς ὅπλοις τῆς τέχνης κατὰ τῶν παθῶν χρώμενοι συνεργοῖς, ὥσπερ τινὰς πολεμίους ἐκ τῶν σωμάτων διώκειν ἐπιχειροῦσιν. Ἰατρικὴ γὰρ τέχνη σωμάτων ἐπίκουρος, καὶ παθῶν ἐπίβουλος. Καὶ τὰς ψυχὰς τοίνυν οἱ μὲν ἐρρωμένας ἔχοντες, καὶ τῇ τῆς εὐσεβείας ὑγεία λαμπρυνομένας, τῶν διδασκαλικῶν φαρμάκων οὐ χρήζουσιν· οἱ δὲ προλήψει πονηρᾷ κατεχόμενοι, καὶ τῶν βδελυρῶν δογμάτων τὴν νόσον δεξάμενοι, καὶ τῷ χρόνῳ τὴν διάθεσιν ἕξιν

---

18 On the use of this metaphor by Christian authors as polemic against paganism, see Agosti 2011:33–50.

19 It is worth noting that for Theodoret pagan religion is based on unreflective preconceptions that constitute the criteria of religious truth. The term that Theodoret twice employs in the *Therapeutikê* is πρόληψις, a technical term that had an important background in Epicurean epistemology. In both passages the seat of προλήψεις is the soul. This is where Theodoret's arguments (*pharmaka*) are applied and are expected to effect the cure. The role of these preconceptions is complex, but for our discussion it is important to stress the fact that, along with feelings and perceptions, they are the prerequisites for any investigation and principles beyond proof that provide the basis for the formation of judgments or beliefs. Apologetics, ethics, and logic are thus inextricably linked. As a result, preconceptions play an important cognitive role. For a detailed discussion of the term πρόληψις, see Asmis 1999:260–294. From *Therapeutikê* 9.73.1: "Ἐπειδὴ τοίνυν καὶ τῶν νόμων καὶ τῶν νομοθετῶν κατάδηλον ἐκ ξυγκρίσεως γεγένηται τὸ διάφορον, καὶ τὰ μὲν ὤφθη λογισμῶν ἀνθρωπίνων εὑρήματα, τὰ δὲ θεόσδοτα καὶ σωτήρια, δέξασθε, ὦ ἄνδρες, τὰ θεσπέσια δῶρα καὶ τὸν μεγαλόδωρον καὶ φιλόδωρον μὴ ἀτιμάσητε χορηγόν. Εἴσεσθε δὲ αὐτῶν τὸ θεοπρεπὲς ἀκριβέστερον, εἰ τούτοις ἐντύχητε τὴν πονηρὰν τῶν ψυχῶν ἐξελάσαντες πρόληψιν" ("Since the difference has now been clearly demonstrated between both the laws and the legislators [by the preceding comparative study]—on the one hand, those that are the products of human device have been shown and, on the other, those that are heavenly, salutary products—receive, my friends, the divine gifts and do not dishonor the One who has donated to us this great and loving largess. And you will recognize their divine dimensions more accurately if you encounter them after expelling wretched prejudice from your souls").

ἐργασάμενοι, πολλῶν μὲν δέονται καθαρτηρίων, τὴν μοχθηρὰν ἐκείνην ὕλην ἀναμοχλεῦσαι δυναμένων, καὶ τὰς ψυχὰς καθαρὰς ἀποφῆναι· πολλῶν δὲ φαρμάκων, τοὺς γεννητικοὺς ἐκείνης πόρους τῷ δραστηρίῳ κλώντων τε καὶ φραττόντων, καὶ τὰς πονηρὰς ὠδῖνας παυόντων. Ἐπειδὴ τοίνυν παγχάλεπος καὶ δυστράπελος τῶν τὴν κτίσιν προνοίας ἀποστερεῖν ἐπιχειρούντων ἡ νόσος, δύο μὲν αὐτοῖς ἤδη φάρμακα προηνέγκαμεν, ἐκ τῶν τῆς κτίσεως μορίων ταῦτα κεράσαντες· ἵνα δὲ πρόρριζον ἀνασπάσωμεν τὴν νόσον, καὶ τέλεον αὐτοὺς τῆς χαλεπῆς ἀπαλλάξωμεν ἀρρωστίας, καὶ τρίτον αὐτοῖς κατασκευάσαι τε καὶ προσενεγκεῖν πειρασόμεθα.

PG 83:588

Those who indeed are sound in body are in no need of the physicians' care. Unimpaired health does not need the assistance of drugs. But those who are attacked by disease are accustomed to call on the assistance of doctors, and avail themselves of the help of the weapons of medical science against sufferings as if they were trying to repel enemies from the human body. For medical skill protects bodies and wars on diseases. Likewise, those who are sound in soul [τὰς ψυχὰς τοίνυν οἱ μὲν ἐρρωμένας ἔχοντες] and enjoy a healthy spiritual life do not need doctrinal remedies. Those, however, who are hidebound by some wretched preconception [προλήψει πονηρᾷ κατεχόμενοι] and are victims of loathsome doctrines, having contracted the disease over a period, are in need of many purgations potent to their soul. They also need many remedies capable by their action of closing and blocking up its productive pores, and of putting an end to the wretched sufferings. Dangerous, indeed, and difficult to deal with is the disease of those who try to deprive creation of Providence. Accordingly, we have already applied two treatments to them compounded from the elements of creation. To eradicate the disease and rid them completely of this troublesome malady, let us try to apply a third preparation for them. [20]

The passage illustrates Theodoret's ability to diagnose in startlingly medical/philosophical terms the symptoms of pagan beliefs and to describe the methods by which they cause disease in the soul. In tune with the general approach that we have seen, two kinds of therapy are applied: the replacement of erroneous judgments by those that are morally correct and the assuaging of physical excess as a precondition for psychosomatic health.

[20] Trans. Halton 1988.

The use of Greek philosophical terminology (particularly Stoic and Epicurean) shows how Theodoret plays off of the intellectual background of the theory of emotions in order to articulate his apologetics.[21] What he shares with the Greek philosophical tradition is the attribution of a cognitive aspect to the emotions.[22] Their disorder causes errors in judgment, which, according to the Stoics, calls for emotional extirpation. Caution must be taken, though, against assimilating Theodoret's approach too closely to any of the above schools, since he makes an eclectic use of them. By his time their teachings have been filtered down and sufficiently interwoven, making it difficult to argue for the reception of a distinctive, singular tradition that descends directly from the Peripatetic, Stoic, or Epicurean school.[23]

How do emotions (πάθη) operate in Theodoret's view? In *Therapeutikê* 5.76–77.1f., he discusses their role, accepting the immortality of the soul and the rule of its rational faculty over the emotions:

μάθετε θείων δογμάτων ἀλήθειαν, σώματος θείαν διάπλασιν, <u>ψυχῆς φύσιν ἀθάνατον καὶ τὸ ταύτης λογικὸν ἡγούμενον τῶν παθῶν καὶ τὰ πάθη ἀναγκαῖα τῇ φύσει καὶ χρήσιμα</u>. Ἥ τε γὰρ ἐπιθυμία προυργιαιτάτη, καὶ ὁ θυμὸς ὡσαύτως, ὁ ταύτης ἀντίπαλος. Δι' ἐκείνην μὲν γὰρ καὶ τῶν θείων ὀριγνώμεθα καὶ τῶν ὁρωμένων ὑπερορῶντες τὰ νοητὰ φανταζόμεθα καὶ ἐπὶ γῆς βαδίζοντες τὸν ἐν οὐρανοῖς δεσπότην ἰδεῖν ἱμειρόμεθα καὶ ἀρετῆς ἐφιέμεθα, καὶ μέντοι καὶ διαζῶμεν καὶ ἐδωδῆς μεταλαγχάνομεν καὶ ποτῶν, καὶ πρὸς τούτοις αὔξεται διὰ τῆς ἐννόμου παιδοποιΐας τὸ γένος.

... learn the truth of the divine teachings: the body's formation by God, the immortal nature of the soul, the reasonable part of which controls the passions, which also have a necessary and useful function to play

---

[21] On the theory of emotions in Aristotle, see Cooper 1999:406–423 and Fortenbaugh 1975. On the theory of emotions in Stoicism, see Brenan 1998:21–70, Frede 1986:93–112, Vögtle 1962, and Hengelbrock 1971.

[22] In the words of Nussbaum 1994: ". . . there is in Greek thought about emotions, from Plato and Aristotle straight on through Epicurus, an agreement that the emotions are not simply blind surges of affect, stirrings or sensations that are identified, and distinguished from one another, by their felt quality alone. Unlike appetites such as thirst and hunger, they have an important cognitive element: they embody ways of interpreting the world. The feelings that go with the experience of emotion are hooked up with and rest upon beliefs or judgments that are their basis or ground, in such a way that the emotion as a whole can appropriately be evaluated as true and false, also as rational and irrational, according to our evaluation of the grounding belief. Since the belief is the ground of the feeling, the feeling, and therefore the emotion as a whole, can be modified as a modification of belief" (369). The literature on this topic is enormous and reflects a very nuanced understanding of its role in Greek philosophy and literature. See Pigeaud 1981, Rodis-Lewis 1970, and Dörrie 1956:3–42.

[23] Borgeaud 2007:189–222, esp. Dillon's comments in the discussion (226–227).

in human nature. The concupiscible part, for instance, has a most important role, as has the irascible, its sparring partner. Thanks to the first we desire eternal things and look down on visible things; thus we imagine the intelligibles and, while still walking this earth, we long to see our Master in the heavens and aspire after virtue. And during our mortal life we have our share of food and drink, and besides these the human race is multiplied by the legitimate procreation.

He construes the role of emotions in terms of antithetical pairs where each holds its opposite in check. Take, for example, desire. It is by means of its correct assignment that people approach God, or perform the important task of procreation. To better describe the *modus operandi* of emotions Theodoret employs an image reminiscent of the platonic charioteer:[24]

Ὁ δέ γε θυμὸς ξυνεργὸς ἐδόθη τῷ λογισμῷ, ἵνα τῆς ἐπιθυμίας κωλύῃ τὴν ἀμετρίαν. Ἐπειδὴ γὰρ καὶ πέρα τῶν κειμένων ὅρων ᾄττειν ἐπιχειρεῖ, ξυνέζευξεν αὐτῇ οἷόν τινα πῶλον τὸν θυμὸν ὁ ποιητὴς ἀνθέλκοντα, ὅταν γε ἐκείνη πέρα τῆς χρείας προβαίνειν βιάζηται. Καὶ καθάπερ ἀντίπαλον μὲν τῷ ψυχρῷ τὸ θερμόν, κεραννύμενα δὲ ἀλλήλοις κρᾶσιν ἀρίστην ἐργάζεται, οὕτως ἡ ἐπιθυμία καὶ ὁ θυμός, ἀλλήλοις κεραννύμενα καὶ ὑπ' ἀλλήλων κολαζόμενα, τῆς ἀρετῆς τὴν ἀρίστην ἀπεργάζεται κρᾶσιν. Ἔχει δὲ τῶν δρωμένων τὸ κράτος ὁ λογισμός, ὥστε καὶ ταύτην ἐπέχειν καὶ τοῦτον αὖ νύττειν, ἢ τοῦτόν γε ἄγχειν καὶ διεγείρειν ἐκείνην. Καὶ γὰρ ἡ ἐπιθυμία τοῦ θυμοῦ παύει τὴν ἀμετρίαν, καὶ ὁ θυμὸς αὖ πάλιν κολάζει τῆς ἐπιθυμίας τὴν ἀπληστίαν. Ταῦτα μὲν οὖν ἀποτελεῖται, τοῦ λογισμοῦ τὰς ἡνίας ἐπιστημόνως κατέχοντος· ἢν δὲ οὗτος, ἢ τῷ χαλαρῷ καὶ λείῳ τῆς ἐπιθυμίας καταθελχθεὶς ἢ τῷ θυμῷ ᾄττοντι παρὰ καιρὸν ξυνεξορμήσας, χαυνοτέρας ἢ προσῆκε τὰς ἡνίας ἐάσῃ, οἱ μὲν ἀτάκτως καθάπερ ἵπποι θέουσιν ἐνδακόντες τὸν χαλινόν, ὁ δὲ συρόμενος φέρεται, καταγέλαστός τε καὶ ἐπονείδιστος τοῖς ὁρῶσι γινόμενος. Ταύτῃ τοι καὶ δίκας εἰσπράττεται, ὡς ἐθελοντὴς ὑπομείνας τὸ πάθος.

Therapeutikê 5.78–79

---

[24] Theodoret's contemporary Isidore of Peluse uses the image of the charioteer to illustrate the effects of balanced and imbalanced passions thus: "ὁ ὑπὸ τῶν ἀνελευθέρων τῆς σαρκὸς παθῶν ἐξανδραποδισθεὶς (ἵνα καὶ παχυτέρῳ χρήσωμαι παραδείγματι), ἔοικεν ἡνιόχῳ, ἐκπεπτωκότι μὲν τοῦ ἅρματος, συρομένῳ δὲ ὑπὸ τῶν ἡνιῶν, τῶν μὴ ἀπολυουσῶν αὐτόν, ἀλλὰ συμπλεκομένων αὐτῷ, δίκην τῆς ῥαθυμίας ἀπαιτουμένῳ. Ἔνθα δὴ τῶν κατὰ φύσιν τἀναντία ἐκβαίνει. Δέον γὰρ τὸ ἅρμα ὑπὸ τῆς τέχνης τοῦ ἡνιόχου ἄγεσθαι καλῶς, ὁ ἡνίοχος ὑπὸ τῶν ἵππων σύρεται κακῶς. Τῆς γὰρ κατὰ φύσιν ἡγεμονίας ἀνατροπή, ἡ παρὰ φύσιν παρατροπή, διὸ χρὴ τὸν νοῦν κυβερνᾶν τὸ σῶμα." Ep. 384, PG 78:1557.

The irascible power has been given as a collaborator of reason, in order to check the immoderate desires. Since the latter tries to bound beyond the set limits, the Creator yoked it to the concupiscence as a colt to hold it back when it forces its way beyond its bounds. Just as heat is the opposite of cold but mixed they produce the best mixture, so the concupiscence and the irascible mixed with one another and checked by each other produce the best temper (*krasin*) of virtue. Reason maintains control over acts so that it can restrain the concupiscible and incite the irascible, or rather throttle the latter and urge on the former. For the concupiscible checks the excesses of the irascible, and the irascible chastises the greediness of the concupiscible. All this is done perfectly if reason skillfully holds on to the reins. But if reason, either through being enchanted by the slack and smooth of the concupiscible or if it is urged on in an untimely fashion by the goading of the irascible, allowing the reins to be slacker than is fitting, the passions, like horses, gallop in a disorderly fashion, champing the bit, and reason, [like] the rider, is dragged along and becomes an object of ridicule and censure to the spectators. For this he is punished because he voluntarily endured the passion.

The function, then, of the emotions is equated with natural and inherent psychological states. Human intellect rules over *thûmos* and *epithumia*, which produce a balance that constitutes virtue (ἀρετή). *Pathê* become diseases when they throw the soul into violent motion that interferes with judgment. Theodoret expresses the ideal harmonization of these mental dispositions in a passage in *On Providence*, a polemic treatise against the pagan notion of divine providence. In an analysis of how virtues operate he says:

Οὐκοῦν φρόνησις μὲν ἔστι τοῦ ἐν ἡμῖν λογικοῦ ἡ ἐγρήγορσις, ὥσπερ ἀμέλει παραφροσύνη καὶ ἀφροσύνη πάλιν, ἡ τούτου μέθη ἐκ τῶν παθῶν τικτομένη, καὶ οἷόν τις νεφέλη γενομένη, καὶ πυκνουμένη, καὶ ἐπιπροσθοῦσα, καὶ συνορᾶν αὐτὸν οὐκ ἐῶσα τὸ δέον. <u>Τοῦ λογικοῦ τοιγαροῦν ἡ ὑγεία φρόνησις ὀνομάζεται. Καὶ σωφροσύνην δὲ πάλιν προσαγορεύομεν, τὴν τῶν παθῶν ἐλευθερίαν.</u> Σῶον γὰρ πάλιν καὶ ἄρτιον τοῦ λογικοῦ τὸ φρόνημα κεκτημένου, χαλᾷ μὲν τὰ πάθη, καὶ ὑπορρεῖ, καὶ σκεδάννυται, καὶ τὸ φλεγμαῖνον αὐτῶν διαλύεται, φέρεται δὲ εὐτάκτως ἐπὶ τῶν ἵππων ὁ ἡνίοχος νοῦς. <u>Τὴν τῶν παθῶν τοίνυν εὐταξίαν, καὶ τοῦ ἡνιόχου τὴν ὑγείαν, σωφροσύνην ὀνομάζομεν.</u> Ἀνδρίαν δὲ καλοῦμεν, τὴν δικαίαν τοῦ θυμοειδοῦς κίνησιν· ὥσπερ αὖ πάλιν θρασύτητα, τὴν ἄδικόν τε καὶ ἄτακτον. Δικαιοσύνην δέ, τὴν ὀρθὴν τῆς ψυχῆς ἡγεμονίαν, καὶ τῶν ὑπηκόων παθῶν τὴν συμμετρίαν. Τοῦ γὰρ ἐπιθυμητικοῦ καὶ θυμοειδοῦς ἡ πρὸς τὸ λογικὸν εὐαρμοστία, καὶ ἡ πρὸς ἄλληλα εὐκρασία, τὴν τῆς δικαιοσύνης ἡμῖν πραγματεύεται κτῆσιν.

PG 83:645–648

Prudence [φρόνησις] is an innate watchfulness of reason, as opposed to folly [παραφροσύνη] and sensuality [ἀφροσύνη] which is reason intoxicated by passion, clouded, darkened, obscured, and prevented from observing what it should. Sound reasoning, then, is called prudence. We define temperance as freedom from the domination of the passions. For when intellect was and is possessed of sound and perfect wisdom, the passions abate, recede and subside, cool down, and the intellect rides securely in the saddle. This ordering of the passions [εὐταξίαν] and the soundness of the ruling mental faculty we call temperance [σωφροσύνην]. Fortitude [ἀνδρίαν] we define as the due movement of passion; on the other hand, unlawful and uncontrolled passion is called audacity. Justice is the right ordering of the soul and the due subordination of the passions. For the possession of justice results to us when concupiscence and anger are harmonized with reason and there is no conflict between them.[25]

---

[25] The passage betrays a familiarity with Greek philosophical understandings of affective order and disorder. There are indications that, for instance, the Stoic philosopher Zeno held a similar view on the analogy between the health of the body and the soul that is cast in medical terms: "Ὥσπερ γὰρ τὴν τοῦ σώματος ὑγίειαν εὐκρασίαν εἶναι τῶν ἐν τῷ σώματι θερμῶν καὶ ψυχρῶν καὶ ξηρῶν καὶ ὑγρῶν, οὕτω καὶ τὴν τῆς ψυχῆς ὑγίειαν εὐκρασίαν εἶναι τῶν ἐν τῇ ψυχῇ δογμάτων. Καὶ ὁμοίως ὥσπερ ἰσχὺς τοῦ σώματος τόνος ἐστὶν ἱκανὸς ἐν νεύροις, οὕτω καὶ ἡ τῆς ψυχῆς ἰσχὺς τόνος ἐστὶν ἱκανὸς ἐν τῷ κρίνειν καὶ πράττειν ἢ μή. Ὥσπερ τε τὸ κάλλος τοῦ σώματός ἐστι συμμετρία τῶν μελῶν καθεστώτων αὐτῷ πρὸς ἄλληλά τε καὶ πρὸς τὸ ὅλον, οὕτω καὶ τὸ τῆς ψυχῆς κάλλος ἐστὶ συμμετρία τοῦ λόγου καὶ τῶν μερῶν αὐτοῦ πρὸς <τὸ> ὅλον τε αὐτῆς καὶ πρὸς ἄλληλα" (Stobaeus 2.7.5).

In a different passage in Compendium of Heretical Falsehoods, PG 83:484–488, Theodoret likens ἀρετή with the right medicine and ἀμετρία 'disproportion' with λώβη 'damage' (usually with medical overtones): "Εὑρίσκομεν δὲ ὅμως πολλοὺς διὰ τούτων κατωρθωκότας τὴν ἀρετήν. Οὔτε οὖν κακὸν τὸ ἀγαθοῦ γιγνόμενον ὄργανον, οὔτ' αὖ πάλιν ἀγαθὸν τὸ ἐργαλεῖον ἑτέρῳ πρὸς πονηρίαν γιγνόμενον. Τὴν μέσην τοίνυν ἔχει τάξιν, καθάπερ τὰ φάρμακα. Καὶ γὰρ τὸ ὄπιον, καὶ τὸ κώνειον, εἰ ἄριστα κριθείη παρὰ τῶν ἰατρῶν, ἀλεξιφάρμακα γίγνεται· εἰ δὲ παρὰ τὸν τῆς τέχνης ληφθῇ λόγον, δηλητήρια καὶ ὀλέθρια. Ἔστι δὲ ὅτε ἄρτος καὶ οἶνος νόσον τοῖς χρωμένοις ἐπάγουσι· λώβην γὰρ ἡ ἀμετρία γεννᾷ. Οὕτω δὴ καὶ τὴν εὐπραξίαν, καὶ τὴν δυσπραγίαν, οἱ μὲν σοφῶς κυβερνῶντες σωτήρια κατασκευάζουσι φάρμακα· οἱ δὲ ἀφρόνως καὶ ἀσυνέτως, ἀφορμὰς ὀλέθρου διὰ τούτων εἰσδέχονται. Ταῦτα μὲν οὖν, καὶ ὅσα τούτοις προσόμοια, εὐκαρπία γῆς, καὶ ἀκαρπία, εὐπλοία τε καὶ ναυαγία, τῆς θείας προνοίας ἐξήρτηται. Διὸ δὴ στέργειν ἅπαντα χρὴ τὰ παρ' αὐτῆς γιγνόμενα, καὶ μὴ πολυπραγμονεῖν τὰς αἰτίας· ἀνέφικτος γὰρ τῶν θείων

Sôphrosunê 'prudence' then, is the ideal state whereby passions are well-ordered, and justice is the proper rule of the soul over the symmetrically ordered emotions.[26]

An important feature in Theodoret's approach is that *logoi* have a therapeutic effect[27] and are accordingly used as an *alexipharmakos therapeia*. But how exactly do they function in the procedure that he follows? In *Therapeutikê* 1.127–128 he describes his approach in the following way:

Καὶ ὥσπερ οἱ τὰ σώματα θεραπεύοντες ἐκ τῶν ἰοβόλων θηρίων ὀνησιφόρα κατασκευάζουσι φάρμακα, καὶ τῶν ἐχιδνῶν τὰ μὲν ἀποβάλλοντες, τὰ δὲ ἕψοντες, πολλὰς διὰ τούτων ἐξελαύνουσι νόσους, <u>οὕτως καὶ ἡμεῖς,</u> <u>τὰ τῶν ὑμετέρων ποιητῶν καὶ ξυγγραφέων καὶ φιλοσόφων πονήματα</u> <u>μεταχειρισάμενοι, τὰ μὲν ὡς δηλητήρια καταλείπομεν, τὰ δὲ τῇ τῆς</u> <u>διδασκαλίας ἐπιστήμῃ διασκευάσαντες, ἀλεξιφάρμακον ὑμῖν θεραπείαν</u>

πηδαλίων ὁ λόγος· ἐπιμελεῖσθαι δὲ τῶν ἐφ' ἡμῖν, καὶ τὴν μὲν κακίαν πάμπαν ἀποσκευάζεσθαι, εἰσοικίζεσθαι δὲ τὴν ἀρετήν, καὶ τοῖς ταύτης μορίοις φαιδρύνεσθαι· καὶ καθάπερ αἱ φιλόκοσμοι γυναῖκες κομμωτικῇ τέχνῃ τὸ σῶμα λαμπρύνουσιν, <u>οὕτω τῆς ψυχῆς καλλωπίζειν τὴν ὥραν τοῖς</u> <u>τῆς σωφροσύνης, καὶ δικαιοσύνης, καὶ ἀνδρείας, καὶ φρονήσεως ἄνθεσιν.</u> Ἐφ' ἡμῖν γὰρ τούτων ἡ κτῆσις" (". . . equally we find many who through these have accomplished virtue. Therefore, the good instrument cannot become evil, neither again can the good instrument become for someone else evil. So then, it has a middle order just as medicine. For opium and hemlock, if it be judged by the physicians, becomes an antidote, but it be taken apart from the reasoning of [physician's] art, [is] destructive and deadly. Sometimes bread and wine bring sickness to those who use [them]. For intemperate usage produces damage. So indeed some who govern wisely prepare the saving medicine both fortunate and misfortunate. But those [who govern] foolishly and stupidly admit the means of destruction through these things. Therefore, these things, and whatever resemble these things, the fruitfulness and the unfruitfulness of the earth, both a fair voyage and a shipwreck, hang upon divine providence. Wherefore it is necessary to be satisfied with all things that happen because of this, and not to investigate the causes. Because the Word of the divine rudders is beyond understanding.

But [it is necessary] to care about [these] things [that happen] to us, and, on the one hand, wholly to get rid of evil, and, on the other, to give entrance to virtue and to brighten up with the parts of this. Just as women who love worldly things take pride in the body with the beautification art, so also we wisely devote [ourselves] to beautify, the season of the soul with the flowers of self-control, righteousness, and fortitude. For the acquiring of these things is up to us," trans. Cope).

26 The term is reminiscent of Aristotle's notion of *sôphrosunê* and relevant terms like *phronêsis*. See Aubenque 1963. For a history of the term *sôphrosunê* and a thorough discussion of its diachronic significance, see North 1966a. In this connection it is interesting to mention Theodoret's remark in his commentary to St. Paul's epistles, where he defines *sôphrosunê* as health of the mind in contrast to *huperifaneia* which is defined as disease of the mind: "Σωφροσύνην δὲ ἐνταῦθα τὴν τῶν φρενῶν ὑγείαν ἐκάλεσε, διδάσκων ὡς ἡ ὑπερηφάνεια νόσος φρενῶν" ("Now, he called a healthy mind sober judgment here to bring out that haughtiness is a disease of the mind," *Commentary on the Fourteen Epistles of St. Paul*, PG 82:188, trans. Hill).

27 There are many stages in the development of this tradition. For the therapeutic effect of *logoi* in Greek philosophy, see Laín Entralgo 1970, Thome 1995, Voelke 1993, esp. chapters 5 and 7, Nussbaum 1986:31–74, and Von Staden 2002:803–822.

προσφέρομεν· καὶ οὓς ἀντιπάλους ἡμῶν ὑπειλήφατε, τούτους τῶν ἡμετέρων λόγων ἀποφαίνομεν ξυνηγόρους καὶ τῆς πίστεως δείκνυμεν διδασκάλους. Οὕτω, ξὺν Θεῷ φάναι, καὶ τὴν ἄλλην ὑμῖν διδασκαλίαν προσοίσομεν.

And just as those who cure the body prepare effective remedies from the venom of wild beasts, even from vipers; they first throw away some parts and boil the rest, and with this they cure many sicknesses. So we take the works of your poets, historians and philosophers. Some parts we reject as dangerous and harmful; other parts we inject with the knowledge of our teaching and offer you these as a preventive treatment. And even those whom you regard as our enemies we show you that they champion our teachings and we make you see that even they teach you the faith. In this way, with God's help, we will present to you the rest of our teaching. [28]

Theodoret's elaborate analogy outlines an approach that is twofold: he seeks to criticize but also to instruct. These two principles permeate the *Therapeutikê*. His critique and refutation of pagan religion is internal. It appeals throughout the work to the reader's own cherished religious and cultural loyalties. And yet it leads to conclusions that very few, if any, would have accepted, at least initially. According to his stated aims, Theodoret sets out to refute false beliefs starting from the convictions of Christianity's opponents. This kind of "homeopathic" therapy is based on the extensive use of opinions—understood as proofs—which are consonant with Christian teaching. He employs testimonies (*martyriai*) taken from Greek philosophers, poets, et al. These proofs, taken from their original context, act as *pharmaka* 'medicine': in this case, prestigious opinions (δόξαι) that are used to refute other opinions hostile to Christianity.[29] Theodoret appropriates these *doxai* and frames them to reflect his own interpretations. They

---

[28] The point is reiterated in several passages throughout the *Therapeutikê*, for instance, in the concluding remark of *Therapeutikê* 12.98: "For this reason I undertook this work, and as if by gathering herbs from all over I have prepared for you a wholesome remedy [φάρμακον]."

[29] In a similar vein Theodoret applies the same "therapeutic" method in the refutation of the heretical views of his interlocutor in the work *Eranistês*. As is his habit in the preface of the work, he exposes the rationale of the *Eranistês*. In *Eranistês* 28.17–21 he refers to the "therapeutic" aim of the treatise: "τρισαθλίαν σφίσιν αὐτοῖς ἐπορίσαντο περιφάνειαν. Καινῶν γὰρ δογμάτων προστάται γενέσθαι ποθήσαντες, ἐκ πολλῶν αἱρέσεων ἠρανίσαντο τὴν ἀσέβειαν καὶ τὴν ὀλέθριον ταύτην συνέθηκαν αἵρεσιν. Ἐγὼ δὲ αὐτοῖς βραχέα διαλεχθῆναι πειράσομαι, καὶ τῆς αὐτῶν χάριν θεραπείας καὶ τῆς τῶν ὑγιαινόντων ἕνεκα προμηθείας." Note here that the causes of the disease are diagnosed as being *perifaneia* 'pride'. Proofs from authoritative fathers of the church are adduced as *pharmaka* suitably adjusted to the needs of the interlocutor with the aim to cure. The *Eranistês* is one more work where Theodoret exhibits an ability to organize in a rigorous, logical way a "therapeutic" discourse. Rational arguments are used in order to refute and persuade.

are carefully selected, applied with specificity and psychological insight, and deployed in such a way as to initiate within the reader a reflection—as rational argument—on the unreflective elements that constitute the pagan underlying belief.

Mastery of external *martyriai* confers on Theodoret's enterprise a greater therapeutic efficiency. These homeopathic[30] arguments/*pharmaka* show that not only has Theodoret not ignored Greek contributions and intuitions, he has a full command and mastery of them with the attendant implication that he knows their intrinsic value well. Instead of imposing his perspective on readers, Theodoret positions himself as helping them to arrive at a balanced and thorough view as opposed to the narrow and partial view of those entrenched in conventional, if cherished, belief systems. Theodoret works systematically through the full range of knowledgeable quotations that address cultural concerns in order to provide a coherent presentation of a Christian view of the world. It is important to stress that the aim at coherence implies, ultimately, rightness of view. If erroneous beliefs can be changed, then the audience may shift from one emotion to another and, with that shift, reform their entire judgment about a given set of circumstances, a premise based on the supposition that beliefs can be created, modified, or taken away by discourse and argument.[31]

Consequently, to grasp how Theodoret conceives of the notion of therapy is to understand in great part how he views the nature and function of rhetoric as well as the nature and function of his apologetic enterprise. If persuasion is the removal or alteration of the wrong emotions—or the fostering of the right emotions—in the audience, then the *Therapeutikê*, with its calculated tone and highly structured character, stands in direct association with Greek rhetorical tradition on the craft of persuasion by appealing to emotions.[32]

Those who are too eagerly and uncritically devoted to Greek *paideia* are constantly referred to in the *protheôria*, as well as in the beginning of the first *dialexis* (among other places), and they form Theodoret's assumed audience.

---

[30] A principle based on Hippocratic medicine; see Müller 1965:225–249. For a similar comment on the "homeopathic" nature of Theodoret's arguments, see Wyss 1959:209.

[31] In the Greek philosophy and rhetorical theory on which Theodoret is drawing, passions are conceived as states or conditions of the soul resulting from what it has experienced. A potent means of inducing or altering these states is *logoi*. Particularly on the rhetorical use of emotions, see Wisse 1992:218–224 and Webb 1997:112–127.

[32] Interestingly enough, Julian, in the letter where he attacks Christians for teaching classical literature, begins thus: "Παιδείαν ὀρθὴν εἶναι νομίζομεν οὐ τὴν ἐν τοῖς ῥήμασιν καὶ τῇ γλώττῃ πολυτελῆ εὐρυθμίαν, ἀλλὰ διάθεσιν ὑγιῆ νοῦν ἐχούσης διανοίας, καὶ ἀληθεῖς δόξας ὑπέρ τε ἀγαθῶν καὶ κακῶν, καλῶν τε καὶ αἰσχρῶν" ("I hold that a proper education results, not in laboriously acquired symmetry of phrases and language, but in a healthy condition of mind that has understanding and true opinions about things good and evil, honorable and base," Ep. 36, trans. Wright [LCL]).

From his comments we can infer that they are committed to the ideas and ways of life that he is refuting and that this commitment forms the basis for their conviction of the superiority of Greek philosophy and culture—intertwined as it is with paganism—over its Christian counterpart.[33]

In a revealing passage Theodoret proceeds to define health and disease:

Ταῦτα δὲ οὐ τηνάλλως ἀδολεσχῶ, ἀλλ' ἀπὸ τῶν ἀνθρωπίνων δεικνύναι τὰ θεῖα πειρώμενος καὶ ἀξιῶν ὑμᾶς, ὦ ἄνδρες, καὶ ἐπ' ἐκείνων τόνδε διατηρῆσαι τὸν ὅρον καὶ ὑγιεῖς μὲν καὶ ἀρτίους ἀποκαλεῖν τοὺς τὴν ἀληθῆ θεολογίαν ἀσπαζομένους, ἣν καὶ ἡ φύσις ἐξ ἀρχῆς παραδέδωκε, καὶ τὰ θεῖα ὕστερον ἐκράτυνε λόγια, ἀναπήρους δ' αὖ προσαγορεύειν μὴ μόνον ἐκείνους, οἳ οὐδένα θεὸν εἶναι νομίζουσιν, ἀλλὰ καὶ τούτους, οἳ εἰς πολλὰ τὸ θεῖον κατεμέρισαν σέβας καὶ τῷ δημιουργῷ τῶν ὅλων τὴν κτίσιν ξυνέταξαν. Οὔκουν μόνοι γε ἄθεοι Διαγόρας ὁ Μιλήσιος καὶ ὁ Κυρηναῖος Θεόδωρος καὶ Εὐήμερος ὁ Τεγεάτης καὶ οἱ τούτοις ἠκολουθηκότες, παντάπασι φάντες μὴ εἶναι θεούς, ὡς ὁ Πλούταρχος ἔφη, ἀλλὰ καὶ Ὅμηρος καὶ Ἡσίοδος καὶ αἱ τῶν φιλοσόφων ξυμμορίαι, παμπόλλους μὲν θεῶν μυθολογήσαντες ὁρμαθούς, ἀνδραποδώδεις δέ τινας καὶ παθῶν ἀνθρωπίνων ἀποφήναντες δούλους.

Therapeutikê 3.3–4

I do not say this for the sake of idle chatter but in an attempt to explain divine matters in human terms, and to beg you, my friends, to preserve on this point this rule: regard as "wholesome" and "sound" [ὑγιεῖς μὲν καὶ ἀρτίους] those who have embraced the true theology—what was given by nature at the beginning of time and confirmed later by the divine oracles—but label as "crippled" [ἀναπήρους], on the other hand, not merely those who deny the existence of God but also those who have divided the worship of the gods into many pieces, and who have placed the Creator and His creation on the same footing. The only atheists are not just Diagoras of Miletus, Theodore of Cyrene, Euhemerus of Tegea, and their devotees, who absolutely deny the existence of gods, as we learn from Plutarch, but also Homer, Hesiod, and the schools of philosophers who in their fables have invented hosts of gods and presented them as totally enslaved to human passions.

It is interesting to note that the criterion for mental health in this context becomes the espousal of the true theology that has existed *ab initio* in nature,

---

33 See Chapter Five.

as opposed to the thinking of those who "divided the divine into many pieces and put the Creator together with the created world" (οἳ εἰς πολλὰ τὸ θεῖον κατεμέρισαν σέβας καὶ τῷ δημιουργῷ τῶν ὅλων τὴν κτίσιν ξυνέταξαν, *Therapeutikê* 3.3).

This illuminates the whole of Theodoret's apologetic approach in the *Therapeutikê*. Pagans are held to be diseased on the basis of the fact that they suffer from emotions that prevent them from acknowledging the true religion, Christianity. Healing the emotions restores the rational faculties of the soul and, by implication, moral reasoning.

In *Dialexis* VII. On the Sacrifices, Theodoret employs the motif of the *Deus medicus*, who administers the laws as *pharmakon* to the Israelites in order to heal them from the disease of the idolatry of the Egyptians:

> Τόδε τὸ φάρμακον ὁ πάνσοφος ἰατρὸς τῇ Αἰγυπτίᾳ προσενήνοχε νόσῳ, θύειν μὲν διὰ τὴν τῶν θυόντων ἀσθένειαν ξυγχωρήσας, τὰ δὲ σεβόμενα παρ' αὐτῶν ἰερατεύειν κελεύσας, ἵνα τῷ θύειν μάθωσι μὴ θεοὺς νομίζειν τὰ ὡς ἱερεῖα θυόμενα.
>
> *Therapeutikê* 7.18–19

> The supremely wise physician [πάνσοφος ἰατρός] found this remedy [φάρμακον] for the Egyptian disease [νόσῳ], namely, to permit them to sacrifice because of their weakness, but ordered them to sacrifice what the Egyptians worshipped in order that by sacrificing these animals they would understand that if they were victims for sacrifice they could not be gods.

Explaining the way God proceeded to cure the disease of idolatry, Theodoret says:

> Δεισιδαίμονας γὰρ αὐτοὺς καὶ γαστριμάργους εἰδώς, πάθει πάθος ἀντέταξε καὶ τῇ δεισιδαιμονίᾳ τὴν γαστριμαργίαν ἀντέστησεν.
>
> *Therapeutikê* 7.20

> Knowing [God] that they [the Israelites] were superstitious and gluttonous, He pitted sickness against sickness [πάθει πάθος] and set superstition against gluttony.

And further:

> Οὐ τοίνυν ἱερείων δεόμενος οὐδὲ κνίσης ὀριγνώμενος, θύειν προσέταξεν
> ὁ Θεός, ἀλλὰ τῶν ἀρρωστούντων θεραπεύων τὰ πάθη. Οὕτω δὴ καὶ τὰ
> τῶν εὐήχων ὀργάνων ἠνέσχετο, οὐ τῇ τούτων ἁρμονίᾳ τερπόμενος,
> ἀλλὰ κατὰ βραχὺ παύων τῶν εἰδώλων τὸν πλάνον.

Therapeutikê 7.21

God enjoined sacrifice not because He needed victims or delighted in
the odor of burning victims, but to heal the ills of the ailing. For the
same reason He put up with melodious instruments, not because He
enjoyed their harmony but to put a quick stop to the error of idolatry.

And concluding the analogy, Theodoret comments:

> Ὡς οὐ δεόμενος θυσιῶν ὁ Θεὸς οὐδὲ καπνῷ καὶ κνίσῃ καὶ τοῖς μουσικοῖς
> ὀργάνοις ἐπιτερπόμενος ταῦτα τελεῖσθαι προσέταξεν, ἀλλὰ τῆς ἐκείνων
> προμηθούμενος ἰατρείας.

Therapeutikê 7.35

God ordered those rites not because He needed sacrifices or delighted
in smoke and smell and musical instruments but to provide for their
healing [ἰατρείας].

This is not the only case where the *Deus medicus* motif is blended with the
broader notion of *therapeia*.[34] The motif was widespread in late antique Christian
writing based on the healing activity of Jesus.[35] Healing constituted one of the
main aspects of Jesus' ministry and one of the main signs of His divinity. Because
of this, the notion of healing became the focal point of an intense debate between
pagans and Christians.[36] Traces of this debate are also present in the *Therapeutikê*:

> Τοῦτο γὰρ δὴ καὶ ὁ Πορφύριος, ἐν οἷς καθ᾽ ἡμῶν ξυνέγραψεν, εἴρηκεν·
> "Νυνὶ δέ" φησι "θαυμάζουσιν, εἰ τοσούτων ἐτῶν κατείληφε νόσος τὴν
> πόλιν, Ἀσκληπιοῦ μὲν ἐπιδημίας καὶ τῶν ἄλλων θεῶν οὐκέτι οὔσης·

---

[34] The theme allows for a considerable variety of applications in Theodoret's work. God, and occa-
sionally Christ, is the healer and the purveyor of *pharmaka*, *Therapeutikê* 7.16.

[35] On this motif and its well-documented pedigree, see Dumeige 1972:115–141 and 1980: 891–901;
Fichtner 1982:1–18. For the importance of this motif in early Christian iconography, see Knipp
1998, Hagen Hein 1974, and, more recently, Dörnemann 2003.

[36] See Ruttimann 1987, Duprez 1970, and Schadewaldt 1967:1755–1761. For the positive attitude of the church fathers towards healing and its relationship to medicine, see Schadewaldt
1965:115–130.

Ἰησοῦ γὰρ τιμωμένου, οὐδεμιᾶς δημοσίας τις θεῶν ὠφελείας ᾔσθετο."
Ταῦτα ὁ πάντων ἡμῖν ἔχθιστος Πορφύριος εἴρηκε, καὶ ἀναφανδὸν
ὡμολόγησεν, ὡς πιστευόμενος ὁ Ἰησοῦς φρούδους ἀπέφηνε τοὺς θεούς,
καὶ μετὰ τὸν σταυρὸν καὶ τὸ σωτήριον πάθος οὐκέτι φενακίζει τοὺς
ἀνθρώπους Ἀσκληπιός, οὐδὲ ἄλλος τις τῶν καλουμένων θεῶν. Ἅπαντα
γὰρ αὐτῶν τὸν ὁρμαθόν, οἷόν τινας νυκτερίδας, τῷ σκότῳ παρέπεμψεν
ἀνατεῖλαν τὸ φῶς.

Therapeutikê 12.96–97

That is exactly what Porphyry said in the writing which he directed
against us: One is astonished today at the fact that for so many years
the city had been the prey of disease when Asclepius and the other
gods were sojourning there, but now that Jesus is held in honor it does
not experience the least public benefit from any of the gods. That is
what Porphyry, our worst enemy, has to say. And he recognized clearly
that once faith in Jesus was established He made all the gods disappear
and after the Cross and His saving passion, neither Asclepius nor any
other of the so-called gods could any longer dupe the people/human
beings. Because the Light has risen and banished the lot of them like
bats to darkness.

Conclusion

Emotions are intrinsic to Theodoret's "therapeutic" enterprise, since his
portrayal of pagan disease is a theoretically based one. His method of employing
medical/philosophical notions to counter those pagan adherents reluctant to
acknowledge the superiority of Christianity has been clearly established.

However, different frames of reference, such as literature, philosophy, and
medicine, can help illuminate more fully what Theodoret attempts to convey.
His use of traditional imagery and Stoic and Platonic vocabulary certainly had
a long pedigree, but its application as a tool in religious conversion displays
striking independence and originality. In contrast to the Greek philosophers,
for whom the cure of the emotions formed only part of a broader investigation toward a moral worldview, Theodoret's view of the cure of the emotions is
central, as it is intimately connected with σωτηρία 'salvation'.

Notions of health and disease become important tools of analysis that enable Theodoret to diagnose the latent, wavering religious loyalties of his audience. They also sharpen the antithesis between Christianity and paganism in a concrete and forceful way by presenting Greek beliefs as the inversion of health.

2

God, Gods, Angels, Heroes, and Demons: Parallel Notions of the Intermediaries

I N *DIALEXEIS* III, VII, AND X, Theodoret sets out to contrast Christianity with Greek religious attitudes concerning the gods, angels, daemons, and the associated phenomena of divination, oracles, and sacrifices. Although these concepts are treated in separate *dialexeis*, each with a distinct thematic emphasis, their interrelatedness is hard to ignore. This accords well with Theodoret's method of structuring his apology in such a way as to create an overlap of interlocking ideas.

In *Dialexis* III. On Angels, Gods, and Demons, Theodoret begins with a systematic analysis of the Greek conceptualization of the gods. He prefaces this analysis with a critique of those Greek philosophers who were atheists.[1] Using a Pauline argument, he attacks pagans for having confused the Creator with his creation, a misconception that is reflected not only in the multiplicity of the gods but also in their nature. Polytheists deified animals and human beings who, according to Theodoret, were not worthy of the honor.

At the same time Theodoret emphatically asserts the impassibility of God.[2] This sets up the crucial contrast between pagan gods and the Christian God, which underlies the *dialexis* and underpins Theodoret's main critique of paganism.[3] In other words, his main argument rests on the opposition of 'passible' versus 'impassible':

---

[1] *Therapeutikê* 3.4–5.

[2] The motif was elaborated by the Stoics and had a long and complex history. It was used by several apologists to discredit the false gods of Greek polytheism. For the history of the idea, see Frohnhofen 1987. For the specific use of this argument made by the apologists, see Pohlenz 1909:128–156, esp. the appendix, "Die Affekte in der christlichen Polemik gegen die Heidengötter."

[3] It is worth noting in this connection that Julian was quick to attack the anthropomorphic features of God in the Bible and to refer to the emotions God experiences to suggest that His nature is passible. In contrast to the passible Biblical God, the god of Plato is impassible "οὐδαμοῦ χαλεπαίνων ὁ θεὸς φαίνεται οὐδὲ ἀγανακτῶν οὐδὲ ὀργιζόμενος οὐδὲ ὀμνύων οὐδ' ἐπ' ἀμφότερα ταχέως ῥέπων [. . .], ὡς ὁ Μωυσῆς φησιν ἐπὶ τοῦ Φινεές" (*Against the Galileans* fr. 33, 3–5). For a

Created objects are not the same as the Creator, nor is their grandeur the same as His. They can be seen and touched and the senses can perceive certain deficiencies. *But the Creator cannot be touched, or seen, or affected in any way, or altered, and He does not admit of circumscription like His creations.*[4]

By means of this sharp dichotomy, Theodoret safeguards divine transcendence and exposes the confusion that prevails in Greek polytheism.[5] If God is impassible, then all deities (demons included) that are prone to emotions, passions, or vices are false. Once this dichotomy is established, Theodoret consistently keeps it in view, putting it forth in support of a number of ancillary arguments.[6] For example, as the fifth symptom in a list of aberrations, he criticizes pagans because "[t]hey have made gods out of the most malevolent demons and, trained by them in the art of magical incantations, have honored them by rites of initiation and sacrifices."[7]

By Theodoret's time Greek notions of angels,[8] demons,[9] oracles, and sacrifices had been the subject of intense debate within circles of later Platonists. Using demonology as a lens through which to bring out the falsity of basic Greek polytheistic attitudes and practices, Theodoret presents the role of demons as operative across a number of important facets of Greek religion, including divination, oracles, and sacrifice.[10] The dual focus of his *Dialexis* III allows him to contrast especially the role of demons with that of the angels.

The main pagan source for criticism here is Porphyry. Theodoret borrows a number of passages from *On the Philosophy from the Oracles* and the *Letter to Anebo*. Then he goes on to quote Porphyry's critique of malevolent demons:[11]

---

     detailed discussion, see Castelli 1983:85–91, Riedweg 1999:55–81, Cook 2004:291–293, and Boulnois 2008:13–25 and 2010:297–313.

[4] *Therapeutikê* 3.16 [emphasis mine].

[5] On the way God's transcendence is debated and defended by Cyril of Alexandria against Julian's critique, see Boulnois 2006:177–196.

[6] Theodoret's list of five ways the Greeks erred in their perception of the divine runs as follows: a) worship of the moon, sun, and stars as gods; b) deification of (immoral) people; c) deification of mythical figures; d) deification of the passible (or irrational part of the soul); e) deification of demons. The list is also found in Eusebius's *Preparation for the Gospel* 5.3.2–7, which is most likely Theodoret's source.

[7] This theme foreshadows *Dialexis* VII. On Sacrifices.

[8] For an overview of the role of angels, see Michl 1962:53–200.

[9] On demons in the ancient world, see Klauser 1976:546–797, s.v. "Geister," esp. 640–668 on daimons ("Hellenistische und kaiserzeitliche Philosophie" by C. Zintzen); Andres 1918:267–322 and Alt 2005:73–90.

[10] For attitudes of the apologists toward demons, see Wey 1957, Monaci Castagno 1996, and Kallis 1976:700–715.

[11] Theodoret attributes this to Porphyry's *On the Philosophy from the Oracles* when in fact it comes from *On Abstinence* 2.41–42, Canivet 2000–2001(I):187n2.

Διὰ μέντοι τῶν ἐναντίων καὶ ἡ πᾶσα χρεία ἐπιτελεῖται. Τούτοις γὰρ μάλιστα τὴν τούτων προεστῶσαν τιμῶσιν οἱ τὰ κακὰ διὰ γοητειῶν διαπραττόμενοι. Πλήρεις γὰρ πάσης φαντασίας καὶ ἀπατῆσαι ἱκανοὶ διὰ τῆς τερατουργίας καὶ διὰ τοῦ φίλτρα καὶ ἐρωτικὰ κατασκευάζειν οἱ κακοδαίμονες. Πᾶσα γὰρ καὶ πλούτων ἐλπὶς καὶ δόξης διὰ τούτων, καὶ μάλιστα ἡ ἀπάτη. Τὸ γὰρ ψεῦδος τούτοις οἰκεῖον· βούλονται γὰρ εἶναι θεοί· καὶ ἡ προεστῶσα αὐτῶν δύναμις δοκεῖ θεὸς εἶναι μέγιστος. Οὗτοι οἱ χαίροντες λοιβῇ τε κνίσῃ τε, δι' ὧν αὐτῶν τὸ σωματικὸν καὶ πνευματικὸν πιαίνεται.

Therapeutikê 3.60–61

But it is through the opposite kind of *daimones* that all sorcery is accomplished, for those who try to achieve bad things through sorcery honour especially these *daimones* and in particular their chief.

These *daimones* are resourceful, full of illusory apparitions/ appearances, and adept at deception through their wonder-working. Unfortunate people, with their help, prepare philtres and love-charms.

For all self-indulgence and hope of riches and fame comes from them, and especially deceit, for lies are appropriate to them. They want to be gods, and the power that rules them wants to be thought the greatest god. These are they who take pleasure in libations and the odor of meat sacrifices on which both the pneumatic and somatic parts of their being are nourished.[12]

The kind of demonology that Theodoret seeks to counter bears the signs of a systematization that had already started taking place with the middle Platonists and was further developed by the Neoplatonists under the influence of the Chaldean Oracles.[13]

These efforts set the tone for Theodoret, leading him to make a connection with certain features of the Homeric gods and, thus, relegate them to the status of demons.[14] Consistent with his habit of directing the flow of his *dialexeis* by means of excerpts, he reinforces his point about the demonic nature of Greek deities with another addition from the *Letter to Anebo*:

Οὐ μόνον δὲ τῇδε τοιούσδε λόγους ξυνέγραψεν, ἀλλὰ κἂν τῇ Πρὸς Ἀνεβὼ τὸν Αἰγύπτιον ἐπιστολῇ τά παραπλήσια τέθεικεν. Λέγει δὲ

[12] Trans. Clark (with adjustments).
[13] Cremer 1969; Johnston 1989:121–126, 136; Alt 2005:73–90.
[14] *Therapeutikê* 3.61.

οὕτως περὶ τῶν θεῶν μὲν καλουμένων, πονηρῶν δὲ ὄντων δαιμόνων·
«Πάνυ με θράττει, πῶς ὡς κρείττους παρακαλούμενοι ἐπιτάττονται ὡς
χείρους, καὶ δίκαιον εἶναι κατηγοροῦντες τὸν θεράποντα κολάζεσθαι
τὰ ἄδικα πράττοντα, αὐτοὶ κελευσθέντες ἄδικα δρᾶν ὑπομένουσι, καὶ
καθαρῷ μὲν μὴ ὄντι ἐξ ἀφροδισίων καλοῦντι οὐχ ὑπακούουσιν, αὐτοὶ
δὲ ἄγειν εἰς παράνομα ἀφροδίσια τοὺς τυχόντας οὐκ ὀκνοῦσι· ἀπὸ
ἐμψύχων μὲν ἀποχῆς κελεύουσι δεῖν εἶναι τοὺς ὑποφήτας, ἵνα μὴ τοῖς
ἀπὸ τῶν σωμάτων ἀτμοῖς χραίνωνται, αὐτοὶ δὲ ἀτμοῖς τοῖς ἀπὸ θυσιῶν
μάλιστα δελεάζονται, καὶ νεκροῦ μὲν ἀθιγῆ δεῖν εἶναι τὸν ἐπόπτην, διὰ
νεκρῶν δὲ ζῴων αἱ θεαγωγίαι ἐκτελοῦνται.

Therapeutikê 3.66

And that is not the only place in his works in which he has so expressed
himself. In his Letter to Anebo the Egyptian, he has recorded similar
sentiments. This is how he speaks of the *so-called gods who in fact are
really wicked demons*: It is very disquieting how those who are invoked
as better give orders as worse: they advocate that it is right to inflict
punishment on a slave who does wrong; but they themselves when
ordered to do unjust acts perform them. They do not listen to the
appeal of one who is unclean because of sexual excesses, yet they
themselves do not shrink from leading anyone they meet into unlawful
sexual activity. They give orders that the priest interpreters must
abstain from eating flesh meat lest they be defiled by the vapors of the
bodies, but they themselves are especially ensnared by the vapors of
sacrifices. Finally, the initiate is forbidden to touch a carcass, but it is
through the corpses of living creatures that the gods are invoked in the
evocations of the gods.

Theodoret's goal here is to exaggerate and exploit the disagreements that
prevailed among the later Neoplatonists on various issues pertaining to religion.[15] However, he sidesteps Porphyry's account of the role of demons in *On
Abstinence*[16] as well as the detailed exchange that takes place between Porphyry,
in his *Letter to Anebo*,[17] and Iamblichus, in *On the Mysteries*, which addresses most
of Porphyry's questions and gives the incentive for Neoplatonic theorizing

---

[15]   See for example Taormina 1999.
[16]   For which, see den Boeft 1977.
[17]   See the edition by Sodano 1957:47–64, esp. the discussion in Appendix I that focuses on the rela-
        tionship between divination and theurgy.

on many important aspects of Greek piety.[18] Theodoret's selective quoting of Porphyry helps present the manipulation of demons as magic. In doing so, he forecloses the possibility of further speculation and renders more specific arguments superfluous.

Theodoret's use of Porphyry is important for a number of reasons. Porphyry was considered one of the most fierce, informed, and eloquent opponents of Christianity.[19] At the same time, he was heavily involved in the apologetic process of resolving the inherent contradictions and inconsistencies of Greek religiosity and harmonizing its different traditions. Furthermore, engaged as Porphyry was in the discussion of the theoretical concerns of Greek religion, he provided Christian apologists with an array of arguments against which they could make skillful rebuttals.[20]

Theodoret's way of dealing with the Greek gods, then, is to relegate them to the realm of demons by substituting Greek daimonology (in the form of such intermediaries as *daimones*, angels, and heroes) with Biblical demonology. This renders intermediaries less ambiguous by imposing the following pattern on their nature: good spirits are angels and adopt the role that the Bible assigns to them; bad or impure spirits are categorized as demons. The implication here is that even the role of the (predominantly good) pagan *daimones* is "demonized" and therefore neutralized.[21]

Angels and daimons (or heroes) were important to Neoplatonists because as intermediaries they provided them with a solution to the problem of mediation.[22] After the rejection of Plotinus' theory of the undescended soul, later

---

[18] Saffrey 2008:489–511; Fowden 1999:82–106 calls it "a summa of polytheist belief"; Clarke 2001.

[19] Theodoret makes a point of this in *Therapeutikê* 10.12ff. when he says: "Therefore, my friends, even if you do not believe us when we are critical of your oracles, at least believe the one who is our worst enemy and your best friend. For he is our implacable enemy, one who wages open war on (our) religion. *Porphyry has affirmed that the demons who preside over the so-called oracles tell lies*" [emphasis mine]. On Porphyry's *Philosophy from Oracles*, see Busine 2005:233–317 and Riedweg 2005:151–201. Porphyry's knowledge of Christianity led some Christians to believe that he was a lapsed Christian. The evidence, with a review of scholarly opinion, is collected in Kinzig 1998:320–332. Kinzig holds the view that "er [viz. Porhyrios] in seiner Jungend einen (nicht näher bestimmten) christlichen Unterricht genossen und mit dem Christentum in einer Form sympathisiert hat, die bei anderen den Anschein erweckte, als 'gehöre er dazu'" (328). See recently Schott 2008b:258–277.

[20] For Porphyry's attitudes toward Greek philosophy and religion, see Zambon 2002 and Speyer 2005:65–84. Porphyry's equivocal stance toward theurgy and the methods by which he sought to resolve the theoretical problems that arose has been analyzed by Smith 1974. The problem has been addressed in a way that does more justice to Poprhyry's inquisitive nature by Smith 1997:29–35. For a new assessment of Pophyry's stance on theurgy, see van Liefferinge 1999:176–211 and Tanaseanu-Döbler 2009:109–155.

[21] For what has been called "*diabolisation du paganisme*," see Lepelley 2002:81–96.

[22] For the pagan belief in angels, see Cumont 1915:159–181. Angels played an important role in the Chaldean Oracles as well. In fact, it has been argued that they prompted Neoplatonic speculation

Neoplatonists were faced with the serious problem of connecting the ontological gap between god and man. In order to fill this gap they placed exceptional emphasis on the multiplication of the intermediary entities as well as on the fixed order (τάξις) in this hierarchy. Daimons (at times conflated with heroes) played an important role in holding together the physical and moral cosmos.[23] No less significant was the belief (found across religions at the time) in the personal daimon or *angelos*, a figure said to oversee the actions and behavior of each person,[24] or the idea that angels protected nations.[25]

Theodoret's polemic requires him to engage—in different *dialexeis*—two of the more crucial aspects of Greek religion where demons played an important role, namely, oracles and sacrifices.[26] *Dialexis X. On True and False Oracles* gives Theodoret the opportunity to return to the activity of demons. He presents them as having usurped from God the right to be honored and as deceiving people into believing that they are God:

> Τὴν γὰρ δὴ τάξιν καταλιπόντες, ἣν ἔλαχον, καὶ τὴν ἡμερωτάτην τοῦ πεποιηκότος ἀποδράσαντες δεσποτείαν, ἥρπασαν μὲν τὴν τυραννίδα, τὸ δὲ θεῖον ὄνομα σεσυληκότες, θεοὺς σφᾶς αὐτοὺς προσηγόρευσαν καὶ τὸ θεῖον σέβας σφίσι προσφέρειν τῶν ἀνθρώπων τοὺς ἀνοήτους ἀνέπεισαν· εἶτα κρατῦναι τὴν δυναστείαν σπουδάζοντες, καὶ προγινώσκειν τὰ μέλλοντα καὶ προλέγειν ἐνεανιεύσαντο, ταύτῃ μάλιστα τοὺς εὐαλώτους

---

on the role of angels. On angels in the Chaldean Oracles, see Lewy 1978:236–237 and Majercik 1989:13–14.

[23] Neoplatonic philosophers developed different classifications of intermediaries and assigned different functions to them. For Iamblichus, see Dillon 1987:899–902. For the development of the idea of the intermediaries, see Rodríguez Moreno 1998 and Rodríguez Moreno 2000:91–100.

[24] The idea is found in Porphyry *To Marcella* 21.6–9. For the personal psychological traits that are determined by the daimon/angel, see Dillon 2001:3–9. The idea of tutelary angels who protect nations and people appears also in in the chapter On Angels from Theodoret's *Compendium of Heretical Falsehoods*: "Τεκμηριοῖ δὲ καὶ ταῦτα, καὶ τὰ ἐν τῷ Δανιὴλ εἰρημένα, καὶ τὰ ὑπὸ τοῦ Κυρίου λεχθέντα, τινὰς μὲν τῶν ἀγγέλων ἐθνῶν προστατεύειν, τινὰς δὲ ἑνὸς ἑκάστου τῶν ἀνθρώπων πεπιστεῦσθαι τὴν ἐπιμέλειαν, ὥστε μὴ σίνεσθαι αὐτοὺς καὶ πημαίνειν τοὺς ἀλάστορας δαίμονας" (PG 83 472 c–d). Julian *Against the Galileans* fr. 26, 2–6 uses the idea of ethnarch gods to account for the diversity of the ἔθνη: "Therefore, as I said, unless for every nation separately some presiding national god (and under him an angel, a demon, a hero, and a peculiar order of spirits which obey and work for the higher powers) established the differences in our laws and characters, you must demonstrate to me how these differences arose by some other agency" (143 a–b, Loeb translation). For a discussion of the passage, see Smith 1995:196 and Curta 2002:3–19.

[25] Bouffartigue 2005:113–126 and Boulnois 2011:803–830; Monaci Castagno 2010:319–333.

[26] For the tendency that is attested in the second- and third-century philosophers to support their philosophy with the authority of Oracles (the existence of Chaldean Oracles and their extensive use by the Neoplatonists is a case in point), see Nock 1928:280–290. For a more thorough, recent analysis of the phenomenon, see Athanassiadi 1993:115–130; Athanassiadi 1999:149–184.

ἀνθρώπους παρακρουόμενοι. Διά τοι τοῦτο πανταχοῦ γῆς τὰ τῆς ἀπάτης κατεσκεύασαν ἐργαστήρια καὶ τὰς μαντικὰς ἐπενόησαν μαγγανείας …

Therapeutikê 10.2–3

For they abandoned the rank [τάξιν] which had been assigned them, ran away from the very gentle overlordship of the Creator, and seized upon tyranny, having appropriated the name of divinity; they called themselves gods and persuaded foolish individuals to offer them divine honor. Then, striving to maintain their power, their latest innovation is to foreknow and foretell the future, in this way deceiving men who are easily led astray. That is why everywhere on earth they founded workshops of deceit and thought up the deception of oracles.[27]

In order to accomplish this, they employ their limited capacity to foresee the future. Even more perniciously, demons serve to invest deities with a wide range of immoral and criminal behavior, such that in myths they appear to provide a justification if not an incentive to similar immoral actions. Theodoret attacks them as follows:

Οὐδὲ γὰρ σωφροσύνης αὐτοὺς καὶ δικαιοσύνης ἐπιμελεῖσθαι προσέταξεν, ἀλλ' ἀκολασταίνειν αὐτοὺς ἀδεῶς καὶ ἀσελγαίνειν καὶ πᾶσαν τολμᾶν ἀνέδην παρανομίαν ἐπέτρεψεν. Τῷ τοι καὶ μάλα ῥᾳδίως τοὺς πλείστους ἐξηνδραπόδισεν. Τό τε γὰρ ἐπίπονον τῆς ἀρετῆς ἀποφυγγάνοντες καὶ τῶν θείων νόμων τοὺς ἱδρῶτας διαδιδράσκοντες, ηὐτομόλησαν εὐπετῶς πρὸς τὸν τὰ ῥᾷστα καὶ θυμήρη νομοθετοῦντα. Τόνδε δὴ οὖν τὸν τρόπον αὐτοὺς δουλωσάμενος, πρῶτον μὲν τὰς περὶ τοῦ Θεοῦ τῶν ὅλων, ἅς ἡ φύσις αὐτοῖς ἐξ ἀρχῆς ἐνέγραψεν, ἐξήλειψε δόξας· ἔπειτα δὲ τὰ πονηρὰ τῶν ψευδωνύμων θεῶν ἐξεπαίδευσε δόγματα καὶ τὸν πολὺν τῶν οὐκ ὄντων ὅμιλον ἀντὶ τοῦ ὄντος ἐδίδαξε προσκυνεῖν, ταύτην ὑποβάθραν καὶ κρηπῖδα τῆς διεφθαρμένης προκαταβαλλόμενος βιοτῆς … τοιόνδε φάρμακον αὐτοῖς ἀναλγησίας ὁ τῆς κακίας ἐμηχανήσατο σοφιστής. Περὶ γὰρ δὴ τῶν καλουμένων θεῶν πονηρὰς αὐτοὺς ἐξεπαίδευσε δόξας· ἀκολάστους γὰρ αὐτοὺς ἀπέφηνε καὶ λαγνιστάτους καὶ παιδοπίπας καὶ γάμων ἐπιβούλους καὶ πατραλοίας καὶ μητραλοίας καὶ μητράσι καὶ ἀδελφαῖς, καὶ μέντοι καὶ θυγατράσιν ἀνέδην μιγνυμένους καὶ τὰς εὐνὰς τὰς ἀλλήλων ληστεύοντας καὶ ἁλισκομένους, καὶ παρὰ μὲν τῶν ἠδικημένων δεσμουμένους, παρὰ δὲ τῶν ἄλλων ἀνέδην γελωμένους,

---

[27] There is an interesting similarity here with question 42 of the *Quaestiones et Responsiones*; see p63n38.

καὶ ταῦτα παρὰ μὲν τῶν οὐρανίων, ὡς αὐτοὶ λέγουσιν, ἐν οὐρανῷ
τολμᾶσθαι καὶ γῇ, παρὰ δὲ τῶν ἐναλίων ἐν θαλάττῃ καὶ γῇ, παρὰ δὲ
τῶν καλουμένων νυμφῶν ἐν ὄρεσι καὶ νάπαις καὶ φάραγξιν.

Therapeutikê 7.2–5

In fact, far from prescribing that they should show concern for temperance and chastity, the demon by contrast has taught them to deliver themselves unrestrainedly to license and debauchery, and every kind of immorality. That is why it has been so easy for him to reduce to slavery the greater part of the human race. In fact, people flee from attempting to live virtuously and tend to run away from the hardship of virtue and the ardors of the divine laws. Instead, they transfer without difficulty to the one who has legalized what is easiest and most pleasant. Having enslaved them in this way, the devil then proceeds to eradicate the ideas that the God of the universe has engraved on them from the beginning. Next he has taught them the perverse doctrines of the false gods and has schooled them to adore this crowd of nonbeings instead of the One who is. Such is the basis and foundation which he has prearranged for the dissolute life. . . . But the charlatan of wickedness has invented a drug to immunize the housebreaker, the footpad, the traitor, and other malefactors. For he has taught them perverse beliefs concerning the so-called gods. He has displayed them as unbridled, extremely sexual and pederastic wreckers of marriages, parricides, ones who sleep with their mothers, sisters, even daughters. He has depicted them as plundering one another's marriage beds, being caught in the act, and then, chained by the wrong party, being shamelessly laughed at by the other deities, and that all these things are dared by the heavenly beings in the heavens and on earth, as they themselves admit, and by marine creatures in the sea and on land, and by the so-called nymphs in mountains, valleys and ravines.

As a result of demonic agency, human beings are misled into believing that by propitiating or worshiping them they can accomplish their aims or achieve goals of dubious value. In an extension of this argument, Theodoret employs the notion of demonic agency to explain divination and its role, in which demons are heavily involved.[28] Here, Theodoret conjures ancient Greek philosophers

---

[28] For a similar emphasis on the role of demons in divination in Iamblichus *On the Mysteries*, see the discussion in Clarke 2001:107–110.

Oenomaus, Plutarch, Diogenianus, and Porphyry to criticize oracles.[29] He draws heavily on Plutarch's *On the Failure of Oracles* as a testimony in order to effect a synchronization according to which the birth of Christ is the central event that vanquishes both demons and divination.[30] Porphyry's views on the constraints placed on the gods by rituals that summon them only confirm Theodoret's point:

Θεασάμενοι τοίνυν πανταχοῦ διατρέχον τῆς ἀληθείας τὸ κήρυγμα, καθάπερ στρατιῶται φυγάδες πολλὰ δεινὰ καὶ παράνομα δεδρακότες, εἶτα τῆς τοῦ βασιλέως αἰσθόμενοι παρουσίας, ἀπέδρασαν καὶ γυμνὰς τὰς ἐνέδρας κατέλιπον. Ὁ δὲ τῶν ὅλων παμβασιλεὺς τὰ τούτων κατέλυσεν ὁρμητήρια· καὶ οὔτε τῆς Κασταλίας προαγορεύει τὸ ὕδωρ, οὔτε Κολοφῶνος ἡ πηγὴ προθεσπίζει, οὐχ ὁ Θεσπρώτιος λέβης μαντεύεται, οὐχ ὁ τρίπους ὁ Κιρραῖος χρησμολογεῖ, οὐ τὸ Δωδωναῖον χαλκεῖον ἀδολεσχεῖ, οὐχ ἡ πολυθρύλητος φθέγγεται δρῦς, ἀλλὰ σιγᾷ μὲν ὁ Δωδωναῖος, σιγᾷ δὲ ὁ Κολοφώνιος καὶ Δήλιος καὶ Πύθιος καὶ Κλάριος καὶ Διδυμαῖος καὶ ἡ Λεβαδία καὶ ὁ Τροφώνιος καὶ ὁ Ἀμφίλοχος καὶ ὁ Ἀμφιάραος καὶ ὁ Ἄμμων καὶ ἡ τῶν Χαλδαίων καὶ Τυρρηνῶν νεκυία.

Therapeutikê 10.45–47

That is why, having seen the proclamation of the truth circulating everywhere, they took to flight like runaway soldiers who have committed many crimes and offenses, and then, when they saw the presence of the King, took to flight and deserted their posts. The sovereign King of the universe has destroyed their onslaughts. The water of Castalia no longer issues prophecies; the bronze of Thesprotia no longer is involved in divination; the tripod of Cirrha no longer issues oracles; the

---

[29] *Therapeutikê* 10.42: "I have made mention of Oenomaos, Porphyry, Plutarch, Diogenianus, and the others because you regard them as worthy of credence in that they speak of what pertains you. As for us, the facts speak for themselves, and in one clear voice facts denounce the oracles as false."

[30] *Therapeutikê* 10.4–5: " Ὅτι δὲ παμπονήρων ἦν δαιμόνων ταῦτα χρηστήρια τὴν θείαν προσηγορίαν σεσυληκότων, ἱκανὴ μὲν τεκμηριῶσαι καὶ ἡ νῦν αὐτοῖς ἐπικειμένη σιγή.Μετὰ γὰρ δὴ τὴν τοῦ Σωτῆρος ἡμῶν ἐπιφάνειαν ἀπέδρασαν οἱ τήνδε τὴν ἐξαπάτην τοῖς ἀνθρώποις προσφέροντες, τοῦ θείου φωτὸς οὐκ ἐνεγκόντες τὴν αἴγλην" ("Sufficient proof that these oracles have been the work of maleficent demons, usurping the name of divinity, is the silence that now engulfs them. In fact, after the appearance of our Savior, those who offered this deception to human beings ran away, for the brilliance of the divine light proved unendurable to them"). On how Theodoret's view that Christ's birth silenced pagan oracles compares with other contemporary Christian views on pagan oracles, see Heyden 2009:216–218. The use of Plutarch's work by Eusebius and Theodoret has been discussed in La Matina 1998:81–110. For Plutarch's attitude towards divination à propos the *On the Failure of Oracles*, see Von Arnim 1921.

bronze of Dodona no longer talks nonsense nor does the much-vaunted oak tree speak any longer. No, the god of Dodona is now silent, the god of Colophon is silent, so is the Pythian, the Clarian, the Didymaean, and the oracle of Lebadaia; Trophonios is silent, so is Amphilochus, Amphiaraos, Ammon, and the necromancy of the Chaldeans and of the citizens of Tyre.

There is a conscious effort in the pedantic accumulation and enumeration of the most prominent oracles to show the magnitude of Christ's victory over demons. It is in this vein that, in a rare instance of an explicit reference revealing a local perspective,[31] Theodoret, in *Therapeutikê* 10.47–48, refers in passing to the memory of a recent event—namely, Julian's removal of Babylas' relics from the Oracle of Apollo at Daphne—and the controversy that it created.[32] This episode is used by Theodoret as proof of God's victory through his martyrs over the Oracle of Apollo.

But, more importantly, what Theodoret attempts to accomplish with his attack on demonic agency in divination is the imposition of a conceptual framework within which the relationship between God and human beings is based on a different mode of [divine] communication.[33] The fact that demons are both passible[34]—a quality that Theodoret extends to Greek gods as well—and malicious renders illicit their agency in accessing the divine.

Theodoret's concern with the issue of angels and demons in the *Therapeutikê* becomes clearer when placed against closely parallel arguments that appear in

---

[31] This is an exception to Theodoret's studied avoidance of references to his local environment that would perhaps threaten to overly localize his apology.

[32] *Therapeutikê* 10.47–48: "Καὶ ὁ Δαφναῖος Ἀπόλλων, τὸν ἡμέτερον παρασκευάσας μετατεθῆναι νεκρόν, οὐρανόθεν ἐδέξατο τὸν σκηπτόν. Οὐ γὰρ εἴα προλέγειν αὐτὸν καὶ ξυνήθως ἀποβουκολεῖν τοὺς ἀνθρώπους τοῦ σταυρωθέντος ὁ μάρτυς, ἀλλὰ καθάπερ ὁ μέγας Παῦλος τῷ τοῦ Πύθωνος ἐπετίμησε πνεύματι, οὕτως ἡ τοῦ μάρτυρος κόνις τὸ τοῦ μάντεως ἐχαλίνωσε ψεῦδος" ("Apollo at Daphne, when he ordered us to transfer our remains [i.e. of Babylas], was struck by a thunderbolt from the heavens. For the martyr of the Crucified did not in fact allow him to make his predictions or to lead men continually astray. But just as the mighty Paul rebuked the spirit of the python, so also the remains of the martyr bridled the falsehood of the oracle"). For a discussion of the incident, see Guinot 1995:323–341 and Shepardson 2009:99–115.

[33] The impact of this demonology can also be clearly seen in the *religionsgeschichtliche* exposition on sacrifice that Theodoret undertakes in *Dialexis* VII. On Sacrifices. There the (biblical) demon is the cause of the misdirected practice of sacrifice.

[34] Contrary to Iamblichus, who states in *On the Mysteries* 1.10 (37.1–3.): "Ἀπαθεῖς τοίνυν εἰσὶ καὶ οἱ δαίμονες καὶ πάντα τὰ συνεπόμενα αὐτοῖς τῶν κρειττόνων γενῶν" and rejects the application of the division passible/impassible to Gods and intermediaries.

Quaestiones et responsiones. More specifically, questions 30,[35] 40,[36] 41,[37] and 42[38] deal with similar problems that are raised by anonymous interlocutor(s) and are a good measure of the pervasive hold that demons, angels, and their activities had on the fifth-century thought-world.[39] In question 24 the figure of Apollonius looms large:

Εἰ θεός ἐστι δημιουργὸς καὶ δεσπότης τῆς κτίσεως, πῶς τὰ Ἀπολλωνίου τελέσματα ἐν τοῖς μέρεσι τῆς κτίσεως δύνανται; Καὶ γὰρ θαλάττης ὁρμὰς καὶ ἀνέμων φορὰς καὶ μυῶν καὶ θηρίων ἐπιδρομάς, ὡς ὁρῶμεν, κωλύουσι. Καὶ εἰ τὰ ὑπὸ τοῦ κυρίου μὲν γινόμενα θαύματα ἐν μόνῃ τῇ διηγήσει φέρεται, τὰ δὲ παρ' ἐκείνου πλεῖστα καὶ ἐπ' αὐτῶν τῶν πραγμάτων δεικνύμενα, πῶς οὐκ ἀπατᾷ τοὺς ὁρῶντας; Καὶ εἰ μὲν κατὰ θείαν τοῦτο συγχώρησιν γέγονε, πῶς ὁδηγὸς εἰς ἑλληνισμὸν οὐ γέγονεν ἡ τοιαύτη συγχώρησις; Εἰ δὲ μὴ τοῦτο, πῶς οὐ δυνάμει τῶν δαιμόνων ἐκεῖνα γεγένηνται; Πάλιν δὲ εἴπερ θεὸς ὡς ἀγαθῷ τῷ γινομένῳ ἡδόμενος ἐκείνῳ συνήργησε, διὰ τί μὴ διὰ προφητῶν ἢ ἀποστόλων τὰ τοιαῦτα γεγένηνται; Εἰ δὲ μὴ ἠρέσκετο ὡς φαύλῳ, τίνος ἕνεκεν τὸ φαῦλον ἢ εὐθὺς οὐκ ἐκώλυσεν ἢ μετὰ βραχὺ οὐ κατέλυσεν, ἀλλ' ἕως αἰῶνος τῶν ἡμερῶν τῆς κτίσεως κρατεῖν συνεχώρησεν;

If God is the Creator and Lord of creation, how do Apollonius' divine acts have an impact on parts of that creation? As we see, they hinder the winds and the inroads of mice and wild beasts. And if the miracles that the Lord performed lay only in the narratives, whereas most of his [Apollonius' miracles] are proven by the facts, how does he [Apollonius] not deceive those watching? And if on the one hand this was done by divine permission, how is it that this divine consent does not lead to Hellenism? If this is not so, how are these things done with the power

---

[35] "If every human being is followed by a guardian angel, as the holy Scripture says, while the number of humans at times decreases or increases just as it happened in the flood and in other misfortune on account of their deeds; the [angels] not being prone to increase or decrease, what function did they serve—God having assigned to them a function from the beginning?"

[36] "If demons dwell constantly in those possessed, how do they incur damage to others? If they do this by departing for a short period of time from the possessed, how, when expelled by means of some invisible power, is it that they (the demons) no longer show signs of their presence?"

[37] "If it is only God's right to give life and strength to the human bodies, how can demons do this, namely, strengthen the bodies of the possessed so as to break their bonds and their chains? He was bound with chains and breaking his bonds he was driven by the demon to the desert."

[38] "If demons govern parts of creation, why, when the oracles were not heeded by the Greeks, did they [demons] bring punishments upon them, whereas when the idols were reverenced they put an end to the punishments and they [demons] provided goods instead? Whence did their power come for either act?"

[39] For context, see MacMullen 1997, despite its tendency to overstate the case.

of the demons? Then again if God played a role in this—pleased because what happened was good—why did these things not happen through the prophets or the apostles? If He was not pleased because this was bad, for what reason did He not immediately hinder it or did put an end to it after a short time but instead allowed it to prevail for the duration of the time of this creation?[40]

The problems posed by the interlocutor illustrate the issues that Theodoret is addressing in his critique of pagan demonology. Miracles presented a challenge to the faithful: Are there many conduits of the divine in the universe? How can God allow the existence of multiple and antithetical ways of access to the divine? Why did He allow the activity of demons, and, if He did not want this, why did he allow the continuation of their activity to the present?[41]

Polemicizing demons, oracles, sacrifices, divination, etc. and making accusations against magic emerge as part of a larger project: Theodoret is concerned with undermining theurgy. As an effort to enhance the communication between humans and the divine, theurgy was breathing new life into religious attitudes across the empire.[42] The fact that Julian became one of its most fervent adherents led to its heightened visibility among philosophers and philosophically inclined pagans.[43]

This, among other reasons, is why Theodoret is so keen to discredit Julian's religiosity, which he does by presenting him in his *Ecclesiastical History* (a good deal of which is informed by polemics against pagans) as dabbling in occult practices. Characteristic of Julian's portrait is Theodoret's recounting of the following incident:

Μετὰ δὲ τὴν σφαγὴν αἱ τῆς ἐκείνου γοητείας ἐφωράθησαν μαγγανεῖαι. Κάρραι γὰρ πόλις ἐστὶν ἔτι καὶ νῦν ἔχουσα τῆς ἀσεβείας τὰ λείψανα

---

[40] On Apollonius' popularity, see Dulière 1970:1970, Dzielska 1986, Hägg 2004:379–404, Jones 2006:49–64, and the Christian polemic against it, Junod 1988:475–482.

[41] Isidore of Peluse is faced with a similar task of explaining the maleficent role of demons when responding to an inquiry by a grammarian, Ophelius: "ἐπειδὴ θαυμάζειν ἔφης, πῶς τινες τῶν ἀλιτηρίων δαιμόνων δίκαιον ἠξίουν εἶναι τὸν θεραπευτὴν αὐτῶν, οἱ δὲ τὰ ἄδικα δρᾶν πραττόμενοι ὑπέμενον· ἡγοῦμαι, ὅτι δίκαιον μὲν ἠξίουν εἶναι τὸν θεραπεύοντα, διότι θεοὶ εἶναι ὑπεκρίνοντο. Ὑπηρέτουν δὲ τὰ ἄδικα διότι πονηροὶ γεγόνασιν ἐκ προαιρέσεως. Ἐπειδὴ γὰρ ᾔδεσαν πολλοὺς τῶν ἀνθρώπων τὴν ἀρετὴν τιμῶντας, τοὺς φιλαρέτους ἀγαπᾶν προσποιούμενοι, ἵν' ἀγαθοὶ νομισθεῖεν εἶναι, μετ' οὐ πολὺ ταῖς ἐναγέσι πράξεσιν ἤλεγχον ἑαυτῶν τὴν ἐπὶ τὰ κακὰ ῥέπουσαν διάνοιαν," Ep. 105, PG 78:1172.

[42] For the legislation against theurgy, see Clerc 1996:57–64 and Desanti 1990. Augustine's sustained engagement with magic and theurgy also comes to mind, on which, see Graf 2002:87–103 and Sfameni Gasparro 1997:48–131.

[43] For Julian's theurgic piety, see Smith 1995 and Van Liefferinge 1999:213–243, both of which are devoted to Julian; Renucci 2000.

διὰ ταύτης ὁ μάταιος τὴν πορείαν ποιούμενος (τὴν γὰρ Ἔδεσαν ὡς εὐσεβείᾳ κοσμουμένην εὐώνυμον καταλελοίπει), εἰς τὸν παρὰ τῶν δυσσεβῶν τιμώμενον σηκὸν εἰσελθὼν καί τινα ἐν τούτω σὺν τοῖς κοινωνοῖς τοῦ μύσους ἐπιτελέσας, κλεῖθρα καὶ σήμαντρα ταῖς θύραις ἐπέθηκε καί τινας ταύταις προσεδρεύειν προσέταξε στρατιώτας, μηδένα εἴσω τῶν θυρῶν γενέσθαι μέχρι τῆς ἐπανόδου κελεύσας. Ἐπειδὴ δὲ ὁ θάνατος ἀπηγγέλθη καὶ εὐσεβὴς βασιλεία τὴν δυσσεβῆ διεδέξατο, εἴσω γενόμενοι τοῦ σηκοῦ εὗρον τὴν ἀξιάγαστον τοῦ βασιλέως ἀνδρείαν τε καὶ σοφίαν καὶ πρὸς τούτοις εὐσέβειαν. Εἶδον γὰρ γύναιον ἐκ τῶν τριχῶν ἠωρημένον, ἐκτεταμένας ἔχον τὰς χεῖρας. ἧς ἀνακείρας ὁ ἀλιτήριος τὴν γαστέρα τὴν νίκην δήπουθεν τὴν κατὰ Περσῶν διὰ τοῦ ἥπατος ἔγνω. Τοῦτο μὲν ἐν Κάρραις ἐφωράθη τὸ μύσος.

Ecclesiastical History 3.26.1–3

After he [Julian] was slain the jugglery of his sorcery was detected [αἱ τῆς ἐκείνου γοητείας ἐφωράθησαν μαγγανεῖαι]. For Carrhae is a city which still retains the relics of his false religion. Julian had left Edessa on his left because it was adorned with the grace of true religion, and while in his vain folly he was journeying through Carrhae, he came to the temple honored by the impious, and after going through certain rites with his companions in defilement, he locked and sealed the doors and stationed sentinels with orders to see that none came in till his return. When news came of his death, and the reign of iniquity was succeeded by one of piety, the shrine was opened, and within was found a proof of the late emperor's *manliness*, *wisdom*, and *piety*. For there was seen a woman hung up on high by the hairs of her head, and with her hands outstretched. The villain had cut open her belly, and so I suppose learnt from her liver his victory over the Persians. This was the abomination [μύσος] discovered at Carrhae.[44]

Having set up the first part of his contrast between pagan gods and demons and the Christian God, Theodoret's *dialexis* turns to its second part, the angels. He draws his attention to an objection and goes on to apostrophize what appears to be an anonymous pagan interlocutor:

Ἀλλὰ γὰρ οἶμαι ὑμᾶς ἐρεῖν, ὡς καὶ ὑμεῖς ἀοράτους τινὰς δυνάμεις φατέ, οὓς καὶ Ἀγγέλους καὶ Ἀρχαγγέλους ὀνομάζετε καὶ προσαγορεύετε

---

[44] See Martin 2008:71–82. For the attitude of late antique historians to Julian, see Nesselrath 2001:15–43.

καὶ Ἀρχὰς καὶ Ἐξουσίας καὶ Κυριότητας καὶ Θρόνους· καὶ ἄλλας
αὖ πάλιν κατὰ τὴν Ἑβραίων γλῶτταν Χερουβὶμ καὶ Σεραφὶμ ἴστε
προσαγορευομένας. Ἀνθ' ὅτου τοίνυν ἡμῖν νεμεσᾶτε, μετὰ τὸν ἀεὶ ὄντα
καὶ ὡσαύτως καὶ κατὰ ταὐτὰ ἔχοντα δευτέρους τινὰς θεούς, καὶ κομιδῇ
γε ἐκείνου ἀποδέοντας, νομίζουσί τε καὶ γεραίρουσιν;

Therapeutikê 3.86–87

But I know well that you are going to say to me: "You also speak of certain
invisible powers whom you call angels and archangels and whom you
salute with the title of Principalities and Powers, Dominations and
Thrones. You know others who in the Hebrew language are called
Cherubim and Seraphim. How, then, can you be angry at us if, next to
Him who is eternal and absolutely identical with Himself, we admit and
venerate secondary gods who are certainly inferior to Him?"

The objection of the anonymous interlocutor is indicative of the variety of ways
that angels were perceived among pagans, Christians, and Jews. This is true
especially in areas like northern Syria,[45] but also in such texts as the *Apokritikos*
of Macarius Magnes (ca. 410), where the pagan interlocutor, in his objection,
blurs the distinction between God and angels:

The difference therefore is not great, whether a man calls them gods
or angels, since their divine nature bears witness to them, as when
Matthew writes thus: "And Jesus answered and said, Ye do err, not
knowing the scriptures, nor the power of God; for in the resurrection
they neither marry nor are given in marriage, but are as the angels
in heaven" (Matt. xxii. 29–30). Since therefore He confesses that the
angels have a share in the divine nature, those who make a suitable
object of reverence for the gods do not think that the god is in the wood

---

[45] The cult of the angels was widely attested in northern Syria, as is shown by Canivet 1980:85–
117; Bowersock 1990:19–20. See also Zanetti 1994:323–349. Recent archaeological discoveries at
the same site have brought to light a Mithraeum with spectacular representations of demonic
figures: Gawlikowski 2000:161–171. These discoveries have enhanced our picture of both the religious landscape assumed by Theodoret and the vitality of paganism. Ample context is provided
also in Peers 2001:8–15, 67–68. Alongside the heavy Neoplatonic emphasis on the role of intermediary entities it is important not to exclude the possibility of an audience that was faced with
challenges posed by the existence of religious groups that presupposed the existence of angels
as well as good and bad spirits. [Theodoret's silence about these in the *Therapeutikê* should be
contrasted with his polemical engagement with Manicheans in a separate (now lost) work, in
his commentaries to the epistles of Saint Paul, and in his accounts of the teachings of Mani and
Marcion in the *Compendium of Heretical Falsehoods*.] See Hutter 2002:287–294. See also Tardieu
1997–1998:596–605.

or stone or bronze from which the image is manufactured, nor do they consider that, if any part of the statue is cut off, it detracts from the power of the god.[46]

Question 158 in the *Quaestiones et Responsiones ad Orthodoxos* deals with a similar issue.[47] This objection gives Theodoret occasion to provide instruction on the nature, role, and importance of angels:[48]

Ἐγὼ δὲ ὁμολογῶ μὲν τὴν θείαν ἡμᾶς διδάξαι γραφήν, εἶναι δή τινας ἀοράτους δυνάμεις, καὶ ὑμνούσας τὸν ποιητὴν καὶ ὑπουργούσας αὐτοῦ τῷ θείῳ βουλήματι· οὐ μὴν θεοὺς τούτους ὀνομάζομεν οὐδὲ θεῖον αὐτοῖς ἀπονέμομεν σέβας οὐδὲ μερίζομεν εἰς τὸν ὄντα Θεὸν καὶ τούτους τὴν θείαν προσκύνησιν, ἀλλὰ τούτους τιμιωτέρους μὲν ἀνθρώπων, ὁμοδούλους δὲ εἶναί φαμεν.

Therapeutikê 3.88–89

I know the sacred Scripture teaches us there certainly exist invisible powers who chant the praises of the creator and who are at the service of His divine will. But we assuredly do not style them "gods" anymore than we assign them divine honor; we do not divide divine honor between the true God and them. But we say, on the one hand, they are more worthy of honor than humans, and, on the other, they are also our fellow slaves.

But there is an interesting dimension adduced at the end of this exposition. Theodoret exploits the opportunity that discussing the nature of angels offers to incorporate a connection to the Syrian ascetics who imitate the angelic life.[49]

---

[46] Trans. Crafer 1919:145. The Greek text can be found in Goulet 2003(II-4):3–5.

[47] "Εἰ ὁ ἄγγελος τοῦ ἀνθρώπου ἀνώτερος καὶ θεοὺς τοὺς ἀνθρώπους ἡ γραφὴ ὀνομάζει, πῶς οὐχ ἁρμόττει καὶ τοὺς ἀγγέλους θεοὺς παρ' ἡμῶν ὀνομάζεσθαι;" See also similar inquiries in questions 44, 45, 46, and 47 in the sixth-century question-and-answer collection of Ps.-Kaisarios in *Caesarii Dialogi quatuor. Die Erotapokriseis*, ed. Riedinger 1989.

[48] A slightly different account of the angels and their nature is found in Theodoret's anti-heretical treatise *Compendium of Heretical Falsehoods*. The fifth chapter of the work is a systematic exposition of fundamental Christian beliefs (Young 1983:288 calls it Theodoret's *De principiis*). The interesting addition in this account is a more explicit reference to the deification of angels by Greek poets and philosophers. "Τοὺς δὲ ἀγγέλους, οὔτε κατὰ τοὺς τῶν Ἑλλήνων ποιητὰς καὶ φιλοσόφους θεοποιοῦμεν, καὶ εἰς θῆλυ καὶ ἄρρεν τὴν ἀσώματον διακρίνομεν φύσιν, καὶ μίξεις ἀκολάστους τῶν ἀοράτων κατηγοροῦμεν δυνάμεων· οὐδὲ κατὰ τοὺς τῶν αἱρετικῶν μύθους ποιητὰς τῆς κτίσεως ὁριζόμεθα, οὔτε μὴν συναϊδίους εἶναί φαμεν τῷ τῶν ὅλων Θεῷ" (*Compendium of Heretical Falsehoods*, PG 83:468).

[49] The motif is firmly rooted in early Christian writers, especially in Syriac Christianity: see Frank 1964. See also Brown 1988:323–338 and Rousseau 2004:323–346.

This effort reflects another of Theodoret's apologetic concerns, the defense of Syrian ascetics from their pagan opponents:

Τὴν ἐκείνων μιμούμενοι πολιτείαν, ὅσοι τῶν ἀνθρώπων τὴν τοῦ Θεοῦ θεραπείαν ἠσπάσαντο, ἔφυγον μὲν τῶν σωμάτων καὶ τὴν ἔννομον κοινωνίαν ὡς τῶν θείων ἀφέλκουσαν, κατέλιπον δὲ καὶ πατρίδα καὶ γένος, ἵνα πᾶσαν εἰς τὰ θεῖα μεταθῶσι τὴν μέριμναν, καὶ μηδεὶς τὸν νοῦν ἐπέχῃ δεσμός, εἰς οὐρανὸν ἀναπτῆναι καὶ τὸ ἀόρατον καὶ ἄρρητον τοῦ Θεοῦ κατοπτεῦσαι γλιχόμενον κάλλος. Τούτων πλήρεις καὶ πόλεις καὶ κῶμαι καὶ τῶν ὀρῶν αἱ ἀκρωνυχίαι καὶ φάραγγες. Καὶ οἱ μὲν κατὰ ξυμμορίας οἰκοῦντες δημιουργοῦσιν ἐν ταῖς ψυχαῖς τὰ τῆς φιλοσοφίας ἀγάλματα, οἱ δέ, κατὰ δύο καὶ τρεῖς διάγοντες, οἱ δὲ καὶ μόνοι καθειργμένοι καὶ τὼ ὀφθαλμὼ τῷ κάλλει τῶν ὁρωμένων ἐπιτέρπεσθαι διακωλύοντες, σχολὴν τῷ νῷ παρέχουσιν ἐπεντρυφᾶν τῇ θεωρίᾳ τῶν νοητῶν. Εἰ δὲ οἱ σώμασι ξυνεζευγμένοι καὶ ὑπὸ πολλῶν καὶ παντοδαπῶν ἐνοχλούμενοι παθημάτων ἀσώματον καὶ ὑψηλὴν καὶ οὐρανίοις πρέπουσαν ἀσπάζονται βιοτήν, τίς ἂν ἐκφράσαι λόγος τῶν ἀσωμάτων φύσεων τὴν ἀπαθῆ πολιτείαν καὶ φροντίδων ἀπηλλαγμένην;

Therapeutikê 3.92–94

Imitating their way of life, so many humans embrace the service of God. For they flee even legitimate carnal intercourse as drawing them away from divine things; they leave fatherland and family behind, so they may devote all their cares to divine things and so no bond may restrain their spirit, eager to fly upward to the heavens to contemplate the invisible and ineffable beauty of God. They [monks] fill the towns and villages, the mountaintops and ravines. Some dwell in communities and carve on their souls the images of wisdom; others live in twos or threes, or even as complete solitaries, withholding their eyes from the enjoyment of visible things and providing leisure to their mind for the enjoyment of the contemplation of intellectual things. Now if those who are attached to a body and are troubled with a host of every kind of passions can embrace with joy a way of life that is incorporeal, elevated, and close to the life of the heavens, how could one describe the life of incorporeal natures, exempt from passions and free from all disturbance?

Theodoret is acutely aware of the weight of his language and imagery. This weight is compounded by the associations he develops earlier in the *dialexis*. The citizenship imagery is particularly important given the ideals and values of contemporary philosophers like Hierocles of Alexandria, who in his praise of heroes (who are conflated with daemons) explains that they are called "heroes because they are, so to speak, 'loving ones', like 'erotics' and lovers of god versed in dialectics, 'raising' us up and bearing us aloft from our sojourn on earth to citizenship with the divine. It is also customary to call them . . . sometimes 'angels' as they bring to light and define for us the guidelines for happiness."[50] Porphyry also asks, in his *Letter to Anebo*, the difference between the soul of the hero and demon and how to distinguish between angels and demons.[51] Iamblichus puts purified souls in an angelic space.[52]

Theodoret alludes to an imagined community (κοινωνία) of the living (and dead, in the case of the martyrs)[53] that transcends earthly limitations and allows citizens of this world to become citizens of heaven.[54] The implications of this dramatic inversion are very important, as the ascetics become conduits of divine power and grace.

Conclusion

Theodoret's critique of various aspects of pagan demonology runs parallel to the Neoplatonic emphasis on the elaboration of the precise nature of demons and angels and their instrumental role in divination and sacrifices. What emerges from Theodoret's treatment of demonic agency, angelology, sacrifice, divination, and the role of oracles is the underlying issue of divine communication and the available channels to it. Christian and pagan belief in intermediaries formed a common spectrum. The fluid conception of these intermediaries and the ambiguity of their roles led to an ambivalence that permeates the texts under

---

[50] Trans. Schibli 2002:192–193. *Commentary on the Golden Verses of the Pythagoreans* 3.6.3–7: "ἥρωες δὲ ὡς ἔρωές τινες ὄντες καὶ ἥρωες οἷον ἐρωτικοὶ καὶ διαλεκτικοὶ ἐρασταὶ τοῦ θεοῦ αἴροντες ἡμᾶς καὶ κουφίζοντες πρὸς τὴν θείαν πολιτείαν ἀπὸ τῆς ἐν γῇ διατριβῆς. τοὺς δὲ αὐτοὺς . . . καλεῖν ἔθος . . . ἔστι δὲ ὅτε καὶ ἀγγέλους ὡς ἐκφαίνοντας καὶ διαστέλλοντας ἡμῖν τοὺς πρὸς εὐζωΐαν κανόνας."

[51] *Letter to Anebo* 1.3a: "Δεῖ δὲ δὴ καὶ τοῦτο προσαποδειχθῆναί σοι, δαίμων ἥρωος καὶ ψυχῆς τίνι κατ' οὐσίαν διαφέρει ἢ κατὰ δύναμιν ἢ ἐνέργειαν"; also 1.4a: "'Ἐπιζητεῖς γάρ, παρουσίας τί τὸ γνώρισμα θεοῦ ἢ ἀγγέλου ἢ ἀρχαγγέλου ἢ δαίμονος ἤ τινος ἄρχοντος ἢ ψυχῆς."

[52] Finamore 2002:425–433.

[53] See the following chapter.

[54] *Therapeutikê* 1.118: "Τοῖς γὰρ δὴ μετασχοῦσι τῆς ἀληθείας καὶ ταύτης ἀξίως βεβιωκόσιν οὐρανὸς εὐτρεπὴς καὶ τὰ τῶν ἀγγέλων ἐνδιαιτήματα· ὁ δὲ ταύτης ἔρημος καὶ ἀτέλεστος καὶ τῶν παναγῶν καὶ θείων ἀμύητος μυστηρίων ἔρημος μὲν τῶνδε τῶν ἀγαθῶν γενήσεται, κολαστηρίοις δὲ διηνεκέσι παραδοθήσεται." See also in the *History of the Monks of Syria* 10: "Ταύτης καὶ νῦν ἀπολαύσαιμι, ζῆν αὐτὸν πιστεύων καὶ τοῖς ἀγγέλοις συγχορεύειν καὶ πλείονι ἢ πάλαι πρὸς τὸν θεὸν παρρησία κεχρῆσθαι. *History of the Monks of Syria* 11: "'Ἐντεῦθεν δὲ ἐκδημήσας καὶ εἰς τὴν ἀγγελικὴν χορείαν μετατεθεὶς κατέλιπε μνήμην οὐ συνταφεῖσαν τῷ σώματι ἀλλ' ἀνθοῦσαν καὶ τεθηλυῖαν καὶ ἄσβεστον εἰς ἀεὶ διαμένουσαν καὶ εἰς ὄνησιν τοῖς βουλομένοις ἀκούσαν."

discussion. Theodoret attempts to restructure this ambivalence into belief along the lines of Biblical teaching. The alternative to Greek daimons and angels that he seeks to establish are Christian angels, whose essence he outlines with catechetical zeal—probably in reaction to a widespread trend among pagans and Christians to revere angels or to confuse them with God. At the same time, the deliberate association between angels and Syrian ascetics that he effects, following a firmly established Christian tradition, implies a broader vision of the κοινωνία among angels, ascetics, and martyrs in the heavenly πολιτεία. This will be taken up in the following chapter on the cult of the martyrs.

3

Greek Heroes and Christian Martyrs:
In Defense of the Friends of God
and Heroes of the Faith

THE ACCOUNT THAT THEODORET provides concerning the practice of honoring martyrs and their relics occupies a central position in his defense of Christianity. In *Dialexis* VIII. On the Cult of the Martyrs, he explains the importance of martyrs by suggesting the parallel notion of heroism and the cult of heroes in Greek religion and culture.[1] A significant portion of the *dialexis* takes as its focus the resistance to notions of heroism. It is worth noting at the outset that pagan accusations act as the incentive for the defense of Christian martyrs.[2] That said, it is important to ask: What was Theodoret's attitude toward Greek heroes? In what way did he present Christian martyrs? What does this tell us about his conception of martyrdom?[3]

---

[1] For a general discussion of the relationship between the cult of heroes and the honor of the saints, see Lucius 1908, Delehaye 1927 and 1933², Speyer 1988:861–877 and 1990:48–66, Klauser 1974:221–229, Kötting 1990:67–80, and Jones 2010:84–92. Baumeister 1988 writes: "*Die Kirche hat nicht etwas Fertiges voll übernommen,* sondern sie hat in einem längerem historischen Prozeß durch Steigerung des Totenkultes die vielfältigen Formen der Heiligenverehrung entwickelt, wobei sie seit dem 4. Jh. im einzelnen sehr wohl Anregungen aus dem Bereich der Heroenverehrung aufgegriffen hat. Die Gemeinsamkeiten zwischen Heroenkult u. Heiligenverehrung erklären sich zunächst daher, daß es sich in beiden Fällen um Steigerungen des Christen u. Nichtchristen gemeinsamen, allgemeinen Totenkultes handelt. Mit direkten Übernahmen *einzelner Formen der Heroen-* in die Heiligenverehrung ist dann seit dem 4. Jh. zu rechnen" (104, emphasis mine). On the background of these practices and beliefs, see Hartmann 2010.

[2] In the prologue, where the main thrust of each *dialexis* is clearly set out, Theodoret writes: "The eighth *dialexis* is concerned with the accusation mounted against those glorifying the martyrs and with the counter-defense. With the assistance of the testimonies of philosophers, historians, and poets, the *dialexis* shows that Greeks honored the dead, not only with libations, but also with sacrifices to their so-called gods, demigods, or heroes, the majority of whom passed their lives in debauchery" (*Therapeutikê*, prologue 11).

[3] Although briefly touched upon by Dihle 1998:104–108, there has been no detailed discussion of the issue. For general accounts of the idea and practice of martyrdom and their historical developments, see Droge Tabor 1992, Bowersock 1995, and Moss 2010.

The *dialexis* begins with a contrast that is set up between the enigmatic nature of Pythagorean precepts and the simplicity of the Christian message. By making effective use of this opposition,[4] which underlies the entire *dialexis*, Theodoret refutes the implied accusation that Christians occupy an inferior social status. Within the teachings of Christianity, unexceptional people perform exceptional deeds motivated solely by their faith in the power of God. The universal appeal of the gospels is used to further bolster the value of the Christian message. However, arguably the most eloquent and forceful proof can be found in the example of the martyrs:

Καὶ οὐχ ἁπλῶς ἔπεισεν, ἀλλὰ τοσαύτην γε πίστιν τοῖς πλείστοις ἐντέθεικεν, ὡς ἥδιστα τὸν ὑπὲρ τῶν δὲ τῶν δογμάτων καταδέξασθαι θάνατον καὶ τοῖς ἀρνηθῆναι κελεύουσιν ἥκιστα μὲν προέσθαι τὰς γλώττας, προτεῖναι δὲ τὰ νῶτα τοῖς ἐθέλουσι μαστιγοῦν καὶ λαμπάσι καὶ ὄνυξι τὰς πλευρὰς καὶ τοὺς αὐχένας ὑποθεῖναι τοῖς ξίφεσι καὶ ἀποτυμπανισθῆναι προθύμως καὶ ἀνασκινδυλευθῆναι, καὶ μέντοι καὶ ἐμπρησθῆναι καὶ θῆρας ἀγρίους ἰδεῖν <u>θοινωμένους</u> τὰ σώματα.

Therapeutikê 8.9

And they [the scriptures of the apostles] have not only persuaded, but have instilled such faith in most people that they have gladly accepted death on behalf of these beliefs, and to those who have ordered them to deny their faith they have not uttered a word but have bared their backs to those who wished to flog them, and submitted their limbs to burning torches and iron hooks, and their heads to the sword. They have let themselves be cudgeled to death and be put in jar and set on fire and saw their bodies be feasted on/devoured by wild animals.

Theodoret builds on a set of oppositions recalling the contradictions with which he punctuates his *dialexis*: divided body/undivided grace, part/whole. In what follows, flowering grace is meant to suggest, on a figurative level, the notional unity and integrity of the body,[5] which, on a literal level, has been dismembered:

---

[4] Theodoret sums up the idea with his usual capacity to produce apophthegmatic statements in his *Ecclesiastical History* by saying: πέφυκε γὰρ τὰ παράδοξα ἕλκειν ἅπαντας ὡς ἐπίπαν πρὸς ἑαυτά ("for the extraordinary is generally sure to draw all men after it," *Ecclesiastical History* 4.27.16–17). For the effective use of paradox in Christian rhetoric, see Cameron 1991:155–188.

[5] A pervasive concern at the time, especially in connection with the resurrection; see Bynum 1995:59–114.

Καὶ αἱ μὲν γενναῖαι τῶν νικηφόρων ψυχαὶ περιπολοῦσι τὸν οὐρανόν, τοῖς ἀσωμάτων χοροῖς ξυγχορεύουσαι· τὰ δὲ σώματα οὐχ εἷς ἑνὸς ἑκάστου κατακρύπτει τάφος, ἀλλὰ πόλεις καὶ κῶμαι ταῦτα <u>διανειμάμεναι</u> σωτῆρας καὶ ψυχῶν καὶ σωμάτων καὶ ἰατροὺς ὀνομάζουσι καὶ ὡς πολιούχους τιμῶσι καὶ φύλακας· καὶ χρώμενοι πρεσβευταῖς πρὸς τὸν τῶν ὅλων δεσπότην, διὰ τούτων τὰς θείας κομίζονται δωρεάς. <u>Καὶ μερισθέντος τοῦ σώματος, ἀμέριστος ἡ χάρις μεμένηκεν,</u> καὶ τὸ σμικρὸν ἐκεῖνο καὶ βραχύτατον λείψανον τὴν ἴσην ἔχει δύναμιν τῷ μηδαμῇ μηδαμῶς διανεμηθέντι μάρτυρι· γὰρ <u>ἐπανθοῦσα χάρις</u> διανέμει τὰ δῶρα, τῇ πίστει τῶν προσιόντων τὴν φιλοτιμίαν μετροῦσα.

Therapeutikê 8.10

And the souls of those valiant victors traverse the heavens and join in chorus with choruses of the immortals. Their bodies are not concealed in the grave of a single individual, but cities and towns have divided their [bodies] among themselves and hail them [the martyrs] and name them saviors and physicians of both bodies and souls, honoring them as protectors and guardians. Although the body has been severed, grace has remained undivided, and this tiny piece of a relic has a power equal to that which the martyr would have had if he had never been dismembered. For grace when it blooms extends its gifts proportionate to the faith of those who pray.[6]

The articulation of this stance provides Theodoret with the opportunity to address one of the pagan objections that inform his portrayal of the martyrs. Turning to his opponents he says: "But as for you, not even all this persuades you to sing the praises of the God of martyrs; on the contrary, you laugh and scoff at the honor accorded the martyrs by the whole world and consider it an abomination to approach their tombs" (Ὑμᾶς δὲ οὐδὲ ταῦτα πείθει τὸν τούτων ὑμνῆσαι Θεόν, ἀλλὰ γελᾶτε καὶ κωμῳδεῖτε τὸ τούτοις παρὰ πάντων προσφερόμενον γέρας καὶ μύσος ὑπολαμβάνετε τὸ πελάζειν τοῖς τάφοις, *Therapeutikê* 8.12).

The honor accorded to the martyrs was met with acerbic criticism by pagans.[7] For example, Eunapius, in his *Lives of the Sophists*, attacks both the monks and their practice of re-sacralizing pagan temples with relics:

Εἶτα ἐπεισῆγον <u>τοῖς ἱεροῖς τόποις</u> τοὺς καλουμένους μοναχούς, ἀνθρώπους μὲν κατὰ τὸ εἶδος, ὁ δὲ βίος αὐτοῖς συώδης, καὶ ἐς τὸ

---

[6]   For the various attitudes of hagiographers towards relics and their cults, see Kaplan 1999:19-38.
[7]   For an overview, see Rinaldi 1998(I):355-364 and 1994:31-82.

ἐμφανὲς ἔπασχόν τε καὶ ἐποίουν μυρία κακὰ καὶ ἄφραστα. ἀλλ᾽ ὅμως τοῦτο μὲν εὐσεβὲς ἐδόκει, τὸ καταφρονεῖν τοῦ θείου· <u>τυραννικὴν</u> <u>γὰρ εἶχεν ἐξουσίαν τότε πᾶς ἄνθρωπος μέλαιναν φορῶν ἐσθῆτα,</u> <u>καὶ δημοσίᾳ βουλόμενος ἀσχημονεῖν·</u> εἰς τοσόνδε ἀρετῆς ἤλασε τὸ ἀνθρώπινον. <u>ἀλλὰ περὶ τούτων μὲν καὶ ἐν τοῖς καθολικοῖς τῆς ἱστορίας</u> <u>συγγράμμασιν εἴρηται.</u> τοὺς δὲ μοναχοὺς τούτους καὶ εἰς τὸν Κάνωβον καθίδρυσαν, ἀντὶ τῶν νοητῶν θεῶν εἰς ἀνδραπόδων θεραπείας, καὶ οὐδὲ χρηστῶν, καταδήσαντες τὸ ἀνθρώπινον. ὀστέα γὰρ καὶ κεφαλὰς τῶν ἐπὶ πολλοῖς ἁμαρτήμασιν ἑαλωκότων συναλίζοντες, οὓς τὸ πολιτικὸν ἐκόλαζε δικαστήριον, θεούς τε ἀπεδείκνυσαν, καὶ προσεκαλινδοῦντο τοῖς ὀστοῖς καὶ κρείττους ὑπελάμβανον εἶναι μολυνόμενοι πρὸς τοῖς τάφοις. <u>μάρτυρες</u> γοῦν ἐκαλοῦντο καὶ διάκονοί τινες καὶ πρέσβεις τῶν αἰτήσεων παρὰ τῶν θεῶν, ἀνδράποδα δεδουλευκότα κακῶς, καὶ μάστιξι καταδεδαπανημένα, καὶ τὰς τῆς μοχθηρίας ὠτειλὰς ἐν τοῖς εἰδώλοις φέροντα· ἀλλ᾽ ὅμως ἡ γῆ φέρει τούτους τοὺς θεούς. τοῦτο γοῦν εἰς μεγάλην πρόνοιαν καὶ <εὐστοχίαν> Ἀντωνίνου συνετέλεσεν, ὅτι πρὸς ἅπαντας ἔφασκεν τὰ ἱερὰ τάφους γενήσεσθαι.

Eunapius *Lives of the Sophists* 6.11

Next, into the sacred places they imported monks, as they called them . . . They settled these monks at Canopus also, and thus they fettered the human race to the worship of slaves, and those not even honest slaves, instead of the true gods. For they collected the bones and skulls of criminals who had been put to death for numerous crimes, men whom the law courts of the city had condemned to punishment, made them out to be gods, haunted their sepulchers, and thought that *they became better by defiling themselves at the graves.* "Martyrs" the dead men were called, and "ministers" of a sort, and "ambassadors" from the gods to carry men's prayers—these slaves in vilest servitude, who had been consumed by stripes and carried on their phantom forms the scars of their villainy. However, these are the gods that earth produces.

Several features bear special mention, if only because they recur in the polemic against the martyrs. Eunapius connects honoring the relics with the Christianizing zeal of the monks, the pollution that the relics incur,[8] and the humiliating death of the martyrs—an allusion to the Roman legal procedure

---

[8] For the notion of pollution and purity as well as the realms of life and activities associated with them in classical Greece, see Parker 1996. For a similar study in early Christianity, see Volp 2002.

that was followed in their trials—and their inferior social status.[9] The latter claims make it incumbent upon Theodoret, as well as most of the Christian authors writing in defense of the martyrs and the monks, to stress the moral dignity of martyrdom, which he does by playing it off against the background of hero-cult.[10]

The pollution to which Eunapius alludes is a moralized one that exists in direct proportion to the social status of the deceased,[11] as well as to those who revere them: in this case, the monks. Purity and pollution were used in classical society to demarcate realms of human activity.[12] In the case of Eunapius, pollution is used to demarcate religions specifically. He implies that, given the inferior social class of the deceased and the humiliating manner in which they die, they are not entitled to the honors that the Christians accord them. This is of crucial importance for our efforts to understand what Theodoret is trying to accomplish.

Julian reiterates the same accusation[13] in his *Against the Galileans* (among other writings),[14] perceptively noting the lack of precedent for honoring the martyrs in the scriptures:

ὅσα δὲ ὑμεῖς ἐξῆς προσευρήκατε, πολλοὺς ἐπεισάγοντες τῷ πάλαι νεκρῷ τοὺς προσφάτους νεκρούς, τίς ἂν πρὸς ἀξίαν βδελύξαιτο; πάντα

---

[9] In a similar vein one of Isidore's correspondents, Dometius, comes to be convinced that the martyr's death was not a defeat: "Ἧττα ἐστιν ὦ σοφώτατε, οὐ τὸ τεθνάναι ἐν πολέμῳ, ἀλλὰ τὸ δεῖσαι τοὺς πολεμίους, καὶ ῥῖψαι τὴν ἀσπίδα· ὃν δὲ ἐπέλιπε τὸ σῶμα τῆς ἀριστείας ἐπιθυμοῦντα ἐν τοῖς τροπαιούχοις ἀναγράφεσθαι, νόμος· ἐπεὶ καὶ τῶν ἀθλητῶν τοὺς ἐν αὐτῇ ἀποθανόντας πάλῃ, μᾶλλον τιμῶσιν οἱ τοὺς ἀγῶνας τούτους διαθέντες τῶν μὴ τοῦτο παθόντων. Εἰ τοίνυν ταῦθ' οὕτως ἔχει, δι' ἣν αἰτίαν νομίζεις τοὺς μάρτυρας τῷ τεθνάναι ἡττᾶσθαι, καὶ μὴ διὰ τοῦτο μᾶλλον ἀνακηρύττεις; Τέλος γὰρ ἐστι τῆς μάχης ταύτης οὐ τὸ σῶμα (ὃ καὶ δοκοῦν ζῆν ἐνέκρωσαν) ἀλλ' τὸ μὴ διαφθεῖραι τὸ τῆς ἀρετῆς κλέος" (Ep. 5, PG 78:1328).

[10] Eusebius, Chrysostom, Cyril of Alexandria, Basil, Asterius of Amaseia. For the critique of heroized men in Greek culture as a shared concern across a number of Christian authors in the fourth and fifth centuries, see Hammerstaedt 1996:76–101.

[11] Precisely the same point is made by Libanius, for whose polemic see Rinaldi 1994:62–64.

[12] Parker 1996:18–31 refers to this phenomenon (when discussing purification) as a science of division.

[13] Asmus 1894:116–145 finds a number of passages that echo Julian's polemic in *Against the Galileans* and makes a good case for the possibility of the *Therapeutikê* being a response to it. However Geffcken 1908:161–195, defending his choice not to discuss Theodoret's *Therapeutikê*, writes: "Man kann von Asmus über Julian und über manches andere recht viel lernen, aber er berücksichtigt etwas zu wenig die Tradition der einzelnen Argumente und glaubt in mancher Replik alter hellenischer, auch von Julian gebrauchter Vorwürfe eine besondere Spitze gegen den Kaiser zu erkennen. Wer damals den lange toten Julian bekämpfte, nannte ihn auch. Eine gelegentliche Bekämpfung, ohne ihn direct zu nennen, ist natürlich nicht ausgeschlossen, aber der Hauptgegner ist er für Theodoret nicht" (188n2).

[14] See Rinaldi 1994:62–64.

ἐπληρώσατε τάφων καὶ μνημάτων, καίτοι οὐκ εἴρηται παρ' ὑμῖν
οὐδαμοῦ τοῖς τάφοις προσκαλινδεῖσθαι καὶ περιέπειν αὐτούς. εἰς τοῦτο
δὲ προεληλύθατε μοχθηρίας, ὥστε οἴεσθαι δεῖν ὑπὲρ τούτου μηδὲ τῶν γε
Ἰησοῦ τοῦ Ναζωραίου ῥημάτων ἀκούειν. ἀκούετε οὖν, ἅ φησιν ἐκεῖνος
περὶ τῶν μνημάτων· "οὐαὶ ὑμῖν, γραμματεῖς καὶ Φαρισαῖοι ὑποκριταί,
ὅτι παρομοιάζετε τάφοις κεκονιαμένοις· ἔξωθεν ὁ τάφος φαίνεται
ὡραῖος, ἔσωθεν δὲ γέμει ὀστέων νεκρῶν καὶ πάσης ἀκαθαρσίας." εἰ
τοίνυν ἀκαθαρσίας Ἰησοῦς ἔφη πλήρεις εἶναι τοὺς τάφους, πῶς ὑμεῖς
ἐπ' αὐτῶν ἐπικαλεῖσθε τὸν θεόν; ... τούτων οὖν οὕτως ἐχόντων, ὑμεῖς
ὑπὲρ τίνος προσκαλινδεῖσθε τοῖς μνήμασι;

Julian Against the Galileans, fr. 81 Masaracchia

. . . but who could detest as they deserve all those doctrines that you
have invented as a sequel, while you keep adding so many corpses
newly dead to the corpse of long ago? *You have filled the whole world with
tombs and sepulchres, and yet in your scriptures it is nowhere said that you
must grovel among tombs and pay them honour.* But you have gone so far in
iniquity that you think you need not listen even the words of Jesus of
Nazareth on this matter. Listen then to what he says about sepulchres:
"Woe unto you, scribes and Pharisees, hypocrites! For ye are like unto
whited sepulchres; outward the tomb appears beautiful, but within it
is full of dead men's bones, and of all uncleanness." *If, then, Jesus said
that sepulchres are full of uncleanness, how can you invoke God at them?* . . .
Therefore, since this is so, why do you grovel among tombs?[15]

The same concern about pollution from the dead is addressed in question 28 of
the *Quaestiones et responsiones*, where, in an objection echoing Julian's criticism,[16]
the unnamed enquirer asks:

---

[15] Trans. Wright.

[16] Rinaldi 1989:478 argues similarly. Isidore of Peluse conjures up the strong reactions and attempts
to assuage the concerns and objections of his correspondent Hierax *clarissimus*, who is clearly
put off by and jeers at the honor paid to the martyr's relics: "Εἰ σκανδαλίζῃ ἐπὶ τῇ κόνει τῶν
μαρτυρικῶν σωμάτων παρ'ἡμῶν τιμωμένῃ διὰ τὴν περὶ τὸν Θεὸν αὐτῶν ἀγάπην καὶ ἔνστασιν,
ἐρώτησον τοὺς ἐξ αὐτῶν τὰς ἰάσεις λαμβάνοντας, καὶ μάθε πόσοις πάθεσι θεραπείας χαρίζονται.
Καὶ οὐ μόνον οὐ σκώψεις τὸ γινόμενον, ἀλλὰ καὶ ζηλώσεις πάντως τὸ κατορθούμενον.
Εἰ δὲ αὐτὸς νεκρῶν ὀστῶν παραιτῇ θίγειν, ὡς γέγραφας, τῶν πονηρῶν ἀνθρώπων καὶ ἐπὶ
κακίᾳ βοηθέντων τὰ λείψανα βδέλυξαι, οὓς ἐν τῷ ναῷ τῆς Ἐφεσίας Ἀρτέμιδος κατώρυξαν
Ἕλληνες σεμνοποιοῦντες τὰ αἴσχιστα, καὶ φαύλων ἀνθρώπων τάφους καὶ κόνεις λοιμοποιοὺς
ἐκθειάζοντες" (Ep. 55, PG 78:217).

Εἰ τὴν τῶν Φαρισαίων ἐσχηματισμένην ὁ κύριος ἐλέγχων εὐλάβειαν ἔλεγεν ὅτι τάφοι κεκονιαμένοι εἰσί, πεπληρωμένοι ὀστέων νεκρῶν καὶ πάσης ἀκαθαρσίας, καὶ ἐν τῷ νόμῳ ὁ ἁπτόμενος νεκροῦ ἀκάθαρτος λέγεται, τί ἄτοπον ἐργάζονται Ἕλληνες τοὺς νεκροὺς καὶ τοὺς τούτων μυσαττόμενοι τάφους, ὑπό τε παλαιᾶς καὶ καινῆς ἀκαθάρτου τοῦ νεκροῦ καλουμένου; πῶς δὲ ἀμφοτέροις ὁ κύριος ἐναντία οὐκ ἔπραξεν, ὅτε τὸν υἱὸν τῆς χήρας ἀνιστῶν ἥψατο τῆς σοροῦ καὶ τὴν θυγατέρα τοῦ Ἰαείρου τῆς χειρὸς ἐκράτησεν; εἰ γὰρ ἀμφότεροι τελευταῖον ἀνέστησαν. ἀλλὰ τὴν ἀφὴν τὰ νεκρὰ ἐδέξαντο σώματα.

If the Lord censuring the piety of the Pharisees as feigned was calling them whitewashed graves, full of dead bones and of every impurity, and (if) according to the Law he who touches a corpse is called unclean, why is it absurd that the Greeks abhor—because of the impurity—the corpses and their graves since a corpse is called unclean by the Old and the New Testament? How did the Lord not act against both [Old and New Testament], when, upon resurrecting the son of the widow, He touched the corpse and held the hand of the daughter of Jaeirus? Even if both were, ultimately, resurrected, their dead bodies were nevertheless touched.

The question gives the anonymous author the opportunity both to discuss the issue of pollution and to rationalize the fear of corpses and their polluting effect:

Τῶν ἀνθρώπων τὰ νεκρὰ σώματα καὶ οἱ τούτων τάφοι μυσάττονται διὰ τὴν ἑπομένην αὐτοῖς βαρεῖαν δυσωδίαν, οὐχ ἁπλῶς διὰ τὴν νέκρωσιν· εἰ γὰρ ἁπλῶς διὰ τὴν νέκρωσιν ἐμυσάττοντο τῶν νεκρῶν τὰ σώματα, οὐκ ἄρα ἐχρῆν τοῖς τῶν ζῴων νεκρῶν σωμάτων μέρεσι κεχρῆσθαι πρὸς τὴν τῶν ζώντων χρείαν, ὡς τοῖς δέρμασι καὶ τοῖς κέρασι καὶ τρίχαις καὶ χολαῖς καὶ τοῖς στέασι καὶ ταῖς σαρξίν, ἅτινα οὐδεὶς λόγος δύναται ὑπεξελεῖν τῆς προσούσης αὐτοῖς νεκρώσεως. εἰ δὲ νεκρὰ μὲν καὶ ταῦτα, οὐ μυσαττόμενα δὲ διὰ τὴν ἐξ αὐτῶν χρείαν, πῶς οὐκ ἔστι τῶν ἀτοπωτάτων τὸ καθαρὰ μὲν ἡγεῖσθαι ταῦτα διὰ τὴν ἐξ αὐτῶν χρείαν, μυσάττεσθαι δὲ τῶν ἁγίων μαρτύρων τὰ σώματα καὶ τοὺς τάφους ὑπὸ Ἑλλήνων, φυλακτικὰ ὄντα ἀνθρώπων τῆς τῶν δαιμόνων ἐπιβουλῆς καὶ ἰαματικὰ νοσημάτων τῶν κατὰ τὴν τῶν ἰατρῶν τέχνην ὄντων ἀνιάτων; παρεικάζει δὲ ὁ κύριος τὴν τῶν Φαρισαίων ἐσχηματισμένην εὐλάβειαν τάφοις κεκονιαμένοις, ὅτι ὥσπερ τῇ αἰσθήσει τῶν ζώντων βδελυκτή ἐστι τῶν νεκρῶν σωμάτων ἡ δυσωδία καὶ ἡ ἀκαθαρσία, οὕτω καὶ ἡ ἐκείνων ἀνομία βδελυκτή ἐστι τῇ νοήσει τῶν εὐσεβῶν, τρόπον τινὰ οὖσα αὕτη ψυχῆς νέκρωσις καὶ δυσωδία καὶ ἀκαθαρσία. ὥσπερ γὰρ χωρισθείσης τῆς ψυχῆς τοῦ σώματος νεκρὸν τὸ σῶμα καὶ δυσῶδες καὶ ἀκάθαρτον, οὕτω χωρισθέντος τοῦ φόβου τοῦ θεοῦ τῆς ψυχῆς νεκρὰ ὑπάρχει ἡ ψυχὴ καὶ δυσώδης καὶ ἀκάθαρτος. κατ᾽ ἐναντίωσιν δὲ πράξας ὁ κύριος οὐδὲν οὔτε τῇ παλαιᾷ οὔτε τῇ καινῇ δείκνυται· οὐκ ἦν γὰρ ὑπὸ τὸν νόμον, ὅτε τοὺς ἐν τῇ ἐρωτήσει ἤγειρε νεκρούς· ἀπὸ γὰρ τοῦ βαπτίσματος ἤρξατο ὁ κύριος τῆς εὐαγγελικῆς πολιτείας, οὔσης ἔξωθεν τῆς τοῦ νόμου φυλακῆς. διὸ οὐκ ἐμιάνθη ἁψάμενος τοῦ νεκροῦ. <u>κατὰ δὲ τὴν καινὴν</u> ἐκεῖνα μόνα ἦν μιαντικὰ ἀνθρώπων, τὰ ἐκ τῆς καρδίας ἐξερχόμενα κακά. τὸ δὲ ἅπτεσθαι νεκροῦ οὐ μιαίνει τὸν ἄνθρωπον.

Quaestiones et responsiones, Q. 28

The corpses of dead people and their graves are abhorred because of the heavy stench that follows them, not just for the fact that they are dead [for their death]. For if the bodies of the dead were abhorred for their death, the body parts of dead animals should not be used for the needs of the living, as is the case with skins, horns and hair and gall-bladder and fat and flesh, by no means can one take away the state of death that inheres in them. For even though these are dead, and are not abhorred because they are needed, how is it not one of the most absurd things to regard them clean because they are needed, and for the Greeks to loath the bodies and the graves of the holy martyrs, protecting as they do from demonic attacks and healing the diseases which according to the art of the doctors are incurable. The Lord compares the feigned piety of the Pharisees to whitewashed graves because just as the stench and the uncleanness of dead bodies is abominable to the living so is their lawlessness abominable to the mind of the pious, this [lawlessness] being in some way the death of the soul and stench and uncleanness. Because, just as when the soul is separated from the body it stinks and is unclean, so the soul separated from the fear of God stinks and is unclean. The Lord did appear to act against the Old or the New Testament. Since his baptism, the Lord began a way of life according to the gospel, which is above the keeping of the Law. This is why He was not defiled by having touched the dead. According to the New Testament the only things defiling humans are the evils coming from the heart. Touching the dead does not defile humans.

This attempt to normalize the practice of honoring the martyrs prompts Theodoret to launch into a survey on notions of heroism and patterns of heroization in Greek culture.[17] Before analyzing the specific arguments that Theodoret employs, it is useful to speculate as to the background that he presumes in his encounter with Hellenic ideals of heroism. The very notion of heroization had, by his time, had a long and complex history. Hero cult was one of the oldest features of Greek culture and religion.[18] It was multifaceted and entailed a number of functions for practitioners.[19] Heroes themselves could be mythical figures—malevolent or benevolent—and they had a daimonic aspect (in the form of souls of the deceased).[20] Moving freely from the simple to the most complex, even literary, aspects of hero worship, Theodoret seems to build on an expanded notion of heroization that encompassed public figures,[21] philosophers, and poets of the past.[22]

Theodoret singles out Hercules,[23] Asclepius, and Dionysus, showing how they acquired the heroic-divine status in Greek culture, but more importantly that they were human beings unworthy of the divine status that they were accorded by the Greeks. He employs the language of disease to describe the misplaced (but very popular) cult of Hercules:

Διέβη δὲ καὶ εἰς τὴν Ἀσίαν τῆς ἐξαπάτης ἡ νόσος· καὶ γὰρ καὶ ἐν Τύρῳ καὶ ἐν ἄλλαις πόλεσι παμπόλλους καὶ μεγίστους αὐτῷ σηκοὺς ᾠκοδόμησαν. Καὶ οὐ μόνον ἐτησίους ἀπένειμαν πανηγύρεις, ἀλλὰ καὶ τετραετηρικοῖς ἀγῶσιν ἐτίμησαν, καὶ ταῦτά γε ἄνδρα εἰδότες, καὶ ἄνδρα οὐ σώφρονα οὐδὲ φιλοσοφίαν ἠγαπηκότα, ἀλλ' ἀκολασίᾳ καὶ λαγνείᾳ ξυνεζηκότα

Therapeutikê 8.15

The disease of this error has reached even to Asia; for instance, in Tyre and in other cities they have constructed for him enormous and

---

[17] This was foreshadowed in *Dialexis* III. On Angels, Gods, and Demons, where we find *in nuce* the outline of what will be more thoroughly developed in *Dialexis* VIII.

[18] For a comprehensive treatment, see Farnell 1921; see also Nock 1944:141–174 and Jones 2010.

[19] For an overview of the range of these functions, see Pirenne-Delforge and Suárez de la Torre 2000.

[20] Soler 2006:441 notes, "A la fin du IV siècle, les textes ne font pas apparaître la célébration de ces fêtes mais Jean Chrysostome met bien l'accent sur la croyance répandue à Antioche selon laquelle les âmes des martyrs seraient des démons."

[21] See Farnell's 1928 definition of the hero as: "a person whose virtue, influence or personality was so powerful in his lifetime or through the peculiar circumstances of his death that his spirit after death is regarded as a supernormal power, claiming to be reverenced and propitiated" (343).

[22] Especially in late antiquity, poets (Homer) and philosophers (Plato predominantly) had been put on the pedestal and revered as cultural heroes. For the "cult of learning," see Zanker 1995:267–331 and Boyancé 1937:231–297.

[23] Malherbe 1988:559–583.

countless sanctuaries.[24] And not satisfied with offering annual celebrations, they have special games every four years in his honor. They are aware that he was a mere man, one who had esteemed neither temperance nor philosophy, but who had spent all his life in debauchery and dissolute conduct.

Having gone through a critique of popular Greek heroes, he turns to the pagans, asking:

Τί δήποτε τοίνυν οἱ τοσούτους νεκροὺς ὠνομακότες θεοὺς νεμεσᾶτε ἡμῖν, <u>οὐ θεοποιοῦσιν</u>, ἀλλὰ τιμῶσι τοὺς μάρτυρας, ὡς Θεοῦ γε <u>μάρτυρας</u> καὶ εὔνους θεράποντας; ἀνθ' ὅτου δὲ μολυσμοῦ τινος μεταλαμβάνειν νομίζετε τὸν ταῖς θήκαις τῶν τεθνεώτων πελάζοντα; ἀνοίας γὰρ ταῦτα καὶ ἀμαθίας ἐσχάτης.

Therapeutikê 8.29–30

Why, then, do you who have given the name of gods to so many of the dead express such indignation at us *who without deifying them* honor our martyrs in that they are witnesses to God and faithful servants? And why do you think that anyone who approaches the tomb of a martyr incurs some sort of pollution/defilement? This is a sign of lack of understanding and ignorance.

This particular issue prompts Theodoret to refer to several cases of famous Greek heroes (Cecrops; Athens, Acrisius; Larissa Cleomachus; Didyma, Lycophrone; Magnesia) who were buried in temples or their sacred precincts.[25] There follows

---

[24] Asterius of Amasea, attacking the same gods in his *Encomium on All the Martyrs* homily, notes in a similar vein: "Οὐ σὺ ὁ τὸν Θηβαῖον Διόνυσον ὡς θεὸν προσκυνῶν–λέγω γὰρ τὴν πατρίδα, ἵνα γνωρίσῃς τὸν ἄνθρωπον-, ἄνδρα γεωργὸν ἀμπέλων καὶ φίλοινον, κωμαστὴν πάροινον, δῆμον ἐπισυρόμενον ἀσχημονοῦντα τῇ μέθῃ, ἐκεῖνα ποιοῦντα ἃ τοὺς ἀσώτους νέους στηλιτεύει ἀκολασταίνοντας, μεθύοντα δὲ μετὰ τοῦ γέροντος τοῦ Σιληνοῦ καὶ τοῖς φιλοσκιρτηταῖς Σατύροις συνδιαιτώμενον καὶ ἱστορίαν μέθης ὄντα τῷ βίῳ; Οὐ σὺ ὁ τῷ ἀνδρὶ Ἡρακλεῖ ὡς θεῷ τὰς θυσίας προσάγων, ἀνθρώπῳ ῥωμαλαίῳ, σῶμα λαχόντι δυνατὸν καὶ ἀνδρεῖον, καὶ σέβεις ἐκεῖνον, ἐπειδὴ ἐν πολλοῖς ἠρίστευσεν καὶ θηρίων περιεγένετο; Τί δὲ πάλιν τὸν Ἀσκληπιὸν τὸν ἐν τῷ νάρθηκι πολλὰ καὶ τῇ σιδηροθήκῃ περινοστήσαντα οὐ σέβεις καὶ τέθηπας; Καὶ οὐκ ἂν ἀρνηθείης ὡς οὐ τοῦτο ποιεῖς. Οἱ γὰρ πανταχοῦ τῆς οἰκουμένης ἀνεστῶτες ναοί, τὰ Ἀσκληπιεῖα λέγω καὶ τὰ Ἡράκλεια καὶ τὰ Διονύσια, ἔλεγχοι ἑστᾶσιν ὑψηλοὶ τῆς σῆς ματαιότητος· καὶ οὕτως ἐγὼ μὲν ἄθῳος ἀπελεύσομαι τοῦ ἐγκλήματος, οὐ γὰρ προσκύνω μάρτυρας οὐδὲ νομίζω θεούς· σὺ δὲ πέφηνας ἐνεχόμενος τοῖς ἐγκλήμασιν, καὶ ταῦτα κατηγορῶν ἑτέρων, ὥσπερ οἱ διὰ κακὸν συνειδὸς προκατηγοροῦντες τῶν ἀνευθύνων. Ἀνθρώπους γὰρ ὡς θεοὺς προσκυνῶν ἐπιδέδειξαι. Ταῦτα πρὸς τὸν ἐθνικὸν ἐκ πολλῶν ὀλίγα" (10.9.11–29 ed. Datema).

[25] This particular argument is discussed [and dismissed] by Volp 2002:253 who writes: "Die von Theodoret bemühten Mythen gehören zu den exotischen Überlieferungen paganer Volkererzählungen, die alles andere als gängige Kultpraxis widerspiegeln. Auf der Grundlage

a passage from the *Iliad* where Achilles does not hesitate to carry the dead body of Patroclus or to take his bones from the pyre to his tent. An additional reference is made to Thucydides' account of the burial and grave of those who fought in the battle of Marathon.[26] Theodoret explicates further:

Ἡμεῖς δέ, ὦ ἄνδρες, οὔτε θυσίας, οὔτε μὴν χοὰς τοῖς μάρτυσιν ἀπονέμομεν, ἀλλ᾽ ὡς θείους καὶ θεοφιλεῖς γεραίρομεν ἄνδρας. Οὕτω γὰρ τοῦ πεποιηκότος καὶ σεσωκότος ἡράσθησαν, ὡς τὴν ὑπὲρ αὐτοῦ σφαγὴν ὑπολαβεῖν ἀξιέραστον.

Therapeutikê 8.34

As for us, my friends, it is not sacrifices or libations we offer to our martyrs;[27] we honor them like *men of God and friends of God*, because they have loved their Creator and Savior to the point of believing nothing is so desirable as to lay down their lives for Him.

The centrality of Christ's sacrifice is the ultimate paradigm for the self-sacrifice of the martyrs.[28] Here, Theodoret expands the notion of friendship with God so that it encompasses the martyrs.[29] He continues:

Εἰ δὲ μάντεις καὶ ἰατροὺς τοσαύτης ἔφησεν ἐκεῖνος ἀξιοῦσθαι τιμῆς, τί ἂν εἴποι τις περὶ τοσαύτην ἐπιδειξαμένων ὑπὲρ εὐσεβείας ἀνδρείαν, οἷς τοὖργον οὐ μόνον ἀνδρείαν, ἀλλὰ καὶ δικαιοσύνην καὶ σωφροσύνην καὶ σοφίαν καὶ φρόνησιν μαρτυρεῖ; τί γὰρ σωφρονέστερον τῶν οὐκ ἀνασχομένων ἐκείνων ἐκστῆναι, ἅπερ ἐξ ἀρχῆς εὖ ἔχειν ὑπέλαβον; τί δὲ δικαιότερον τῶν τὰς θείας εὐεργεσίας ἀμειψαμένων σφαγῇ καὶ τὰ σώματα ἐκδεδωκότων ὑπὲρ τοῦ τὸ σῶμα παραδεδωκότος σταυρῷ;

Therapeutikê 8.37

---

dieser Legenden läßt sich nicht auf eine laxe Handhabung der Bestattungsverbote in den Tempelbezirken historischer Zeit schliessen. Im Gegenteil, die Tatsache, dass er gezwungen ist, seine Beispiele aus der mythischen Götterwelt zu beziehen, untermauert die Historizität dieser Verbote für gewöhnliche Sterbliche. Vor allem aber zeigt dieser Passus, dass es zu Theodorets Zeit zahlreiche Christen gegeben hat, die in der Anwesenheit von Leichen in Gottesdiensträumen eine Gefährdung der Sakramente und eine Verunreinigung der christlichen Altäre sahen." See also Hartmann 2010:500.

[26] On the role of relics in ancient Greek culture, see Pfister 1909–1912, Lacroix 1989:58–99, Zografou 2005:123–145, and Hartmann 2010:52–592.

[27] For a recent study, see Ekroth 2002.

[28] Moss 2010.

[29] The idea of friendship with God is treated more fully in *Therapeutikê* 12.19–20, which is devoted to the defense of Christianity as the ultimate practical virtue. Theodoret's use of the concept of θεοφιλία owes as much to the biblical tradition as it does to the Greek philosophical one; see Chapter Four.

Now if this author [viz. Empedocles[30]] says that seers and physicians deserve such great *honor*, what should be said of those who have given proof of such great fortitude in defense of their religion and whose deeds give testimony not just to their manliness but to their *justice* also, and to their *temperance, wisdom and prudence?* What is more prudent than that those people should stand up for those principles which they had maintained were correct from the start? What is more just than that those should requite the divine blessings by their own lives and should deliver up their bodies for Him who delivered his for them on the cross?

Concepts like honor (timê) that have an indisputable cultural weight are deployed to give dignity to the moral struggle of the martyrs. Furthermore, Theodoret skillfully assimilates into the portrayal of the martyrs such moral virtues as ἀνδρεία 'manliness', δικαιοσύνη 'justice', σωφροσύνη 'temperance', σοφία 'wisdom', and φρόνησις 'prudence', which were current in Greek philosophy from the time of Plato.[31] What to pagan eyes may have looked like a humiliating death emerges as a noble and forceful practice of precisely those virtues that brought the martyrs close to God.

In a similar vein, martyrs form part of an argument closely allied with the political and ethnographic argument that Theodoret sets forth in *Dialexis IX. On the Laws.* In *Therapeutikê* 9.30, by way of a hypothetical question, Theodoret says: "And if one supposed that it is the piety of the emperors that has confirmed the teaching of the fishermen, that only goes to show the strength of this same teaching." The underlying criticism here is of the notion that Christianity succeeded thanks to imperial patronage and support. Martyrs are adduced as proof that, long before any imperial patronage, Christians were prepared to lay down their lives for their beliefs. Their unflinching courage is the sign of the power of the "laws of the fishermen."

To better buttress his claim about the autonomous value of the church, which is not coextensive with the empire,[32] Theodoret introduces a historical

---

[30] For Empedocles' views on intermediaries, see Detienne 1959:1–17.

[31] North 1966b:165–183. For the notion of manliness (ἀνδρεία) in Greek culture, see Bartsch 1968 and, more recently, the contributions in Rosen and Sluiter 2003.

[32] For a similar line of thought, see the reply to Q. 146 in *QRO*, where an inquirer asks about the numerical superiority of the pagans, heretics, and Jews taken together: "To rule earthly things in the present life in the manner of a king, is not the legacy of true Christians ... He who wants to know the power of the true Christians has to look to the future condition. For the power in the present over things material is not a recompense for the faith of the Christians, but rather a [form of public] service according to God's plan (*diataxis*) for the constitution of a well-ordered human polity that has been handed down to people, sometimes to Christians, sometimes to heretics, and sometimes to the Greeks. For as long as the Christians struggle for the sake of

dimension. Referring to the persecutions of the early Christians by Roman emperors,[33] he draws an analogy to the contemporary persecutions in Persia,[34] where Christianity was still making headway despite merciless persecution:

Ἵνα δὲ τοῦτο ὑμῖν ἐκδηλότερον γένηται, τὰ παρὰ Περσῶν νῦν τολμώμενα καταμάθετε. Ποῖον γάρ τοι εἶδος σφαγῆς κατὰ τῶν εὐσεβούντων οὐκ ἐπινενόηται τούτοις; οὐκ ἐκδοραί, οὐκ ἐκτομαὶ χειρῶν καὶ ποδῶν, καὶ ὤτων καὶ ῥινῶν κολοβώσεις, καὶ δεσμοὶ πρὸς ὑπερβολὴν ὀδύνης ἐξευρημένοι, καὶ ὀρύγματα κεχριμένα μὲν εἰς ἀκρίβειαν, μυῶν δὲ τῶν μεγίστων ἀνάπλεα τοὺς δεδεμένους θοιναζομένων; ἀλλ᾿ ὅμως τοσαύτας καὶ τούτων πολλαπλασίας κατὰ τῶν εὐσεβούντων τιμωρίας ἐξευρηκότες, αἰκίζονται μὲν καὶ κολοβοῦσι τὰ σώματα καὶ παντάπασι διαφθείρουσι, τὸν δέ γε τῆς πίστεως οὐ ληστεύουσι θησαυρόν. Καὶ τοῖς μὲν ἄλλοις αὐτῶν νόμοις ἅπαντας ὑποκύπτειν τοὺς ὑπηκόους καταναγκάζουσι, τοὺς δὲ τῶν ἁλιέων ἐξαρνηθῆναι τοὺς πεπιστευκότας οὐ πείθουσιν.

Therapeutikê 9.32–33

To make this clearer to you, learn of the enormities attempted just now by the Persians. What extremes of slaughter have they not devised against the faithful? Have they not resorted to flaying, cutting off of hands and feet, mutilation of ears and noses? They have devised chains of most exquisite cruelty, and trenches carefully greased and filled with huge rats to feast on those who were chained. And yet, in devising such punishments and others like them against the Christians they may have mutilated and maltreated their bodies and sometimes even destroyed them totally, but they have not robbed the treasure of their faith. And while they force all of their subjects to obey their laws, they do not convince those who believe in the laws of the fishermen to reject/deny them.

---

virtue and they walk on the "narrow" and "hard path" [Matthew 7:14], they are set before all [lie exposed] (*prokeimenoi*) as assistance to anyone who wants to press them into service they are not considered rulers."

[33] To this historical dimension Theodoret adds the recent persecutions by Julian, on which see Scorza Barcellona 1995:53–83. See also Penella 1993:31–43.

[34] Dignas 2007:223–255; Van Rompay 1995:363–375; on Theodoret's reference to these persecutions in his *Ecclesiastical History*, see Leppin 2009:154–158.

In this formulation, the more the church is persecuted, the more it thrives.[35] The heroic death of Christians is a powerful statement of the value of their beliefs at a time when people expected spectacular demonstrations of faith.[36] John Chrysostom, apostrophizing a pagan fictive speaker, suggests this:

Ἀλλ' οὐ τούτοις προσέχουσιν Ἕλληνες. Μὴ γάρ μοι, φησίν, εἴπης τὸν ἐκτὸς τοῦ πάθους φιλοσοφοῦντα, τοῦτο γὰρ οὐδὲν μέγα οὐδὲ θαυμαστόν, ἀλλὰ δεῖξόν μοι τὸν ἐν αὐτῷ τῷ πάθει φιλοσοφοῦντα, καὶ τότε πιστεύσω τῇ ἀναστάσει.

On the Letter to the Hebrews 4.5, PG 63:43

But to these things the pagans give no heed. For [one will say] do not tell me of him who is philosophical when out of the affliction, for this is nothing great or surprising—show me a man who in the very affliction itself is philosophical, and then I will believe the resurrection.

No less significant is the activity of the monks who are actively engaged in the Christianization of the countryside and who bear living testimony to their tenets.[37] By Theodoret's time the notion of martyrdom had been extended to include monks as well.[38] The relics of the martyrs also led to new forms of religiosity and helped to re-sacralize the sacred *loci* by becoming focal points of local piety.[39]

---

[35] Reflecting on the history of the persecutions Theodoret says: "Οὐ χρὴ δὲ θαυμάζειν ὅτι τῆς ἐκείνων θηριωδίας καὶ δυσσεβείας ἀνέχεται τῶν ὅλων ὁ πρύτανις. καὶ γὰρ πρὸ τῆς Κωνσταντίνου τοῦ μεγάλου βασιλείας ὅσοι Ῥωμαίων ἐγένοντο βασιλεῖς κατὰ τῶν θιασωτῶν τῆς ἀληθείας ἐλύττησαν. Διοκλητιανὸς δὲ ἐν τῇ τοῦ σωτηρίου πάθους ἡμέρᾳ τὰς ἐν ἁπάσῃ τῇ Ῥωμαίων ἡγεμονίᾳ κατέλυσεν ἐκκλησίας· ἀλλ' ἐννέα διεληλυθότων ἐτῶν αὐταὶ μὲν ἤνθησαν καὶ πολλαπλάσιον ἐδέξαντο μέγεθός τε καὶ κάλλος, ἐκεῖνος δὲ μετὰ τῆς δυσσεβείας ἀπέσβη. καὶ τοὺς πολέμους δὲ τούτους προείρηκεν ὁ δεσπότης καὶ τὸ τῆς ἐκκλησίας ἀήττητον. καὶ αὐτὰ δὲ ἡμᾶς διδάσκει τὰ πράγματα ὡς πλείονα ἡμῖν τῆς εἰρήνης ὁ πόλεμος πορίζει τὴν ὠφέλειαν· ἡ μὲν γὰρ ἁβροὺς ἡμᾶς καὶ ἀνειμένους καὶ δειλοὺς ἀπεργάζεται, ὁ δὲ πόλεμος τά τε φρονήματα παραθήγει καὶ τῶν παρόντων ὡς ῥεόντων παρασκευάζει καταφρονεῖν. ἀλλὰ ταῦτα μὲν καὶ ἐν ἑτέραις πραγματείαις πολλάκις εἰρήκαμεν" (*Ecclesiastical History* 5.39.24–26 [347, 4–17]). A similar thought appears in the answer to question 74 of the *Quaestiones et responsiones*: "ἀλλ' αἱ βάσανοι αὗται, αἷς πάλαι χρησάμενος ὁ ἑλληνισμὸς καὶ προσδοκήσας ἐν αὐταῖς ἄλυτον φυλάττειν ἑαυτόν, τὸν μὲν ἑλληνισμὸν ἔλυσαν, τὸν δὲ χριστιανισμὸν ἔστησαν κατὰ κράτος." For a collection of texts that illustrate this idea, see Pellegrino 1955–56:371–442. Trompf 2000:213–252.

[36] Nock refers to the "theatricality" of the accounts of martyrdom as a shared feature in the Greco-Roman literature, especially the novel; see Nock 1933:197 and Potter 1993:53–88.

[37] This is a period during which the notion of martyrdom is extended to the ascetics as well as to those who suffered persecutions by rival Christian factions and heretics.

[38] Malone 1950; Baumeister 1988:104, 136–139.

[39] *Therapeutikê* 8.69: "In fact the master has replaced your gods with the remains of his martyrs, declaring your gods banished and reassigning the honor formerly given to them to the martyrs."

This brings us to a different aspect of the practice of honoring the martyrs, which, a few decades earlier, John Chrysostom had made one of the focal points of his apologetics.[40] For Theodoret, the mention of Hellenic festivals celebrating heroes gives an opportunity to refer, in one passage,[41] to the festivals celebrating the honor accorded to the saints:

Τοὺς γὰρ οἰκείους νεκροὺς ὁ δεσπότης ἀντεισῆξε τοῖς ὑμετέροις θεοῖς, καὶ τοὺς μὲν φρούδους ἀπέφηνε, τούτοις δὲ τὸ ἐκείνων ἀπένειμε γέρας. Ἀντὶ γὰρ δὴ τῶν Πανδίων καὶ Διασίων καὶ Διονυσίων καὶ τῶν ἄλλων ὑμῶν ἑορτῶν Πέτρου καὶ Παύλου καὶ Θωμᾶ καὶ Σεργίου καὶ Μαρκέλλου καὶ Λεοντίου καὶ Ἀντωνίνου καὶ Μαυρικίου καὶ τῶν ἄλλων μαρτύρων ἐπιτελοῦνται δημοθοινίαι· καὶ ἀντὶ τῆς πάλαι πομπείας καὶ αἰσχρουργίας καὶ αἰσχρορημοσύνης σώφρονες ἑορτάζονται πανηγύρεις, οὐ μέθην ἔχουσαι καὶ κῶμον καὶ γέλωτα, ἀλλ' ὕμνους θείους καὶ ἱερῶν λογίων ἀκρόασιν καὶ προσευχὴν ἀξιεπαίνοις κοσμουμένην δακρύοις.

Therapeutikê 8.69

In fact the master *has replaced your gods with the remains of his martyrs*, declaring your gods banished and reassigning the honor formerly given to them to the martyrs. Instead of the festivals of Pandia, Diasia, Dionysia, and all the others are the public holy-days of Peter, Antoninus, Mauricius, and the other martyrs. And instead of the pagan processions with their rites and appropriate obscenities are the chaste festivals which are not characterized by drunkenness, or revelry, or

---

For a nuanced discussion of this phenomenon, see Markus 1990:139–155. Theodoret accords the same sacralizing role to ascetics who were actively engaged in the Christianization of the countryside and whose "abodes . . . sanctify the mountain tops and populate deserts which had previously been uninhabited" (*Therapeutikê* 6.87). Further support can be gained from the *Religious History*, where a number of monks actually reside in the remains of pagan temples and have dramatic encounters with the demons who inhabit them. For a more developed analysis of the text, see Trombley 1993–1994(I):109–147; see also Caseau 2001:61–123. On the representation of temple destruction in contemporary historiography, see Gotter 2008:43–89; on the state of the temples in the process of the Christianization of the empire, see contributions in Lavan and Murlyan 2011.

[40] Soler 2006:395–396 writes: "A Antioche, le culte des martyrs joue un rôle majeure dans les rivalités entre les différentes factions chrétiennes et dans la christianisation massive de la cité, à l' époque de la predication de Jean Chrysostome. C' est sur ces saints hommes et femmes, défunts, témoins du Christ et de leur foi en lui, que Jean Chrysostome s'appuie essentiellement pour conduire le chrétiens sur la voie d' un christianisme nicéen, pour consolider l' emprise du clergé mélécien qu' il représente, sur la cité et enfin, pour tenter de modifier les pratiques festives des Antiochiens."

[41] Theodoret mentions Greek festivals celebrating heroes in many other occasions in other *dialexeis* and works.

laughter, but by sacred chant, listening to sacred eloquence, a prayer adorned with laudable tears.

Theodoret sees these σώφρονες πανηγύρεις 'festivals' as an additional context for not only the display of piety but also for the creation of a new community based on a new relationship with the divine. It is to this spiritual communion (foreshadowed in *Dialexis* III. On Angels, Gods, and Demons), consisting of choruses of angels, the earthly angelic ascetics (or living martyrs), and the dead martyrs, that Theodoret's audience is encouraged to aspire.[42] The festivals of the martyrs helped infuse time-honored patterns of religiosity with a new and fervent sacrality.[43] The formation of a close association with the martyrs, through the recounting of their passion or contact with their relics, effected expectations among the faithful:[44]

Εἰς δὲ τούτους οὐχ ἅπαξ ἢ δίς γε τοῦ ἔτους ἢ πεντάκις φοιτῶμεν, ἀλλὰ πολλάκις μὲν πανηγύρεις ἐπιτελοῦμεν, πολλάκις δὲ ἡμέρας ἑκάστης τῷ τούτων δεσπότῃ τοὺς ὕμνους προσφέρομεν. Καὶ οἱ μὲν ὑγιαίνοντες αἰτοῦσι τῆς ὑγείας τὴν φυλακήν, οἱ δέ τινι νόσῳ παλαίοντες τὴν τῶν παθημάτων ἀπαλλαγήν· αἰτοῦσι δὲ καὶ ἄγονοι παῖδας, καὶ στέριφαι παρακαλοῦσι γενέσθαι μητέρες, καὶ οἱ τῆσδε τῆς δωρεᾶς ἀπολαύσαντες ἀξιοῦσιν ἄρτια σφίσι φυλαχθῆναι τὰ δῶρα· καὶ οἱ μὲν εἴς τινα ἀποδημίαν στελλόμενοι λιπαροῦσι τούτους ξυνοδοιπόρους γενέσθαι καὶ τῆς ὁδοῦ ἡγεμόνας· οἱ δὲ τῆς ἐπανόδου τετυχηκότες τὴν τῆς χάριτος ὁμολογίαν προσφέρουσιν, οὐχ ὡς θεοῖς αὐτοῖς προσιόντες, ἀλλ ὡς

---

[42] This is evident also in the practice of the *depositio ad sanctos*, attested in both East and West, for which see Duval 1988:73–83, esp. Syria.

[43] See Brown 1981 and 2000c:1–24; see also Pasquato 1981:207–241, esp. 234–238.

[44] In his *Homily on the Martyrs*, John Chrysostom states: "Ἀλλὰ βούλει τρυφᾶν; παράμενε τῷ τάφῳ τοῦ μάρτυρος, ἔκχεε πηγὰς δακρύων ἐκεῖ, σύντριψον τὴν διάνοιαν, ἆρον εὐλογίαν ἀπὸ τοῦ τάφου· λαβὼν αὐτὴν συνήγορον ἐν ταῖς εὐχαῖς, ἐνδιάτριβε ἀεὶ τοῖς διηγήμασι τῶν παλαισμάτων ἐκείνου· περιπλάκηθι τὴν σορόν, προσηλώθητι τῇ λάρνακι· οὐχὶ τὰ ὀστᾶ μόνον τῶν μαρτύρων, ἀλλὰ καὶ οἱ τάφοι αὐτῶν, καὶ αἱ λάρνακες πολλὴν βρύουσιν εὐλογίαν. Λάβε ἔλαιον ἅγιον, καὶ κατάχρισόν σου ὅλον τὸ σῶμα, τὴν γλῶτταν, τὰ χείλη, τὸν τράχηλον, τοὺς ὀφθαλμούς, καὶ οὐδέποτε ἐμπεσῇ εἰς τὸ ναυάγιον τῆς μέθης. Τὸ γὰρ ἔλαιον διὰ τῆς εὐωδίας ἀναμιμνήσκει σε τῶν ἄθλων τῶν μαρτύρων, καὶ πᾶσαν ἀκολασίαν χαλινοῖ, καὶ κατέχει ἐν πολλῇ καρτερίᾳ, καὶ περιγίνεται τῶν τῆς ψυχῆς νοσημάτων. Ἀλλὰ κήποις ἐνδιατρίψαι βούλει, καὶ λειμῶσι καὶ παραδείσοις;" (PG 50:664–665). Soler 2006:443 emphasizes this aspect thus: "L' exhortation addressée aux fidèles à se mettre sous la protection d' un saint particulier montre certainement la volonté de l' Église chrétienne de remplacer la croyance au génies et aux divinités tutélaires de l' individu par celle aux saints martyrs intercesseurs; elle montre aussi que les chrétiens, en tout cas à Antioche, avaient un rapport privilégié à tel ou tel saint, sans que là encore, il ait été besoin que de *Passions* et des *Miracles* de saints rédigés et codifiés étaient accessibles aux chrétines qui pouvaient être édifiés par leur lecture."

θείους ἀνθρώπους ἀντιβολοῦντες καὶ γενέσθαι πρεσβευτὰς ὑπὲρ σφῶν παρακαλοῦντες.

Therapeutikê 8.63

And we make pilgrimage to them, not once or twice or five times a year, but frequently, and celebrate holy days often spending whole days in singing hymns to the lord of martyrs. And those in good health petition protection of their health, while those struggling with some ailment ask for relief from their maladies. Those who are childless pray for offspring, and the barren pray to become child-bearing, while those who already possess this gift pray for the protection of this gift. Those who are sent on a foreign trip beseech the martyrs to be their fellow travelers and guides on their journey home, and those who have a chance to return offer expressions of their gratitude. They do not approach the martyrs for help as gods but invoke them as men of God and pray to them to be divine ambassadors for them.

We have here a rare moment where several perspectives and aims overlap and intersect. There is more at work than Theodoret's personal touch, given what he tells us about the way he was conceived:[45] he becomes the living witness of the outcome of holy men's prayer. His very name bears constant testimony to this.[46] But it is also a moment wherein a society "fabrique les saints dont elle a besoin: (du martyr à l'anachorète, de l'évêque fondateur au roi souffrant, du missionaire au contemplatif"),[47] and, conversely, wherein "de même que la société chrétienne, ou ses élites spirituelles, produit les images de saints en qui elle reconnait son idéal, de la même façon, cet idéal rejaillit sur la société qu'il informe."[48]

Theodoret places emphasis on the number of offerings that show the manifold workings of the power of God; they "proclaim the power of the martyrs

---

[45] The details are to be found in *Religious History* 13.15–18.

[46] The name Theodoret literally means 'given as gift from God'.

[47] Tilliette 1991:5. It is to Theodoret that we owe what will become the birth of a cult. In his *Ecclesiastical History* he sets the scene for the *translatio* and the προσκύνησις of Chrysostom's remains: "At a later time the actual remains of the great doctor were conveyed to the imperial city, and once again the faithful crowd turning the sea as it were into land by their close packed boats, covered the mouth of the Bosphorus toward the Propontis with their torches. The precious possession was brought into Constantinople by the present emperor, who received the name of his grandfather and preserved his piety undefiled. After first gazing upon the bier he laid his head against it, and prayed for his parents and for pardon on them who had ignorantly sinned" (*Ecclesiastical History* 5.36.10–18).

[48] Tilliette 1991:6; on the process in general, see Bozóky 2006:1–118.

who repose there, and this power guarantees that their God is the true God" (*Therapeutikê* 8.65). They are the visible proof of the invisible grace of God.

Theodoret conjures up the image of Socrates (the intellectual hero manqué[49] *par excellence*) to support the idea of martyrdom.[50] By means of a bold and deftly assembled collage,[51] he juxtaposes quotations from Empedocles, Heracleitus, Hesiod, and Plato in order to prove the preexistence of similar ideas in Greek culture.[52] It should be noted that the texts that Theodoret pieces together are also central to the history of Greek demonology.[53]

Anaxarchos and Zeno the Eleatic supply the stock of exempla[54] that would suggest the existence of Greek "martyrs"[55] who bear witness to their tenets by way of their actions. From those that Theodoret adduces, he concludes, "Nonetheless, not one of these has been judged worthy of the same honor as that given to the martyrs" (*Therapeutikê* 8.59). Famous generals (Miltiades, Kimon, Pericles, Themistocles, Aristides, Brasidas, Argesilaus, Lysander, Pelopidas, Epameinondas, Scipio the Elder, Scipio the Younger, Cato, Sulla, Marius, Caesar);

---

[49] Theodoret concludes his reference to Socrates thus: ". . . but he failed to attain the honor accorded to the martyrs. Those who were present at his discourse erected no sanctuary to him, nor did they dedicate a sacred enclosure to him, nor assign him any festival. However wise and courageous he had become, they left him unrewarded and inflicted on him an unjust death" (*Therapeutikê* 8.56).

[50] Socrates provided an ideal model for the apologists. His *exemplum* was variously used to make a number of points. For the particularly rich use of Socrates by Christians, see Döring 1979; see also Giannantoni 1986, Droge and Tabor 1992:17–51, and Edwards 2007:127–142.

[51] On the face of it, the use of these authors in the collage is odd. However, Theodoret is interested in the thematic appropriateness of the quotations and the logic that they evince. By invoking these parallel *doxai*, he wants to affect the reader's mode of reasoning and thus create a *shared inferencing*. In other words, he seeks to fuse the reader's knowledge of the logic of these texts with the new religious phenomenon associated with the cult of the martyrs. A more developed analysis will be made in Chapter Five.

[52] See Butterweck 1995; see also van Henten and Avemarie 2002:9–41.

[53] Kidd 1995:217–240; Algra 2011:71–96.

[54] Known from a literature of stoic origin that emphasized the heroic resistance to tyrants, which became widespread in the early imperial period. See Ronconi 1940:3–32; Huttner 2009:295–320.

[55] There has been a long discussion about the semantic development of the term. For a review of these discussions, see Rordorf 1986:381–403. Rordorf is too quick to dismiss the affinities with the Greek philosophical notion of the martyr. In n14 of the above article he qualifies this by stating that he does not preclude an influence from Epictetus, whose philosophy, however, "serait d'ailleurs difficile de dire par quel canal la philosophie d' Epictète aurait passé dans la tradition chrétienne." For the reception of Epictetus by Christians, see Spanneut 1960:830–854. Rordorf ignores an important article by Delatte that suggests precisely these affinities. The idea of the martyr seems to have been circulating in Cynic philosophical circles in the first century AD. For a careful discussion of the semantic nuances of the term in Cynic philosophers and the semantic affinities between Greek philosophical use of the term and the Christian use, see Delatte 1953:166–186.

kings (Cyrus, Darius, Alexander the Great);[56] and emperors (Augustus, Vespasian, Trajan, Hadrian, Antoninus) join the list of the heroized men[57] whose ephemeral fame does not measure up to that of the martyrs. Finally, he observes, "once dead nothing distinguished them from anybody else."[58]

On the contrary, the martyrs stand for the inversion of this ideal of worldly fame. Theodoret provides a stark contrast when he asks, "Let us inquire, therefore, who these were who merited such a grace and where they originated. Were they well-known and illustrious, who could boast a distinguished pedigree or an ocean of wealth? Did they acquire fame because of some power and influence?" Then he returns to the elaboration of the paradox of the otherworldly status of martyrs:

Οὐδαμῶς, ὦ ἄνδρες. Τούτων γὰρ οὐδενὸς μετεσχήκασιν, ἀλλ' ἰδιῶται ἦσαν ἢ στρατιῶται, τινὲς δε αὐτῶν καὶ οἰκέται γεγένηνται καὶ θεραπαινίδες, ἐν ἀσθενέσι δ' ἄγαν σώμασι γενναίως ἀγωνισάμεναι· καὶ

---

[56] There are indications that Alexander especially enjoyed a considerable reputation in Antioch. John Chrysostom inveighs against the practice of wearing talismans with the image of Alexander thus: "Τί ἄν τις εἴποι περὶ τῶν ἐπῳδαῖς καὶ περιάπτοις κεχρημένων, καὶ νομίσματα χαλκᾶ Ἀλεξάνδρου τοῦ Μακεδόνος ταῖς κεφαλαῖς καὶ τοῖς ποσὶ περιδεσμούντων; Αὗται αἱ ἐλπίδες ἡμῶν, εἰπέ μοι, ἵνα μετὰ σταυρὸν καὶ θάνατον Δεσποτικὸν εἰς Ἕλληνος βασιλέως εἰκόνα τὰς ἐλπίδας τῆς σωτηρίας ἔχωμεν; Οὐκ οἶδας πόσα κατώρθωσεν ὁ σταυρός; τὸν θάνατον κατέλυσε, τὴν ἁμαρτίαν ἔσβεσε, τὸν ἄδην ἄχρηστον ἐποίησε, τοῦ διαβόλου τὴν δύναμιν ἐξέλυσε, καὶ εἰς σώματος ὑγίειαν οὐκ ἔστιν ἀξιόπιστος; τὴν οἰκουμένην ἀνέστησεν ἅπασαν, καὶ σὺ αὐτῷ οὐ θαρρεῖς; καὶ τίνος ἂν ἄξιος εἴης, εἰπέ μοι; Οὐ περίαπτα δὲ μόνον, ἀλλὰ καὶ ἐπῳδὰς σαυτῷ περιάγεις, γρᾴδια μεθύοντα καὶ παραπαίοντα εἰς τὴν οἰκίαν σου εἰσάγων· καὶ οὐκ αἰσχύνῃ οὐδὲ ἐρυθριᾷς μετὰ τοσαύτην φιλοσοφίαν πρὸς ταῦτα ἐπτοημένος;"

("And what is one to say about them who use charms and amulets, and encircle their heads and feet with golden coins of Alexander of Macedon. Are these our hopes, tell me, that after the cross and death of our Master, we should place our hopes of salvation on an image of a Greek king? Do you not know what great result the cross has achieved? It has abolished death, has extinguished sin, has made Hades useless, has undone the power of the devil, and is it not worth trusting for the health of the body? It has raised up the whole world, and do you not take courage in it? And what would you be worthy to suffer, tell me? Thou dost not only have amulets always with you, but incantations bringing drunken and half-witted old women into your house, and are you not ashamed, and do you not blush, after so great philosophy, to be terrified at such things?" *Instructions to Catechumens*, PG 49:240). On Alexander the Great's popularity in antiquity, see Cracco Ruggini 1965:3–80. For the attitude of the church fathers toward Alexander, see Straub 1972:178–194 and Klein 1987–1988:925–989.

[57] On the divinization of public figures, see the discussion in Rufus Fears 1988:1047–1093; Beaujeu 1973:101–136. The case of Julian was particularly interesting in the general context of the cult of the martyrs. Nock 1957(II):115–123 writes: "Julian's admirers were familiar with Christian belief in the efficacious aid of martyrs and saints in general, and many of them would know how Constantine's burial associated him with the homage paid to the Apostles . . . Was it not easy for convinced pagans to believe that no less supernatural efficacy attached to their sainted leader than was imputed to St. Babylas?" (123). See also Straub 1972:159–177. But see comments by Bowersock 1982(III):171–182, with notes at 238–241.

[58] *Therapeutikê* 8.60.

αἱ μὲν σωφρόνως ἕλκουσαι τὸν τοῦ γάμου ζυγόν, αἱ δὲ τί γάμος οὐκ ἐπιστάμεναι. Ἀκούω δὲ ἔγωγέ τινας καὶ τῇ σκηνῇ ξυντραφέντας καὶ ἐξαπίνης τοῖς ἀγωνισταῖς ξυνταχθέντας καὶ ἀξιονίκους γεγενημένους καὶ τῶν στεφάνων τετυχηκότας καὶ μετὰ τὴν ἀνάρρησιν σφόδρα δεδιττομένους τοὺς δαίμονας, οἷς ἦσαν ὑποχείριοι πάλαι· πολλοὶ δὲ καὶ ἱερεῖς καὶ νεωκόροι τὰ κατὰ τῆς ἀσεβείας ἀνέστησαν τρόποια. Ἐκ τοιούτων ἀνδρῶν καὶ γυναικῶν ξυνέστησαν οἱ τῶν μαρτύρων χοροί.

Therapeutikê 8.66–67

Not at all my friends. None of the above. They were lay people and soldiers; some of them were female domestics and servants who contended nobly with very weak constitutions. Of these some bore chastely the yoke of marriage; others were unaware of what marriage was. And I hear that some of the men who had long been in the military camp suddenly enrolled in the ranks of the combatant and, once victorious and in possession of their crowns, after their public proclamation they became an enormous menace to the very demons to whom they had previously been subject. Many priests and sacristans of temples erected trophies gained in their fight against impiety. It is from the ranks of these poor men and women that the choruses of martyrs are composed.

Theodoret emphasizes the anonymity and low social status of the martyrs in order to reinforce their otherworldliness. The significance of such a dramatic reversal in a status-conscious society is not expected to be overlooked. In this way Theodoret delineates the contrast between Greco-Roman notions of heroism and those associated with the Christian martyrs.

Conclusion

We have seen how Theodoret's defense of honoring the martyrs is shaped partly by his response to pagan criticisms. The hero-cult, in its myriad cultural manifestations, offers the most appropriate analogue against which to situate the idea of the honor accorded to Christian martyrs. While he criticizes the elevation of mortals (who at times are full of vices) to the status of gods, he endows Christian martyrs with the right to be honored for having died an honorable death. He insists on the difference between honoring the martyrs and worshiping them, which he considers a pagan attitude. At the same time, it is crucial for Theodoret to show that the church of his day produced martyrs because he considers martyrdom the touchstone of Christianity. More importantly, in his effort to normalize the practice of honoring the martyrs, Theodoret seeks to create an intellectual, spiritual, and religious context for the practice.

To be sure, Theodoret stops short of calling the martyrs heroes. Nevertheless, he implicitly imbues them with qualities reminiscent of the Greek heroes. In fact, the culturally pervasive image of the hero is reconceptualized and employed to serve the practice of honoring them.

4

Christianity as the Universal Practical Virtue

THE PRESENTATION OF CHRISTIANITY as a way of life maintains a significant thematic resonance throughout Theodoret's *Therapeutikê*. Following the long line of Christian authors who from an early stage offered Christianity as a response to pagan polemic, his motivation lay in the conviction that Christianity encompassed and surpassed all that ancient philosophy had attempted to accomplish. While Theodoret devotes an entire *dialexis* to the topic (XII. On Practical Virtue), discussions that touch upon and reiterate it are scattered in several other *dialexeis*. These references complement *Dialexis* XII, but serve at the same time to bolster other arguments. Theodoret's overall presentation hinges on such different facets of Christianity as its asceticism, the martyrs and their honor,[1] and the universality of the Biblical laws. In what follows, I will analyze the main arguments that Theodoret deploys and explore the goals of his approach.

In *Dialexis* XII we encounter Theodoret's most sustained effort to present the ascetics in a form that recommends itself to the ethical traditions, moral sense, and practical reason of the Greek world. In order to accomplish this, Theodoret redeploys elements from Greek, mainly philosophical, culture to contrast Christian ascetics with the pagan philosophers. The ascetics emerge as the true philosophers because they espouse the true philosophy, Christianity.[2]

---

[1] This theme is treated in the previous chapter.

[2] For general accounts, see Hadot 1995 and 2002. For more lexicographically oriented studies, see Malingrey 1961. But see the strictures by Barnes 2002a:293–306, who argues, among other things, for more lexicographical rigor. Bardy 1949:108 writes: "Déjà pour les Grecs, les philosophes étaient à la fois les maîtres qui enseignaient une doctrine et des modèles qui en pratiquaient les règles. Le christianisme a commencé par s'opposer à la philosophie païenne et par la consommer. *Mais dès le milieu du second siècle, un certain nombre de ses fidèles ont appris à le regarder comme une philosophie supérieure, si bien que les meilleurs d'entre eux ont fini par être considérés comme de vrais philosophes, voire comme les seuls vrais*" [emphasis mine]. In a telling passage in *History of the Monks of Syria*—a work that continues the same apologetic program in defense of asceticism—Theodoret writes: "Ὁ τοίνυν τῷ ὄντι φιλόσοφος καὶ φιλόθεος ἂν εἰκότως καλοῖτο. Ὁ δὲ φιλόθεος τῶν ἄλλων ἁπάντων ὑπερφρονῶν καὶ τὸν ἐρώμενον μόνον ὁρῶν, πάντων ὁμοῦ

From Theodoret's comments we can infer his determination to defend monks and their way of life against a number of accusations,[3] among which was the failure of certain of them to live up to the high ethical standards that their vocation demanded. In *Therapeutikê* 12.33.1–12 he writes:

Ἀλλ' ὑμεῖς τοὺς μὲν οὕτως ἀγωνιζομένους οὔτε θεωρεῖν οὔτε θαυμάζειν ἐθέλετε. Εἰ δέ τινας ἴδοιτε τὸ μὲν πρόσχημα τοῦτο περικειμένους, οὐ πάντα δὲ ξυνομολογοῦντα τῷ σχήματι βίον ἀσπαζομένους, εὐθὺς εἰς λοιδορίαν κινεῖτε τὴν γλῶτταν. Καὶ εἰ μὲν ἐκείνους ἐβάλλετε μόνους, εἶχεν ἄν τινα τὸ γινόμενον λόγον· ἐπειδὴ δὲ μετ' ἐκείνων καὶ τοὺς ἄντικρυς ἐναντίως διακειμένους ἐκείνοις καὶ ἀληθῶς φιλοσοφοῦντας κωμῳδεῖν πειρᾶσθε καὶ διασύρειν, τὸν ἀδικώτατον ὑμῶν δῆλον ποιεῖτε σκοπόν. Οὐ γὰρ τοῖς πονηροῖς ἀπεχθάνεσθε, ἀλλὰ τὸν ἀξιέπαινον διαβάλλετε βίον, ὅμοιον ποιοῦντες, ὥσπερ ἂν εἴ τις πίθηκον ἰδὼν μιμούμενον ἄνθρωπον, δι' ἐκείνην τὴν μίμησιν καὶ τῶν ἀνθρώπων μισήσοι τὴν φύσιν.

Therapeutikê 12.33

But you are reluctant to view or marvel at those engaged in such contests. If you see some who partially surround themselves with this appearance but whose lives do not completely conform to the pattern, you immediately wag your tongues in abuse. And if you exclude only those, that would be somehow understandable. But when you go beyond those and try to abuse those who are very different and who are true devotees of philosophy, you show how totally unjust your objection is. For then you are not excoriating the wicked, but slandering the life that is worthy of emulation, acting like one who sees a monkey imitating a human and, because of this act of imitation, decides to hate humanity.

It is difficult to determine the identity of the alleged "pseudo-monks" to whom Theodoret refers.[4] However, there is overwhelming evidence that pagans

---

τὴν ἐκείνου προτίθησι θεραπείαν, ἐκεῖνα μόνα καὶ λέγων καὶ πράττων καὶ λογιζόμενος ἃ τὸν ἀγαπώμενον ἀρέσκει καὶ θεραπεύει, καὶ μυσαττόμενος ἅπαντα ὅσα ἐκεῖνος ἀπαγορεύει."

[3] A collection of the criticisms can also be found in Rinaldi 1994:31–82.

[4] In the same *dialexis* Theodoret returns to this problem by adding the following comment: "Τί δήποτε τοίνυν χαλεπαίνετε, παρ' ἡμῖν ὁρῶντές τινας ψευδομένους, ὃν ἐπαγγέλλονται βίον; ἀνθ' ὅτου δὲ μὴ θαυμάζετε τοὺς τὸν ὑπερφυᾶ βίον ἠγαπηκότας καὶ ἐν σώματι μὲν ἀγωνιζομένους, τὴν ἀσώματον δὲ πολιτείαν ἐζηλωκότας; Πᾶν γὰρ τοὐναντίον ἔδει ποιεῖν· τοὺς μὲν ἄγαν θαυμάζειν ὡς ὑπεραλλομένους τὰ τῆς φύσεως σκάμματα, τοῖς δὲ νέμειν τινὰ ξυγγνώμην, ὡς ὑπὸ τῶν ἐμφύτων κατασυρομένοις παθῶν" ("Why, then, do you find it so hard to put up with the fact that you see some people in our community being untrue to the way of life which they profess? Why do you not rather marvel at those who have embraced the supernatural life and wage this contest in the body while pursuing with zeal a way of life that is incorporeal? But you had to do something

and a number of Christians put up resistance to asceticism. John Chrysostom, writing a few decades earlier, summarizes the attitudes of both:

Ἡ δὲ τοῦ γέλωτος τούτου καὶ τῆς κωμῳδίας ὑπόθεσις, τῶν εἰς τοὺς ἁγίους ἄνδρας εἰργασμένων ἐστὶ τὰ διηγήματα. Καθάπερ γάρ τινες πολεμισταὶ πολλὰς ἠνυκότες μάχας, καὶ τρόπαια στήσαντες, τὰς ἑαυτῶν ἀριστείας διηγούμενοι χαίρουσιν, οὕτω δὴ καὶ οὗτοι γάννυνται ἐπὶ τοῖς τολμήμασι τοῖς ἑαυτῶν· καὶ ἀκούσῃ τοῦ μὲν λέγοντος ὅτι, Ἐγὼ πρῶτος καὶ χεῖρας ἐπέβαλον ἐπὶ δεῖνα τὸν μοναχὸν, καὶ πληγὰς ἐνέτεινα· ἑτέρου δὲ ὅτι, Τὸ καταγώγιον πρὸ τῶν ἄλλων εὗρον αὐτός. Ἀλλὰ τὸν δικαστὴν ἐγὼ μᾶλλον τῶν ἄλλων παρώξυνα, φησὶν ἕτερος· ἄλλος τὸ δεσμωτήριον καὶ τὰ ἐν τῷ δεσμωτηρίῳ δεινὰ, καὶ τὸ διὰ τῆς ἀγορᾶς ἑλκύσαι τοὺς ἁγίους ἐκείνους ἐν ἐγκωμίου τίθεται μέρει· καὶ ἄλλος ἄλλο. Εἶτα πάντες ἀνακαγχάζουσιν ἐπὶ τούτοις. Καὶ ταῦτα, μὲν ἐν τοῖς τῶν Χριστιανῶν συνεδρίοις· οἱ δὲ Ἕλληνες καὶ τούτους γελῶσι, καὶ τοὺς ὑπ᾽αὐτῶν γελωμένους· τοὺς μὲν ἐφ᾽ οἷς ἔδρασαν, τοὺς δὲ ἐφ᾽ οἷς ἔπαθον.

Against the Opponents of Monastic Life, PG 47:322

The subject of their laughter and jests are these stories of attacks against the holy men. Just as warriors, who have won many battles and erected monuments, love to tell of their exploits, so also do these people rejoice over their rush deeds. You will hear one saying: "I was the first to lay hands on so-and-so monk, and I struck him." Another says: "I found his hut before anyone else." "But I stirred on the judge more than the rest," says a third. Yet another boasts of the prison and the terrors of the prison, and claims praise for having dragged these holy men through the marketplace. And on and on it goes. Then everyone breaks out in laughter at them. *And these things happen in the gatherings of the Christians!* And the pagans laugh both at the scoffers and at those

---

quite different, on the one hand, excessively marveling at them because they transcended the limits of human nature and on the other hand, having indulgence for those who have been [laid waste, ravaged, dragged away] by their natural passions," *Therapeutikê* 12.37–38). Theodoret seems to be faced with the same situation that his predecessor John Chrysostom criticizes in Antioch. For a detailed discussion of the phenomenon, see Caner 2002, esp. 158–205. Caner has effectively demonstrated the existence of deviant itinerant monks who did not conform to the rules of society and created problems among Christians. In all likelihood Theodoret refers to this phenomenon, which was widespread in Antioch. See also Fitschen 1998:60–69, where Theodoret is discussed.

who are scoffed at, at the former because of what they do, and at the latter because of what they suffer.[5]

Both Chrysostom and Theodoret are reacting to criticism against asceticism that emerged in the writings of Eunapius, among others, who had attacked monks on a number of occasions, most prominently in the *Lives of the Sophists*, where he refers to them as follows:

> . . . μοναχούς, ἀνθρώπους μὲν κατὰ τὸ εἶδος, ὁ δὲ βίος αὐτοῖς συώδης, καὶ ἐς τὸ ἐμφανὲς ἔπασχόν τε καὶ ἐποίουν μυρία κακὰ καὶ ἄφραστα. ἀλλ' ὅμως τοῦτο μὲν εὐσεβὲς ἐδόκει, τὸ καταφρονεῖν τοῦ θείου· τυραννικὴν γὰρ εἶχεν ἐξουσίαν τότε πᾶς ἄνθρωπος μέλαιναν φορῶν ἐσθῆτα, καὶ δημοσίᾳ βουλόμενος ἀσχημονεῖν· εἰς τοσόνδε ἀρετῆς ἤλασε τὸ ἀνθρώπινον.

Lives of the Sophists 472–473

> . . . men in appearance but [who] led the lives of swine, and openly did and allowed countless unspeakable crimes. But this they accounted piety, to show contempt for things divine. For in those days every man who wore a black robe[6] and consented to behave in unseemly fashion in public possessed the power of a tyrant, to such a pitch of virtue had the human race advanced!

In his *Universal History* Eunapius alludes to the role that monks played in the barbarian invasion of Greece.[7]

Julian is equally harsh when, in the context of a letter to the priest Theodorus, he refers to the monks in the following words:

> ἐπίδωσιν ἀτακτοῦντάς τινας, αὐτίκα μάλα κολάζουσιν· ἐπὶ δὲ τοὺς οὐ προσιόντας τοῖς θεοῖς ἐστι τὸ τῶν πονηρῶν δαιμόνων τεταγμένον φῦλον, ὑφ' ὧν οἱ πολλοὶ παροιστρούμενοι τῶν ἀθέων ἀναπείθονται θανατᾶν, ὡς ἀναπτησόμενοι πρὸς τὸν οὐρανόν, ὅταν ἀπορρήξωσι τὴν ψυχὴν βιαίως. Εἰσὶ δὲ οἳ καὶ τὰς ἐρημίας ἀντὶ τῶν πόλεων διώκουσιν, ὄντος ἀνθρώπου φύσει πολιτικοῦ ζῴου καὶ ἡμέρου, δαίμοσιν ἐκδεδομένοι πονηροῖς, ὑφ' ὧν εἰς ταύτην ἄγονται τὴν μισανθρωπίαν. Ἤδη δὲ καὶ δεσμὰ καὶ κλοιοὺς ἐξεῦρον οἱ πολλοὶ τούτων· οὕτω πανταχόθεν αὐτοὺς

---

5   Trans. D. Hunter.
6   See Oppenheim 1931.
7   For a discussion of the evidence, see Cracco Ruggini 1972:177–300, esp. 288–300.

ὁ κακὸς συνελαύνει δαίμων, ᾧ δεδώκασιν ἑκόντες ἑαυτούς, ἀποστάντες
τῶν ἀϊδίων καὶ σωτήρων θεῶν·

Ep. 89b[8]

Only that they chastise, then and there, any whom they see rebelling
against their king. And the tribe of evil demons is appointed to punish
those who do not worship the gods, and stung to madness by them
many atheists are induced to court death in the belief that they will
fly up to heaven when they have brought their lives to a violent end.
Some men there are also who, though man is naturally a social and
civilized being, seek out desert places instead of cities, since they have
been given over to evil demons and are led by them into this hatred of
their kind. And many of them have even devised fetters and stocks to
wear; to such a degree does the evil demon, to whom they have of their
own accord given themselves, abet them in all ways after they have
rebelled against the everlasting and saving gods.

In light of such criticism, it is worth looking closely into the way that
Theodoret presents his ascetics. The parallel that he employs in *Therapeutikê*
12.5–6 is to crafts (τέχναι), and by doing so he clearly implies that the ascetic
life is a τέχνη βίου:[9]

Χρὴ δὲ οὐ μόνον εἰδέναι, τί προσήκει περὶ τοῦ θείου δοξάζειν, ἀλλὰ
καὶ κατὰ τοὺς ἐκείνου πολιτεύεσθαι νόμους. Ὥσπερ γὰρ οἱ ζωγραφικὴν
ἢ σκυτοτομικὴν ἢ ἄλλην τινὰ παιδευόμενοι τέχνην, οὐχ ὅπως μόνον
ἐπίστωνται ταῦτα μανθάνειν σπουδάζουσιν, ἀλλ' ἵνα καὶ χειρουργῶσι
καὶ μιμητὰς σφᾶς αὐτοὺς τῶν διδασκάλων τοῖς ἔργοις δεικνύωσιν, οὕτω
δεῖ καὶ τῆς εὐσεβείας τοὺς ἐραστὰς μὴ μόνον θεολογίαν καὶ φυσιολογίαν
παιδεύεσθαι, ἀλλὰ καὶ τοὺς τῆς πρακτικῆς ἀρετῆς ἐκπαιδεύεσθαι
νόμους καὶ τούτους φυλάττειν εἰς δύναμιν καὶ <u>πρὸς τούτους πειρᾶσθαι
τῆς ψυχῆς ἐκτυποῦν καὶ διασκευάζειν τὸ εἶδος</u>.

Therapeutikê 12.6

8 Vol. 2 Bidez/296 vol. 2 Wright. Trans. Wright.
9 See also Iamblichus *Protrepticus* 6.3–10: "ὥστε εἴπερ ψυχὴ μὲν σώματος ἄμεινον (ἀρχικώτερον
γὰρ τὴν φύσιν ἐστί), περὶ δὲ σῶμα τέχναι καὶ φρονήσεις εἰσὶν ἰατρική τε καὶ γυμναστική (ταύτας
γὰρ ἡμεῖς ἐπιστήμας τίθεμεν καὶ κεκτῆσθαί τινας αὐτάς φαμεν), δῆλον ὅτι καὶ περὶ ψυχὴν καὶ τὰς
ψυχῆς ἀρετάς ἐστί τις ἐπιμέλεια καὶ τέχνη, καὶ δυνατοὶ λαβεῖν αὐτήν ἐσμεν, εἴπερ γε καὶ τῶν μετ'
ἀγνοίας πλείονος καὶ γνῶναι χαλεπωτέρων."

But it is not enough to know what it is appropriate to think about the divinity; one's life must be organized according to its laws. In fact, just like those who are taught painting, or shoemaking or any other craft, do not seek to be proficient merely for the sake of knowledge, but to produce something with their hands and to show in their works imitations of these masters, so too it is necessary that those who love religion should not confine themselves to the study of theology and natural philosophy, but should also study the laws of practical virtue and observe them to the best of their ability, and should try to fashion the type of their soul in accordance with these laws.

The soul is the seat of the struggle for perfection. It is the soul and its εἶδος that Theodoret sets out to describe, praise, and defend. A finely tuned soul is a living statue of the Lawgiver.[10]

The dense clustering of platonizing vocabulary is keyed by rich interpretative implications. In *Therapeutikê* 12.53–56 Theodoret employs the notion of ἐπιμέλεια 'care of the soul',[11] which is made to agree with the apostle Paul's advice in Romans 13:12–14, followed by the comment: "In fact we should not give such care to the body as to risk it dominating the soul, but so that it should collaborate with the soul, and in dependence upon it, so that it recognizes its least signs (νεύμασιν)."[12]

A more developed presentation of the ascetics as philosophers is found in the no less apologetic *History of the Monks of Syria*.[13] Theodoret's ascetics are

---

[10] *Therapeutikê* 12.7: "Ὁ γὰρ δὴ οὕτω ῥυθμίζων τε καὶ διαμορφῶν τὴν ψυχὴν οὐ μόνον τῶν θείων νόμων τοὺς χαρακτῆρας ἐκμάττεται, ἀλλὰ καὶ αὐτοῦ γε τοῦ νομοθέτου ζῶσά τις εἰκὼν καὶ λογικὴ γίνεται."

[11] The first Christian author to consciously appropriate the idea of the cultivation of the self into Christianity was Clement of Alexandria. In doing so, he set in motion a tradition on which Theodoret drew in order to present his ascetics. For Clement of Alexandria's transformation of notion of the *epimeleia eautou*, see Maier 1994:719–745. For a parallel emphasis on care of the soul in Greek philosophical texts, cf. Iamblichus *Protrepticus* 16: "Ἄλλαι ἔφοδοι ἀπὸ τοῦ τέλους τῆς παιδείας προτρέπουσαι ἐπὶ τὴν συγγενῆ πρὸς τὸ παιδεύεσθαι φιλοσοφίαν, τό τε ἔργον ὁμοῦ τῆς φιλοσοφίας ἐπιδεικνύουσαι καὶ τὴν ὅλην αὐτῆς ἐπιμέλειαν περὶ τὰς ἀρίστας ἐνεργείας τῶν τῆς ψυχῆς δυνάμεων."

[12] This line of thought would recur in the *Compendium of Heretical Falsehoods* (PG 83:488) in a passage on the importance of harmony in the soul: "ἐπιμελεῖσθαι δὲ τῶν ἐφ' ἡμῖν, καὶ τὴν μὲν κακίαν πάμπαν ἀποσκευάζεσθαι, εἰσοικίζεσθαι δὲ τὴν ἀρετήν, καὶ τοῖς ταύτης μορίοις φαιδρύνεσθαι· καὶ καθάπερ αἱ φιλόκοσμοι γυναῖκες κομμωτικῇ τέχνῃ τὸ σῶμα λαμπρύνουσιν, οὕτω τῆς ψυχῆς καλλωπίζειν τὴν ὥραν τοῖς τῆς σωφροσύνης, καὶ δικαιοσύνης, καὶ ἀνδρείας, καὶ φρονήσεως ἄνθεσιν."

[13] Canivet 1977: ". . . Mais il est probable que le monument qu'il dresse à la gloire des moines pour l'édification des fidèles est écrit aussi avec l'intention apologétique de faire oublier les travers qui nuisent à leur reputation. Déjà quelque vingt ans plus tôt, la Thérapeutique faisait des anachorètes les prototypes de la vie chrétienne pour démontrer aux païens la supériorité de

dear to God (θεοφιλεῖς) because they are presented to embody and practice ideals similar to those that God espouses. The ultimate goal of these ascetics is union with God, which requires that they be in a permanent state of alertness (ἐγρήγορσις) with their souls properly maintained (ἐπιμέλεια).[14] The aim is to show the "philosopher" in the process of *askêsis* and to make visible the mental struggle involved, the triumph of the mind over the body. To that end, Theodoret presents Eusebius of Teleda, who "had so taught virtue to each of the parts of his body that they performed what reason alone enjoined."[15] As an indication of the γαλήνη of his soul, the result of the power of his intense concentration, Eusebius is described thus: "During the entire cycle of a week that we spent with this man of God, we saw his face remain without any change, not now relaxed and now contracted with sternness. Likewise his look was not at times grim and cheerful at others, but his eyes always preserved the orderliness [εὐκοσμία]; they were sufficient proof of the calm of his soul."[16] Likewise, Theodoret says of Acepsimas: "turning into himself and contemplating God [τὸν θεὸν φανταζόμενος], he received consolation from this [ἐκεῖθεν ψυχαγωγίαν ἐδέχετο], in accordance with the prophecy that says, 'Take delight in the Lord,

---

leur conception de l' existence" (76). A good case has also been made by Gaşpar 2000:151–178, 211–240. Gaşpar dwells mainly on the study of epic terminology.

[14] These concepts belong to what Hadot 1995:81–125 and 126–144 calls "spiritual exercises." Hadot writes: "Along with its absorption of spiritual exercises, Christianity acquired a specific style of life, spiritual attitude, and tonality, which had been absent from primitive Christianity, this fact is highly significant: it shows that if Christianity was able to be assimilated to a philosophy, the reason was that philosophy itself was already, above all else, a way of being and a style of life" (1995:129–130). Hadot continues: "A result of this [*viz.* the introduction of certain Greek philosophical spiritual techniques into Christian spirituality] was that the Christian ideal was described, and in part, practiced, by borrowing models and vocabulary from the Greek philosophical tradition. Thanks to its literary and philosophical qualities, this tendency became dominant, and it was through this agency that the heritage of ancient spiritual exercises was transmitted to Christian spirituality" (140).

[15] *Religious History* 4.5.21–23: "Οὕτω δὲ τῶν τοῦ σώματος μορίων ἕκαστον τὴν ἀρετὴν ἐξεπαίδευσεν ὡς ἐκεῖνα δρᾶν ἃ μόνος ὁ λογισμὸς ἐπιτρέπει."

[16] *Religious History* 4.5.10.4–13: "'Άπαντα τοίνυν τῆς ἑβδομάδος τὸν κύκλον παρὰ τῷδε τῷ θείῳ διαγαγόντες, ἐθεώμεθα πρόσωπον οὐδεμίαν μεταβολὴν δεχόμενον, οὐδὲ νῦν μὲν διαχεόμενον, νῦν δὲ σκυθρωπότητι συναγόμενον καὶ τὸ ὄμμα δέ γε ὡσαύτως οὐκ ἄλλοτε μὲν βλοσυρόν, χαροπὸν δὲ ἄλλοτε, ἀλλ' ἐπὶ τῆς αὐτῆς ἀεὶ τοὺς ὀφθαλμοὺς μένοντας εὐκοσμίας· ἱκανοὶ δὲ οὗτοι τεκμηριῶσαι τῆς ψυχῆς τὴν γαλήνην. Ἀλλ' εἰκός τινα νομίσαι τοιοῦτον αὐτὸν ἑωρᾶσθαι μηδεμιᾶς παρακινούσης αἰτίας."

and may he grant you the requests of your heart.'"[17] The ideas and practices of the care of the self recur with the word *phrontistêrion* 'house of contemplation'.[18]

The ideal of *philia* between God and human beings can be summed up in the following words from *Therapeutikê* 12.8: "He imitates, as far as possible, the God of the universe. He desires what God desires, and likewise hates what his Master hates. Now what pleases and displeases God is taught in clear terms in the divine laws."[19] There follows a long list of quotations from the Bible in support of this claim. After this piece of instruction, Theodoret offers the following from Plato: "So he who would be loved by such being must himself become such to the utmost of his might, and so, by this argument, he who is temperate among us is loved by God [καὶ κατὰ τοῦτον τὸν τρόπον ὁ μὲν σώφρων ἡμῶν θεῷ φίλος· ὅμοιος γάρ], for he is like God, whereas he who is not temperate is not like God" (Plato *Laws* 5.716c–d). In this manner, Theodoret correlates the biblical notion of *philia* with the platonic *philia* between God and human beings.[20] Continuing in a similar vein, he cites the favorite platonic *topos* of ὁμοίωσις θεῷ invoked in the quotation from *Theaetetus*: "Evils can never be done away with, for the good must always have its contrary, nor have they any place in the world of the gods but they must haunt this region of our mortal nature. That is why we should make all speed to take flight from this world to the other, and flight means becoming like to God insofar as is possible," followed by a small exegesis of the passage in which the addition "flight means becoming like God" and the qualification "insofar as this is possible" are particularly praised.[21]

Theodoret's stated intent is to show that "Plato has depicted the mode of existence of our philosophers [*viz.* ascetics] because he certainly did not

---

[17] *Religious History* 15.1.4–6: "ἀλλ'εἰς ἑαυτὸν νεύων καὶ τὸν θεὸν φανταζόμενος ἐκεῖθεν ψυχαγωγίαν ἐδέχετο κατὰ τὴν προφητείαν." Compare with Marinus' description of Proclus: "And thus the soul of the blessed man, collecting itself from every side and gathering itself, all but departed from the body, even while it seemed to be still detained by it. For its thinking was not the political kind that consists in acting well with regard to matters that could be otherwise, but knowing in itself, pure and simple, a reversion to itself without any share in the impressions of the body" (*Life of Proclus* 21.1–5, trans. Edwards).

[18] *Religious History* 2: "ἀλλὰ καὶ τοῖς ἐν τῇ Συρίᾳ τῆς φιλοσοφίας φροντιστηρίοις."

[19] *Therapeutikê* 12.8: "Μιμεῖται δέ, ὡς ἔνεστι, τὸν τῶν ὅλων Θεὸν ὁ ποθῶν ἐκεῖνα καὶ ἐχθραίνων ὁμοίως, ἅπερ καὶ αὐτὸς ὁ δεσπότης ἐχθραίνει τε καὶ φιλεῖ. Τίνα δὲ αὐτῷ δυσμενῆ, καὶ τίνα αὖ προσφιλῆ, διαρρήδην οἱ θεῖοι διδάσκουσι νόμοι."

[20] For the historical background, see Vidal 1959:161–184, who denies the existence of *philia* between God and human beings in Greek classical literature. Far more nuanced and comprehensive for classical Greek culture is Dirlmeier 1935:57–77, 176–193. For a diachronic approach that includes Christian authors, see the excellent study by Peterson 1923:161–202. More recently the idea is discussed by Konstan 1996:87–113.

[21] On the significance of the idea for pagans and Christians, see Merki 1952.

find such types among the Greeks."[22] In fact, Theodoret asserts that Plato had prefigured an ascetic way of life in his *Republic* that would not be fulfilled until Theodoret's time, in the way of life of his holy men,[23] since "among the Greeks who cultivate philosophy no one of them has built a mountain shack and occupied it; a sufficient proof of that is provided by the writings of antiquity, and this is corroborated by you in your hostility to those who opt for such a life."[24]

It is interesting to see how heavily Theodoret relies on Plato for his defense of the ascetics. But in so doing he is in tune with a widespread tendency in Greek philosophical literature of the time,[25] in which the ideal of *philia* with God figured prominently. Iamblichus—under Pythagorean influence[26]—refers in *On the Mysteries* to *philia* that connects the creator with his creation.[27] The same notion is behind the term θεοφιλῶς, which Hierocles reserves for the wise man (*sophos*):

> ὅθεν καὶ μόνος ἱερεὺς ὁ σοφὸς λέγεται, μόνος θεοφιλῶς, μόνος εἰδὼς
> εὔξασθαι. μόνος γὰρ οἶδε τιμᾶν ὁ τὴν ἀξίαν μὴ συγχέων τῶν τιμωμένων
> καὶ ὁ προηγουμένως ἱερεῖον ἑαυτὸν προσάγων καὶ ἄγαλμα θεῖον
> τεκταίνων τὴν ἑαυτοῦ ψυχὴν καὶ ναὸν εἰς ὑποδοχὴν τοῦ θείου φωτὸς
> τὸν ἑαυτοῦ κατασκευάζων νοῦν.

Commentary on the Golden Verses of the Pythagoreans 1.18.8–13

. . . hence 'the wise man alone is called a priest, he alone a friend of god, he alone an expert in prayer.' Only he knows how to pay honour who

---

[22] *Therapeutikê* 12.26.1-2: "Ἐν δὲ τούτοις ὁ Πλάτων τὴν τῶν ἡμετέρων φιλοσόφων ἐζωγράφησε πολιτείαν· οὐ γὰρ δή τις παρ' ἐκείνοις τοιοῦτος ἐγένετο."

[23] There is an interesting affinity between this statement and Theodoret's aim in the prologue to the *Religious History*, where he uses the metaphor of painting the souls: "Ἡμεῖς δὲ βίον μὲν συγγράφομεν φιλοσοφίας διδάσκαλον καὶ τὴν ἐν οὐρανοῖς πολιτείαν ἐζηλωκότα· <u>ζωγραφοῦμεν δὲ</u> οὐ τῶν σωμάτων τοὺς χαρακτῆρας, οὐδὲ τὰ τούτων ἐκτυπώματα τοῖς ἀγνοοῦσιν ἐπιδείκνυμεν, <u>ἀλλὰ τῶν ἀοράτων ψυχῶν τὰς ἰδέας σκιογραφοῦμεν</u>, καὶ πολέμους ἀθεάτους καὶ συμπλοκὰς ἀφανεῖς ἐπιδείκνυμεν."

[24] *Therapeutikê* 12.29: "Ὅτι δὲ τῶν παρ' Ἕλλησι πεφιλοσοφηκότων οὐδεὶς ἐν ὄρει σηκὸν δειμάμενος ᾤκησεν, ἱκανὰ μὲν καὶ τὰ παλαιὰ δηλῶσαι ξυγγράμματα, μαρτυρεῖτε δὲ καὶ ὑμεῖς, τοῖς τοιοῦτον μετιοῦσι νεμεσῶντες τὸν βίον" ("But among the Greeks who cultivate philosophy no one of them has built a mountain shack and occupied it; a sufficient proof of that is provided by the writings of antiquity, and this is corroborated by you in your hostility to those who opt for such a life").

[25] On the use of Plato for the legitimization of new interpretations in philosophy in late antiquity, see Erler 2001:313–326.

[26] Pizzolato 1993:18–21; Staab 2002:426–434.

[27] *On the Mysteries* 5.12.216.4–8: "κοινωνίαν ἀπεργάζεται, καὶ ἡμᾶς διὰ τῶν αὐτῶν τρόπων ἀπολύει τῶν τῆς γενέσεως δεσμῶν καὶ ἀφομοιοῖ τοῖς θεοῖς, πρός τε τὴν φιλίαν αὐτῶν ἐπιτηδείους ἐργάζεται, καὶ περιάγει τὴν ἔνυλον ἡμῖν φύσιν ἐπὶ τὴν ἄυλον." Also *On the Mysteries* 5.26.238.7–8: "Ἐν τρισὶ δὲ τούτοις ὅροις, ἐν οἷς τὰ θεῖα πάντα μετρεῖται, τὴν πρὸς θεοὺς ἡμῶν φιλίαν συναρμόσασα." See also Van Liefferinge 1999:59–60, 88.

does not confuse the worth of those being honoured and who renders above all himself as a sacrifice, crafting his own soul into a divine sculpture and making his own intellect a temple for the reception of the divine light[28]

And Marinus uses it to describe Proclus' god-favored life:

In the *Life of Proclus* in Proclus's dream "the god thought the happy man worthy of such grace [τοσαύτης εὐμενείας ἠξίωσεν] that he also appeared and, in the way that one pronounces an encomium of someone in the theatre, he said in an actor's tone with his hand extended in a gesture—I shall declare the very words of the god—'Proclus is the glory of the city. '" Marinus goes on to add: "Now what greater testimony could there be than that the man who was happy in everything was also dear to the gods [καὶ τίς ἂν εἴη μαρτυρία ταύτης μείζων περὶ τῆς θεοφιλείας]? Yet on account of his great fellow-feeling [συμπάθειαν] with the divine, he was always moved to tears if ever he told us his memories of the things that he had seen, and the divine encomium that had been spoken to him."[29]

Life of Proclus 32.31–42

Aiming to show that Christian ascetics realized that to which Greek philosophy could only aspire, Theodoret relies heavily on anecdotal biography. A number of episodes from the lives of Greek philosophers are carefully deployed, the intent being that readers might either criticize or endorse the philosopher depending on the attitude presented. The most prominent figure to appear is Socrates, who, despite his stature, fails to live up to the high standards of the philosophical life.[30] If the most accomplished philosopher is incapable of living up to his vocation, then all other Greek philosophers must by necessity fail as well. This conditional paves the way for the following claim:

Οἱ δὲ τῆς εὐαγγελικῆς ἐρασθέντες φιλοσοφίας πόρρωθεν τῶν πολιτικῶν θορύβων γεγένηνται· τὰς δὲ τῶν ὀρῶν ἀκρωνυχίας κατειληφότες ἢ τῶν ἐν ἐρήμοις χωρίοις ἀγαπήσαντες βίον, τῇ θεωρίᾳ τῶν θείων καὶ

---

[28] Trans. Schibli.
[29] Trans. Edwards.
[30] *Therapeutikê* 12:57–69. Other philosophers are singled out for criticism(*Therapeutikê* 12.47–51), such as Antisthenes, Diogenes of Sinope, Crates (the Cynic), Aristippus of Cyrene, Aristocles, and Plato (*Therapeutikê* 12:70–72). See Krueger 1993:29–49 for a discussion of Theodoret's attitude. See also Goulet-Cazé and Goulet 1993. In Plato's case Theodoret is drawing on a long-standing tradition of criticism against Plato by other Greek authors. For a collection of all the testimonia, see Dixsaut 1995 and 2007.

τῷ ταύτῃ ξυνηρμοσμένῳ σφᾶς αὐτοὺς ἀπεκλήρωσαν βίῳ, οὐ γυναικῶν
καὶ παίδων καὶ κτημάτων ἐπιμελούμενοι, ἀλλὰ τὰς ψυχὰς κατά γε τὸν
κανόνα τῶν θείων διευθύνοντες νόμων καὶ οἷόν τινες ἄριστοι ζωγράφοι
πρὸς τὰ ἀρχέτυπα τῆς ἀρετῆς τὰς νοερὰς αὐτῶν ζωγραφοῦντες εἰκόνας.

Therapeutikê 12.27

But those who have become enamored of the philosophy of the Gospel
have distanced themselves from political troubles. For having installed
themselves on mountain tops, or enjoying the life in desert places,
they have chosen a life spent in contemplating divine things and their
chosen lot in life is in harmonizing themselves with this contemplation, with no care for wives, children, and material possessions, but
directing their souls in accordance with the canon of divine laws and,
like the best artists, they paint their spiritual image after the best
models of virtue.

Moreover, Greek philosophers failed to agree on a number of important issues,
a fact not overlooked by Theodoret, who exploits these disagreements in
Therapeutikê 5.44–49.[31] The failure—moral and otherwise—of Greek philosophers illustrates that the superiority of Christianity is based on the practice of
virtue rather than cultural affiliation. Consequently, when Theodoret claims
that ascetics fulfilled what Plato had only prefigured in his *Republic*, he relies
on Plato's emphasis on moral virtue as the ultimate criterion for philosophy.[32]

---

[31] *Therapeutikê* 5.44–49: "Such is the squabbling and conflict of the historians, philosophers, and
poets concerning the soul and body, and the composition itself of the human being, some cham-
pioning one view, others another, each side elaborating opinions the opposite of their opponents. For they had no desire to learn truth but, being slaves of empty fame and renown, desired
instead to be hailed as inventors of new opinions. And, for this very reason, they have endured
great error, as successors overthrew the opinions of their elders. After the death of Thales,
Anaximander espoused different principles, and after the death of Anaximander, Anaximenes
did the same thing. Likewise Anaxagoras. And Aristotle openly broke with Plato during the
latter's lifetime, set himself in opposition to the Academy, showing no respect for the school
from which he had so eagerly benefited, showing no regard for the renown of his distinguished
teacher, with no deference toward his intellectual rigor, but impudently setting himself up as
his adversary, and espousing principles which, far from being better, were much inferior to his.
Plato, for instance, had asserted that the soul was immortal; Aristotle called it mortal. Plato
had maintained that God exercised providence over the universe; Aristotle, to judge by his
words, excluded the world from divine government, for he said that God's rule over the universe
extended as far as the moon and that the rest came under the sway of destiny. Aristotle has
introduced other novelties of which it seems to me superfluous to talk at the moment. It is only
to be expected that the philosophers would have destroyed one another's systems, since falsehood is not merely the enemy of truth but its own enemy as well, while truth is consistent with
itself and has only falsehood as an enemy."

[32] See Kamtekar 2002:1–13, esp. 9.

In this way, the argument can be used to cut across the cultural criteria (Greek in particular) upon which his readers' sense of virtue was based.[33] Theodoret conjures up the figure of Anacharsis to buttress this claim further:

> Καὶ γὰρ Ἀνάχαρσιν θαυμάζουσιν, ἄνδρα Σκύθην, οὐκ Ἀθηναῖον οὐδὲ Ἀργεῖον οὐδέ γε Κορίνθιον οὐδὲ Τεγεάτην ἢ Σπαρτιάτην, καὶ τοὺς Βραχμᾶνας ὑπεράγανται, Ἰνδοὺς ὄντας, οὐ Δωριέας οὐδὲ Αἰολέας οὐδέ γε Ἴωνας· ἐπαινοῦσι δὲ καὶ Αἰγυπτίους ὡς σοφωτάτους· πολλὰς γάρ τοι καὶ παρὰ τούτων ἔμαθον ἐπιστήμας. Οὔκουν ἡ τῶν γλωττῶν ἑτερότης πημαίνει τὴν φύσιν

Therapeutikê 5.58–59[34]

They admire Anacharsis, a Scythian, who was not from Athens, or Argos, or Corinth, or Tegea, or Sparta, and they are ardent admirers of the Brahmans who are Indians, not Dorians, nor Aeolians, nor Ionians.

---

[33] See for instance *Therapeutikê* 1.25, where Theodoret, criticizing those who "refuse to accept the truth from men who have received it as gift of God," gives a long list of philosophers who did not come from mainland Greece, and continues: "If however you assert that even though these men were born and raised outside of Greece they were nevertheless users of the Greek language, then first acknowledge that there are wise men born among the non-Greeks. For you hold in esteem for their wisdom Zalmoxis, who came from Thrace, and Anacharsis from Scythia, and the Brahmans enjoy great renown with you, although they are Indians, not Greeks." Elsewhere he states: "καὶ γὰρ καὶ ἐν Ἕλλησι καὶ ἐν βαρβάροις ἔστιν ἰδεῖν καὶ ἀρετῆς φροντιστὰς καὶ κακίας ἐργάτας" (*Therapeutikê* 5.58).

[34] See also *Therapeutikê* 12.44–46, where Anacharsis is one of the stock exempla of "barbarian" practical virtue: "Καὶ γὰρ Ἑλλάνικος ἐν ταῖς ἱστορίαις ἔφη τοὺς Ὑπερβορέους οἰκεῖν μὲν ὑπὲρ τὰ Ῥίπαια ὄρη, ἀσκεῖν δὲ δικαιοσύνην, μὴ κρηφαγοῦντας, ἀλλ᾽ ἀκροδρύοις χρωμένους. Καὶ τοὺς Βραχμᾶνας ἱστοροῦσιν ἕτεροι ἐν ταῖς ὕλαις διάγειν, φύλλοις τὸ σῶμα καλύπτοντας. Καὶ Ἀνάχαρσιν δὲ τὸν Σκύθην φιλόσοφον γεγενῆσθαί φασιν· οὕτως δὲ αὐτὸν ὁ τῆς φιλοσοφίας ἐπυρπόλησεν ἔρως, ὡς ὀνομαστότατον γενέσθαι καὶ παρὰ πᾶσιν ἀοίδιμον. Οὐ γὰρ μόνον ἐγρηγορὼς πρὸς τὰ τῆς ψυχῆς ἠγωνίζετο πάθη, ἀλλὰ καὶ καθεύδων τὰ τῆς ἐγκρατείας παρεδήλου σημεῖα· εἰώθει γὰρ τῇ μὲν λαιᾷ τὰ αἰδοῖα κατέχειν, τῇ δεξιᾷ δὲ τὰ χείλη ξυνέχειν, ταύτῃ πη δηλῶν, ὡς πολλῷ μείζων ἐστὶν ἡ ἀγωνία τῆς γλώττης καὶ μείζονος ἐπικουρίας εἰς ἀσφάλειαν δεῖται. Καὶ Χείρωνα δὲ τὸν Κένταυρον Ἕρμιππός φησιν ὁ Βηρύτιος δικαιοσύνης γενέσθαι διδάσκαλον, καὶ Ὅμηρος δὲ αὐτὸν δικαιότατον τῶν Κενταύρων ἐκάλεσεν" ("For example, Hellanicus reports in his Histories that the Hyperboreans dwell beyond the Ripaean mountains and lead a life of justice. They do not eat meat but live on hard-shelled fruits. According to other historians, the Brahmans who live in forests, cover their bodies with leaves. They say that the Scythian Anacharsis was a philosopher. He was at this juncture so inflamed with love for philosophy that his fame and renown had spread far and wide. Not only did he war against the passions of the soul while he was awake. Even when he was asleep he showed signs of his continence. For instance, he was in the habit of holding his private parts with his left hand, and of pressing his lips with his right hand, showing that the battle against the tongue is tougher and needs more help to attain victory. Chiron, the Centaur, according to Hermippus of Berytus, was a teacher of justice and Homer called him the most just of the Centaurs"). For an overview of the use of Anacharsis in Greek literature, see Kindstrand 1981 and, more recently, Ungefehr-Kortus 1996.

They praise the Egyptians as very wise people; in fact, they have learned from them many of their sciences. Differences in languages, then, have not caused any injury to the human condition.

Let us turn now to Theodoret's related defense of Christianity as *the* way of life. Theodoret considers the *universal application* of divine laws as a sign of their intrinsic value.[35] This becomes apparent in *Dialexis* IX. On Laws, where he makes a more systematic case. More specifically, it is the universal appeal of the biblical *nomoi* (understood as rules that shape and direct religious and ethical conduct)[36] that overshadows those that preceded them.[37]

Introducing a historical dimension, Theodoret reflects on the dissipation of the older constitutions and "the memory of the much heralded legislators" that "was extinguished, and the laws of the Romans now govern the Greek cities" (*Therapeutikê* 9.17). On the contrary, Christian *nomoi*, in his view, are intrinsically superior not only to the Greco-Roman ones but also to those of other *ethnē*.[38] Using the example of Persians, he illustrates the change that the practice of the "laws of the fishermen" has brought about:

Καὶ τοῖς μὲν ἄλλοις αὐτῶν νόμοις ἅπαντας ὑποκύπτειν τοὺς ὑπηκόους καταναγκάζουσι, τοὺς δὲ τῶν ἁλιέων ἐξαρνηθῆναι τοὺς πεπιστευκότας οὐ πείθουσιν. Ἀλλὰ κατὰ τοὺς Ζαράδου πάλαι Πέρσαι πολιτευόμενοι νόμους καὶ μητράσι καὶ ἀδελφαῖς ἀδεῶς καὶ μέντοι καὶ θυγατράσι μιγνύμενοι καὶ νόμον ἔννομον τὴν παρανομίαν νομίζοντες, ἐπειδὴ τῆς τῶν ἁλιέων νομοθεσίας ἐπήκουσαν, τοὺς μὲν Ζαράδου νόμους ὡς παρανομίαν ἐπάτησαν, τὴν εὐαγγελικὴν δὲ σωφροσύνην ἠγάπησαν· καὶ κυσὶ καὶ οἰωνοῖς τοὺς νεκροὺς προτιθέναι παρ᾽ ἐκείνου μεμαθηκότες, νῦν τοῦτο δρᾶν οἱ πιστεύσαντες οὐκ ἀνέχονται, ἀλλὰ τῇ γῇ κατακρύπτουσι καὶ τῶν τοῦτο δρᾶν ἀπαγορευόντων οὐ φροντίζουσιν νόμων οὐδὲ

---

[35] While this *topos* goes back to the earliest Christian authors, it had a particular resonance for Theodoret's time: Maiburg 1983:38–53.

[36] The most sustained engagement in *Dialexis* IX. On the Laws is with Plato's *Laws*. For the use of the citations, see Des Places 1944:27–40, repr. 1955:171–184, and 1956:325–336. Theodoret, not unlike Clement of Alexandria, is interested in Plato's *Laws* as an ethical treatise. This is because—as Rizzerio 1997:73 puts it in the case of Clement: "s' il fait suivre la *République* du Timée et les *Lois* de l' *Epinomis*, c'est sans doute parce qu' il croit que le politique aussi bien que la science de la législation *ont comme fonction ultime d' introduire à l'étude des réalités célestes et, de là, d' élever l'homme jusqu' à la pratique de la connaisance la plus haute que celui-ci puisse exercer: la philosophie et la contemplation*" [emphasis mine].

[37] For the background of this debate, see Remus 1987:133-150; see also the remarks of Maas 2003:152–188.

[38] As an apologetic motif it can be traced already in Hellenistic Judaism and the defense of the Torah as laws superior to the Greek ones. For a detailed account of the origins of the motif, see Heid 1996:49–65. See also the discussion by Troianos 1992:47–62.

πεφρίκασι τὴν τῶν κολαζόντων ὠμότητα· πλέον γάρ που δεδοίκασι τὸ
τοῦ Χριστοῦ δικαστήριον· καὶ τὰ ὁρώμενα γελῶντες ὀνειροπολοῦσι τὰ
μὴ φαινόμενα καὶ δειμαίνουσιν. Καὶ τούσδε τοὺς νόμους παρ' ἀνδρῶν
Γαλιλαίων ἐδέξαντο.

Therapeutikê 9.33

However, while compelling their subjects to be submissive to their
other laws, they did not persuade the faithful to abjure the laws of the
fishermen. The Persians who were once ruled by the laws of Zoroaster
had no scruple about marrying their mothers, their sisters, and even
their daughters, thinking that such immoral conduct was perfectly
legitimate. But when they heard of the legislation of the fishermen they
trampled on the laws of Zoroaster as immoral, and embraced evangelical moderation. They had also learned from Zoroaster to expose their
dead to dogs and birds of prey; today those who have been converted
to the true faith do not put up with such conduct, but inter their dead
in the ground, and ignore those laws which prohibit this practice and
in no way fear the savagery of those who would punish them. They are
much more in fear of the court of justice of Christ. They laugh at visible
things and are haunted by fear of what is not visible. *And these laws they
received from the Galilaeans.*

In *Therapeutikê* 5.60–61 *epimeleia aretês*, which is not confined to the Greeks,
resurfaces, reinforcing Theodoret's argument about the universal appeal of the
divine teachings:

Τοιγάρτοι ξυνομολογοῦσι καὶ οἱ Ἕλληνες, καὶ παρὰ τοῖς βαρβάροις <u>εἶναί
τινα ἐπιμέλειαν ἀρετῆς</u>, καὶ μὴ κωλύειν τήνδε τὴν κτῆσιν τῆς φωνῆς τὸ
διάφορον. Καὶ γὰρ ἅπαντες τῆς ἀληθείας οἱ κήρυκες, προφῆταί φημι
καὶ ἀπόστολοι, τῆς μὲν Ἑλληνικῆς οὐ μετέλαχον εὐγλωττίας, <u>ἔμπλεοι
δὲ τῆς ἀληθινῆς ὄντες σοφίας</u>, πᾶσι τοῖς ἔθνεσι, καὶ Ἑλληνικοῖς καὶ
βαρβαρικοῖς, τὴν θείαν διδασκαλίαν προσήνεγκαν καὶ πᾶσαν γῆν καὶ
θάλατταν τῶν ἀρετῆς πέρι καὶ εὐσεβείας ξυγγραμμάτων ἐνέπλησαν.
Καὶ νῦν ἅπαντες τῶν φιλοσόφων τοὺς λήρους καταλιπόντες τοῖς τῶν
ἁλιέων καὶ τελωνῶν ἐντρυφῶσι μαθήμασι καὶ τὰ τοῦ σκυτοτόμου
ξυγγράμματα περιέπουσι·

Therapeutikê 5.60–61

Consequently, the Greeks also share the view that among the non-Greeks there is a concern for virtue [εἶναί τινα ἐπιμέλειαν ἀρετῆς], and that language differences do not impede its acquisition. And indeed all the heralds of virtue—I mean the prophets and apostles—did not share in a knowledge of Greek eloquence, but, being full of divine wisdom [ἔμπλεοι δὲ τῆς ἀληθινῆς ὄντες σοφίας], they carried the divine teaching to all nations, Greek and non-Greek, and they filled every land and every sea with their writings on virtue and religion. And now all the philosophers, abandoning their own trivialities, take delight in the teachings of the fishermen, the tax-gatherers, and they pay great heed to the writings of the tent-maker.

The defense of biblical law should be seen as one side of a debate, the inception of which could already be found in the critique of Celsus.[39] Christians had created an unwelcome innovation in society that ran against established religious customs and *nomoi*.[40] Julian, following the same reasoning, attacked Christians (referring to them disparagingly as Galilaeans) as a religious group that, despite its Jewish origins, did not possess any ancient credentials.[41] Instead, it combined the atheism of the Jews and the indolence of the Greeks.[42] Furthermore, it came from a small and forgotten place in Palestine of no relevance for the empire, and it was espoused by people "of the baser sort, shopkeepers, tax-gatherers, dancers and libertines."[43]

In this way Julian attempted to localize and confine any significance that Christianity had acquired and to remind Christians of their marginal place in society and culture.[44] To this end, he relied on the notion of minor gods

---

[39] See Andresen 1955; Droge 1989; Wilken 1984; Remus 1987:133–150.

[40] Andresen 1955:189 defines the concept of religious as: "die Haltung des Menschen in Kult und Frömmigkeit, indem die religiöse Einstellung des Einzelnen an eine alte Überlieferung gebunden wird, die mit den kultischen Satzungen der Völker sich bis in die Gegenwart lebendig erhalten hat." Porphyry reiterated this criticism, as shown recently by Cook 2011:231–275

[41] See Scicolone 1981:223–236.

[42] *Against the Galileans* fr. 3, 8–14 (Wright [LCL]): "For they have not accepted a single admirable or important doctrine of those that are held either by us Hellenes or by the Hebrews who derived them from Moses; but from both religions they have gathered what has been engrafted like powers of evil, as it were, on these nations—atheism from the Jewish levity, and a sordid and slovenly way of living from our indolence and vulgarity; and they desire that his should be called the noblest worship of the gods."

[43] *Against the Galileans* fr. 58, 25–27.

[44] Scicolone 1982:71–80. Theodoret's awareness of the offensive use of the term "Galilean" by Julian appears more clearly in *Ecclesiastical History* 3.21.5–9: "τοὺς δὲ Χριστιανοὺς Γαλιλαίους ὠνόμαζεν, ἀτιμίαν αὐτοῖς ἐκ τῆς προσηγορίας προσάψειν ἡγούμενος. ἔδει δὲ αὐτὸν σκοπῆσαι

or demons, who were said to preside over different nations, with the intention of showing that the god of the Old Testament was one of national-ethnic significance, but by no means universal.[45]

Christianity as practical virtue, then, was able to cut across *ethnic* differences, customs (*nomoi*), languages, and social classes because it was premised on the *practice* of the divine laws that lead to practical virtue. Thus Theodoret clarifies:

> Καὶ ἔστιν ἰδεῖν ταῦτα εἰδότας τὰ δόγματα οὐ μόνους γε τῆς ἐκκλησίας τοὺς διδασκάλους, ἀλλὰ καὶ σκυτοτόμους καὶ χαλκοτύπους καὶ ταλασιουργοὺς καὶ τοὺς ἄλλους ἀποχειροβιώτους· καὶ γυναῖκας ὡσαύτως οὐ μόνον τὰς λόγων μετεσχηκυίας, ἀλλὰ καὶ χερνήτιδας καὶ ἀκεστρίας, καὶ μέντοι καὶ θεραπαίνας· καὶ οὐ μόνον ἀστοί, ἀλλὰ καὶ χωριτικοὶ τήνδε τὴν γνῶσιν ἐσχήκασι· καὶ ἔστιν εὑρεῖν καὶ σκαπανέας καὶ βοηλάτας καὶ φυτουργοὺς καὶ περὶ τῆς θείας διαλεγομένους Τριάδος καὶ περὶ τῆς τῶν ὅλων δημιουργίας καὶ τὴν ἀνθρωπείαν φύσιν εἰδότας Ἀριστοτέλους πολλῷ μᾶλλον καὶ Πλάτωνος.

Therapeutikê 5.68–69

. . . it is possible to see that those who know these teachings are not merely the leaders of the church, but also workers in leather, coppersmiths, weavers, and other manual workers. And women also, not just those who are educated but those also who are mere weavers, seamstresses, and daily laborers. This knowledge is possessed not just by city dwellers but by country folk. And it is possible to find agricultural workers, drovers, and gardeners engaged in discussions on the blessed Trinity, and knowing much more than Aristotle or Plato about the Creator of the universe and the composition of human nature.

λόγοις ἐντεθραμμένον, ὡς ἥκιστα δόξῃ λυμαίνεται προσηγορίας ἐναλλαγή. οὐδὲ γὰρ εἰ Σωκράτης ὠνομάσθη Κριτίας καὶ Φάλαρις ὁ Πυθαγόρας προσηγορεύθη, λώβης ἂν μετέσχον τινὸς ἐκ τῆς τῶν ὀνομάτων μεταβολῆς· οὐδέ γε ὁ Νηρεὺς Θερσίτης ἐπικληθεὶς ἀπώλεσεν ἂν ὃ παρὰ τῆς φύσεως ἐδέξατο κάλλος. ἀλλὰ τούτων οὐδὲν ὁ ταῦτα πεπαιδευμένος εἰς νοῦν λαβών, ἐκ τῆς οὐδαμόθεν ἡμῖν ἁρμοττούσης προσηγορίας πημαίνειν ἡμᾶς ὑπέλαβε·" ("for so he [Julian] called the Christians [sc. Galileans], thinking thus to bring discredit on them. But, man of education as he was, he ought to have bethought him that no mischief is done to reputation by change of name, for even had Socrates been called Critias and Pythagoras Phalaris they would have incurred no disgrace from the change of name—nor yet would Nireus if he had been named Thersites have lost the comeliness with which nature had gifted him. *Julian had learned about these things, but laid none of them to heart, and supposed that he could wrong us by using an inappropriate title*," trans. NPNF [emphasis mine]).

[45] Bouffartigue 1992:380–382 and 2005:113–126 and Boulnois 2011:803–830 explain the ethnographic argument that Julian is deploying against Christian universality claims.

The twist that Theodoret adds here is that to hold Christian beliefs is tantamount to holding a philosophical position (understood in the broadest sense), which is also inextricably interwoven with the daily practice of those beliefs. Further support for this can be gained from Chrysostom who, again, helps illustrate the nature of the problem that Theodoret is facing.[46] In a passage from his *Homilies on the Letter to the Romans*—worth quoting *in extenso*—he supplies important context:

Τί οὖν πρὸς τὸν Ἕλληνα εἴπω, φησί; Ταῦτα τὰ εἰρημένα. Καὶ σκόπει μὴ τί εἴπῃς πρὸς τὸν Ἕλληνα μόνον, ἀλλὰ καὶ πῶς αὐτὸν διορθώσῃ. Ὅταν σου τὸν βίον ἐξετάζων σκανδαλίζηται ἐκεῖθεν, ἐνταῦθα φρόντισον τί εἴπῃς. Ὑπὲρ μὲν γὰρ ἐκείνου, κἂν σκανδαλίζηται, σὺ λόγον οὐ δώσεις· ἀπὸ δὲ τοῦ βίου τοῦ σοῦ ἐὰν βλαβῇ, κίνδυνον ὑποστήσῃ τὸν ἔσχατον. Ὅταν ἴδῃ σε περὶ βασιλείας φιλοσοφοῦντα, καὶ πρὸς τὰ παρόντα ἐπτοημένον, καὶ περὶ γεέννης δεδοικότα, καὶ τὰ ἐνταῦθα τρέμοντα δεινά, τότε φρόντισον. Ὅταν ταῦτα ὁρῶν ἐγκαλῇ, καὶ λέγῃ· Εἰ βασιλείας ἐρᾷς, τί τῶν παρόντων οὐχ ὑπερορᾷς; εἰ δικαστήριον προσδοκᾷς φοβερόν, τί τῶν ἐνταῦθα δεινῶν οὐ καταφρονεῖς; εἰ ἀθανασίαν ἐλπίζεις, τί τοῦ θανάτου οὐ καταγελᾷς; ὅταν ταῦτα λέγῃ, μερίμνησον τί ἀπολογήσῃ. Ὅταν ἴδῃ σε τρέμοντα ζημίαν χρημάτων τὸν τοὺς οὐρανοὺς προσδοκῶντα, καὶ περιχαρῆ γενόμενον ὑπὲρ ἑνὸς ὀβολοῦ, καὶ τὴν ψυχὴν πάλιν προέμενον ὑπὲρ ἀργυρίου ὀλίγου, τότε φρόντισον· ταῦτα γάρ ἐστι, ταῦτα τὰ τὸν Ἕλληνα σκανδαλίζοντα. Ὥστε εἰ φροντίζεις σεαυτοῦ τῆς σωτηρίας, ὑπὲρ τούτων ἀπολογοῦ, μὴ διὰ ῥημάτων, ἀλλὰ διὰ πραγμάτων. Δι᾽ ἐκεῖνο μὲν γὰρ τὸ ζήτημα οὐδείς ποτε ἐβλασφήμησε τὸν Θεόν, διὰ δὲ τὸν πονηρὸν βίον μυρίαι πανταχοῦ βλασφημίαι. Τοῦτο τοίνυν διόρθου· ἐπεὶ πάλιν ἐρεῖ σοι ὁ Ἕλλην· Πόθεν μάθω, ὅτι δυνατὰ ἐπέταξεν ὁ Θεός; ἰδοὺ γὰρ σὺ Χριστιανὸς ὢν ἐκ προγόνων καὶ ἐντρεφόμενος τῇ καλῇ ταύτῃ θρησκείᾳ, οὐδὲν τοιοῦτον ποιεῖς. Τί οὖν ἐρεῖς; Πάντως ἐρεῖς, ὅτι Δείξω σοι ἑτέρους ποιοῦντας, μοναχοὺς ἐν ἐρημίαις καθημένους. Εἶτα οὐκ αἰσχύνῃ Χριστιανὸς μὲν εἶναι ὁμολογῶν, πρὸς δὲ ἑτέρους πέμπων, ὡς οὐ δυνάμενος δεῖξαι, ὅτι τὰ Χριστιανῶν ἐπιδείκνυσαι; Καὶ γὰρ καὶ ἐκεῖνος εὐθέως ἐρεῖ· Οὐκοῦν ποία μοι ἀνάγκη βαδίζειν ἐπὶ τὰ ὄρη, καὶ τὰς ἐρημίας διώκειν; Εἰ γὰρ μὴ δυνατὸν ἐν μέσαις στρεφόμενον πόλεσι φιλοσοφεῖν, πολλὴ τῆς

---

[46] For the hiatus between Chrysostom's aspirations in creating a Christian society and his congregations' practice of Christianity, see Sandwell 2010:523–542. While Chrysostom's measure of Christianization cannot be used as the only criterion by which to judge how Christian society had become, the importance of religion in shaping society in late antiquity is not in doubt. It is highly questionable to read the modern construct of 'secularism' back to the ancient society, which operated with different assumptions and models of diffuse religiosity firmly embedded in the civic and social structure.

πολιτείας ταύτης ἡ κατηγορία γένοιτ' ἄν, εἰ μέλλοιμεν τὰς πόλεις ἐκλιπόντες, ἐπὶ τὰς ἐρήμους τρέχειν. Ἀλλὰ δεῖξόν μοι ἄνθρωπον γυναῖκα ἔχοντα καὶ παιδία καὶ οἰκίαν, καὶ φιλοσοφοῦντα. Τί οὖν πρὸς ταῦτα ἐροῦμεν; οὐκ ἀνάγκη κάτω κύπτειν καὶ αἰσχύνεσθαι; Οὐδὲ γὰρ ὁ Χριστὸς οὕτως ἐκέλευσεν· ἀλλὰ πῶς; Λαμψάτω τὸ φῶς ὑμῶν ἔμπροσθεν τῶν ἀνθρώπων, οὐχὶ τῶν ὀρῶν οὐδὲ τῆς ἐρημίας καὶ τῆς ἀβάτου. Καὶ ταῦτα λέγω, οὐ κακίζων τοὺς κατειληφότας τὰ ὄρη, ἀλλὰ θρηνῶν τοὺς κατοικοῦντας τὰς πόλεις, ὅτι τὴν ἀρετὴν ἐντεῦθεν ἐξήλασαν. Διό, παρακαλῶ, τὴν φιλοσοφίαν τὴν ἐκεῖθεν καὶ ἐνταῦθα εἰσαγάγωμεν, ἵνα αἱ πόλεις γένωνται πόλεις· ταῦτα τὸν Ἕλληνα ὀρθῶσαι δύναται, ταῦτα ἀπαλλάξαι μυρίων σκανδάλων. Ὥστε, εἰ βούλει κἀκεῖνον ἐλευθερῶσαι σκανδάλου, καὶ αὐτὸς μυρίων ἀπολαῦσαι μισθῶν, τὸν βίον διόρθου <u>τὸν σαυτοῦ, καὶ πάντοθεν ἀπολάμπειν ποίει, Ὅπως ἴδωσιν οἱ ἄνθρωποι τὰ καλὰ ἔργα ὑμῶν, καὶ δοξάζωσι τὸν Πατέρα τὸν ἐν τοῖς οὐρανοῖς.</u>

Homilies on the Letter to the Romans 26, PG 60:642–644

What am I to say to the Gentile? He asks. Why, the same that I have been saying. And look not merely to what you shall say to the Gentile, but also to the means of amending yourself. When he is offended by examining into your life, then consider what you will say. For if he be offended, you will not be called to a reckoning for him, but if it be your way of life by which he is injured, you will have to undergo the greatest danger. When he sees you philosophizing about the kingdom, and fluttering at the things of this life, and at once afraid about hell, and trembling at the calamities of this life, then lay it to mind. When he sees this, and accuses you, and says, If you are in love with the Kingdom, how is it thou dost not look down upon the things of this life? If you are expecting the awful judgment, why do you not despise the terrors of this world? If you hope for immortality, why do you not think scorn of death? When he says this, be thou anxious what defence you will make. When he sees you trembling at the thought of losing your money, you that expectest the heavens, and exceedingly glad about a single penny, and selling your soul again for a little money, then lay it to mind. For these are the things, just these, that make the Gentiles stumble. And so, if you are thoughtful about your salvation, make your defence on these not by words, but by actions. For it is not through that question that anybody ever blasphemed God, but through men's bad lives it is, that there are thousands of blasphemies in all quarters. Set him right then. For the Gentile will next ask you, How am I to know that God's commands are feasible? For thou that art of Christian extraction, and hast been brought up in this fine religion, dost not do anything of the kind. And what will you tell him? You will be sure to say, I will show you others that do; monks that dwell in the deserts. And are you not ashamed to confess to being a Christian, and yet to send to others, as unable to show that you display the temper of a Christian?

For he also will say directly, What need have I to go to the mountains, and to hunt up the deserts? For if there is no possibility for a person who is living in the midst of cities to be a disciple, this is a sad imputation on this rule of conduct, that we are to leave the cities, and run to the deserts. But show me a man who has a wife, and children, and family, and yet pursues wisdom. What are we then to say to all this? Must we not hang down our heads, and be ashamed? For Christ gave us no such commandment; but what? "Let your light shine before men" [Matthew 5:16], not mountains, and deserts, and wildernesses, and out-of-the-way places. And this I say, not as abusing those who have taken up with the mountains, but as bewailing those that dwell in cities, because they have banished virtue from thence. Wherefore I beseech you let us introduce the discipline they have there here also, that the cities may become cities indeed. This will improve the Gentile. This will free him from countless offenses. And so if you would set him free from scandal, and yourself enjoy rewards without number, set your own life in order, and make it shine forth upon all sides, "that men may see your good works, and glorify your Father which is in heaven."[47]

Chrysostom engages in a simulated dialogue with a fictive Greek interlocutor. His criticisms are conjured up vividly (Fuentes Gonzalez's *"adversaire methodique"* comes to mind)[48] to set the issue before the eyes of the readers (or, in this case, most likely listeners). The life of Christians —far from perfect—gives incentive to pagan criticism. The message is unambiguous: Christians living exemplary lives and practicing their beliefs amount to the best "apology" for Christianity: "Ὥστε εἰ φροντίζεις σεαυτοῦ τῆς σωτηρίας, ὑπὲρ τούτων ἀπολογοῦ, μὴ διὰ ῥημάτων, ἀλλὰ διὰ πραγμάτων" ("And so, if you are thoughtful about your salvation, make your defence on these, not by words, but by actions").[49]

---

47 Trans. Jackson (*Nicene and Post-Nicene Fathers*, 2nd Series, Vol. 3, 1892).
48 See Chapter Five on Theodoret's rhetoric for a discussion of this method of argumentation.
49 *Homilies on the Letter to the Romans* 26, PG 60:642. Isidore of Peluse, goading his correspondent Palladius to continue to set an example to non-Christians, makes the similar point that Christianity has prevailed because, in the eyes of non-Christians, Christians practice what they believe by leading exemplary lives: "ὅτι μὲν οὐδεπώποτε ὅπου περὶ τῆς θείας θρησκείας εἰπεῖν

Chrysostom clearly alludes to the unmistakeable complacency of Christians who think that the ascetics can fulfill the ideals of Christian philosophy, allowing them to continue in their moral laxity. But Chrysostom—very much like Theodoret—considers the practice of Christian philosophy by ascetics as of a piece with urban morality, which he seeks to reform.

At the same time, the pagan criticisms of the anti-civic nature of asceticism accord with the objections of Libanius and Julian. Thus, when Chrysostom defends Christianity as a practical virtue that should be accomplished in solitude as well as in the cities,[50] he stresses the unity of these beliefs and addresses a tension between ascetic and urban morality. As if replying, then, to a pagan's criticism, " Ἀλλὰ δεῖξόν μοι ἄνθρωπον γυναῖκα ἔχοντα καὶ παιδία καὶ οἰκίαν,καὶ φιλοσοφοῦντα," ("But show me a man who has a wife, and children, and family, and yet pursues wisdom"),[51] Theodoret elucidates the thought, rounding off his point at the same time:

Καὶ ἔστιν ἰδεῖν ταῦτα εἰδότας τὰ δόγματα οὐ μόνους γε τῆς ἐκκλησίας τοὺς διδασκάλους, ἀλλὰ καὶ σκυτοτόμους καὶ χαλκοτύπους καὶ ταλασιουργοὺς καὶ τοὺς ἄλλους ἀποχειροβιώτους· καὶ γυναῖκας ὡσαύτως οὐ μόνον τὰς λόγων μετεσχηκυίας, ἀλλὰ καὶ χερνήτιδας καὶ ἀκεστρίας, καὶ μέντοι καὶ θεραπαίνας· καὶ οὐ μόνον ἀστοί, ἀλλὰ καὶ χωριτικοὶ τήνδε τὴν γνῶσιν ἐσχήκασι· καὶ ἔστιν εὑρεῖν καὶ σκαπανέας καὶ βοηλάτας καὶ φυτουργοὺς καὶ περὶ τῆς θείας διαλεγομένους Τριάδος καὶ περὶ τῆς τῶν ὅλων δημιουργίας καὶ τὴν ἀνθρωπείαν φύσιν εἰδότας Ἀριστοτέλους πολλῷ μᾶλλον καὶ Πλάτωνος, καὶ μέντοι καὶ ἀρετῆς ἐπιμελουμένους καὶ κακίαν ἐκκλίνοντας καὶ τὰ κολαστήρια δεδιότας τὰ προσδοκώμενα καὶ τὸ θεῖον δικαστήριον ἀνενδοιάστως προσμένοντας καὶ τῆς αἰωνίου πέρι καὶ ἀνωλέθρου φιλοσοφοῦντας ζωῆς καὶ τῆς τῶν οὐρανῶν ἕνεκα βασιλείας πάντα πόνον ἀσπαστῶς αἱρουμένους, καὶ ταῦτα οὐ παρ' ἄλλου του μεμαθηκότας, ἀλλὰ παρ' ἐκείνων, οὓς ὑμεῖς βαρβαροφώνους ἀποκαλεῖτε.

Therapeutikê 5.68–70

ἐδέησεν, ἡττήθημεν, οὐδ'ἀναισχυντεῖν ἐδόξαμεν, ἀλλ' ἀπάντων κρατοῦμεν καὶ περίεσμεν τῷ λόγῳ, παντί που δῆλον. Ὅτι δὲ πάντες, οὐχ οἷς λέγομεν, ἀλλ'οἷς πράττομεν προσέχουσι, καὶ ἀπὸ τούτων φέρουσι τὴν ψῆφον, καὶ εἰ μὴ φανερῶς, ἀλλὰ κατὰ γνώμην μετ'ἐξουσίας ἀποφαίνονται, καὶ τοῦτο εἰδέναι χρή. Οὐκοῦν χρὴ σύνδρομον τῷ λόγῳ ἔχειν τὸν βίον, καὶ συμβαίνουσαν τῷ δόγματι τὴν πολιτείαν, ἵνα μή, λόγοις νικῶντες, τοῖς πράγμασιν ἡττώμεθα" (Ep. 180, PG 78:633).

50 In the same vein Theodoret notes the case of Maësymas: "One can learn from them that those who choose to practice philosophy are harmed not at all by life in towns and villages; for this man and those like him responsible for the service of God have shown that it is possible even for those who go about among many to attain the very summit of virtues."

51 *Homilies on the Letter to the Romans* 26, PG 60:644.

And it is possible to see that those who know these teachings are not merely the leaders of the church, but also workers in leather, copper-smiths, weavers, and other manual workers. And women also, not just those who are educated, but those also who are mere weavers, seam-stresses, and daily laborers. This knowledge is possessed not just by city dwellers but by country folk. And it is possible to find agricultural workers, drovers, and gardeners engaged in discussions on the blessed Trinity, and knowing much more than Aristotle or Plato about the Creator of the universe and the composition of human nature. These people are *concerned about virtue* [ἀρετῆς ἐπιμελουμένους] and avoidance of vice; they fear future punishments and await without the least skepticism the final judgment; they philosophize about eternity and immortality, and they freely accept all sorts of difficulties for the sake of the kingdom of heaven and these things they have learned, not from somebody else, but from those whom you call barbarians because of their speech.[52]

Theodoret alludes here to a primarily linguistic dimension of barbarism (which is the primary understanding and use of the term). However, because Greek language was bound up with identity, the allusion extends well beyond

---

[52] Chrysostom on a similar occasion writes: "Οὐ γὰρ ἐν γωνίᾳ μιᾷ γράψαντες αὐτὰ κατώρυξαν, ἀλλὰ πανταχοῦ γῆς καὶ θαλάττης ἥπλωσαν ὑπὸ ταῖς πάντων ἀκοαῖς· καὶ ἐχθρῶν παρόντων ταῦτα ἀνεγινώσκετο, καθάπερ καὶ νῦν, καὶ οὐδένα οὐδὲν τῶν εἰρημένων ἐσκανδάλισε. Καὶ μάλα εἰκότως· θεία γὰρ δύναμις ἦν ἡ πάντα ἐπιοῦσα καὶ κατορθοῦσα παρὰ πᾶσιν. Ἐπεὶ εἰ μὴ τοῦτο ἦν, πῶς ὁ τελώνης, καὶ ὁ ἁλιεύς, καὶ ὁ ἀγράμματος τοιαῦτα ἐφιλοσόφει; Ἃ γὰρ οὐδὲ ὄναρ οἱ ἔξωθεν φαντασθῆναι ἠδυνήθησάν ποτε, ταῦτα οὗτοι μετὰ πολλῆς τῆς πληροφορίας καὶ ἀπαγγέλλουσι καὶ πείθουσι· καὶ οὐχὶ ζῶντες μόνον, ἀλλὰ καὶ τελευτήσαντες· οὐδὲ δύο καὶ εἴκοσιν ἀνθρώπους, οὐδὲ ἑκατὸν καὶ χιλίους καὶ μυρίους, ἀλλὰ πόλεις καὶ ἔθνη καὶ δήμους, καὶ γῆν καὶ θάλασσαν, καὶ Ἑλλάδα καὶ βάρβαρον, καὶ τὴν οἰκουμένην καὶ τὴν ἀοίκητον·... Τὰ δὲ τῶν ἁλιέων, ἐλαυνομένων, μαστιζομένων, κινδυνευόντων, καὶ ἰδιῶται καὶ σοφοί, καὶ δοῦλοι καὶ ἐλεύθεροι, καὶ βασιλεῖς καὶ στρατιῶται, καὶ βάρβαροι καὶ Ἕλληνες, μετὰ πάσης ἐδέξαντο τῆς εὐνοίας" ("For they did not write these things in one corner and bury them, but everywhere, by sea and by land, they unfolded them in the ears of all, and these things were read in the presence of enemies, even as they are now, and none of the things which they said offended any one. And very naturally, for it was a divine power that pervaded all, and made it to prosper with all men.

For if it had not been so, how could the publican, and the fisherman, and the unlearned, have attained to such philosophy? For things, which they that are without have never been able to imagine, no not in a dream, are by these men with great certainty both published and made convincing, and not in their lives only, but even after death: neither to two men, nor twenty men, nor an hundred, nor a thousand, nor ten thousand, but to cities, nations, and people, both to land and sea, in the land both of Greeks and barbarians, both inhabited and desert;

... But these doctrines of the fishermen, chased as they were, scourged and in jeopardy, both learned and unlearned, both bond and free, both kings and private soldiers, both barbarians and Greeks, have received with all good will," *Homily on Matthew* PG 57:18).

the linguistic realm to a broader spectrum of cultural manifestations. This requires Theodoret to add a moral argument to the linguistic dimension:

Ἀλλ' οὐκ ἐβουλήθη πέντε ἢ δέκα ἢ πεντεκαίδεκα ἢ ἑκατὸν ἢ δὶς τοσούτους τῶν σωτηρίων ἀπολαῦσαι ναμάτων, ἀλλὰ πάντας ἀνθρώπους, καὶ Ἕλληνας καὶ βαρβάρους, καὶ τοὺς λόγοις ἐντεθραμμένους καὶ τοὺς λόγων οὐ γεγευμένους, καὶ σκυτέας καὶ ὑφάντας καὶ χαλκοτύπους καὶ τοὺς ἄλλους, ὅσοι τὰς τέχνας μεταχειρίζουσι, καὶ πρὸς τούτοις καὶ οἰκέτας καὶ προσαίτας καὶ γηπόνους καὶ ἀλσοκόμους καὶ γυναῖκας ὡσαύτως, τάς τε πλούτῳ περιρρεομένας καὶ τὰς πόνῳ ξυνεζευγμένας καὶ ἐκ χειρῶν βιοτεύειν ἠναγκασμένας. Τούτου δὴ εἵνεκα ἁλιεῦσι καὶ τελώναις καὶ σκυτοτόμῳ χρησάμενος ὑπουργοῖς, προσενήνοχε τοῖς ἀνθρώποις τὰ σωτήρια καὶ θεῖα μαθήματα, τὰς μὲν γλώττας αὐτῶν, ἃς ἐξ ἀρχῆς ἔλαχον, οὐκ ἀμείψας, τὰ δέ γε διειδῆ καὶ διαυγῆ τῆς σοφίας νάματα διὰ τούτων προχέας.

Therapeutikê 8.3-4

But [the source of Wisdom] did not wish for merely five, ten, fifteen, a hundred, or two hundred, to benefit from the streams of salvation, but rather everybody, Greeks and non-Greeks, and those nourished in rhetoric as well as those with no taste for speeches: shoemakers, weavers, coppersmiths, and all craftsmen, and besides these, maids and mendicants, tillers of fields and tenders of the groves, and besides women, both those swimming in riches and those yoked to toil and forced to make a living by manual labor. That is why, with the fishermen, the publicans, and the tent-maker for collaborators, [Wisdom] has brought to humanity its saving and divine teachings, not in exchanges with them in their maternal tongue, which they always had, but by pouring on them the limpid, translucent streams of wisdom.

The dissociation of message from the language in which it is conveyed suggests a refocusing of the importance of language—as well as of the identity with which it is bound—and a rethinking, on the basis of meaning, that the teachings (and their practice) have for human beings regardless of their culture.[53]

---

[53] Isidore of Peluse argues similarly when addressing his correspondent Ophelius scholasticus: "οὔτε τοὺς λεξιθήρας, οὔτε τοὺς ῥήτορας, οὔτε τοὺς διαλεκτικούς, οὔτε τοὺς ἐπὶ τῇ τῶν λόγων δεινότητι ἐναβρυνομένους, σοφοὺς κλητέον, ἀλλὰ τοὺς ἐπὶ τῇ πρακτικῇ φιλοσοφίᾳ διαλάμποντας. Εἰ δὲ κοσμοίη τούτους καὶ ἡ λογικὴ σοφωτέρους ὀνομαστέον. Εἰ δὲ καὶ ἡ θεωρητικὴ (φημὶ δὴ ἡ εὐσέβεια, ἣν μόνην κυρίως σοφίαν ὁριζόμεθα), σοφωτάτους προσαγορευτέον. Τὴν μὲν ὥσπερ θεμέλιον καὶ οἰκοδομὴν εἶναι, τὴν δὲ ὡς ἐγκαλλώπισμα, τὴν δὲ ὡς κορωνίδα. Ὥσπερ

The implications of this argument are that Greek philosophers, despite their fame (they failed to convince even their own pupils),[54] remained associated with Greek culture and were therefore confined within the limits of Greek culture in a rapidly expanding multiethnic Christianity.[55]

It is hard to underestimate the importance of Theodoret's view of Christianity, in its relationship with the *oikoumenê*, as a practical universal

---

οὖν θεμελίου μὴ ὑπάρχοντος, μηδ'οἰκοδομίας, οὔτε τὰ κοσμοῦντα, οὔτε τὰ στεφανοῦντα χώραν ἔχει· οὕτω καὶ ἀρετῆς μὴ ὑπαρχούσης, ἡ λογικὴ καὶ ἡ θεωρητικὴ οὐχ ἕξει" (Ep. 201, PG 78:645).

54 *Therapeutikê* 5.46–49.

55 *Therapeutikê* 5.66: " Ἀλλὰ τούτων μὲν τῶν δογμάτων οὐδένα διδάσκαλον ἡμῖν ἐπιδεῖξαι δυνήσεσθε, ἡμεῖς δὲ τῶν ἀποστολικῶν καὶ προφητικῶν δογμάτων τὸ κράτος ἐναργῶς ἐπιδείκνυμεν πᾶσα γὰρ ἡ ὑφήλιος τῶνδε τῶν λόγων ἀνάπλεως. Καὶ ἡ Ἑβραίων φωνὴ οὐ μόνον εἰς τὴν Ἑλλήνων μετεβλήθη, ἀλλὰ καὶ εἰς τὴν Ῥωμαίων καὶ Αἰγυπτίων καὶ Περσῶν καὶ Ἰνδῶν καὶ Ἀρμενίων καὶ Σκυθῶν καὶ Σαυρομάτων καὶ ξυλλήβδην εἰπεῖν εἰς ἁπάσας τάς γλώττας, αἷς ἅπαντα τὰ ἔθνη κεχρημένα διατελεῖ" ("Now you will be unable to show us one teacher of these teachings whereas we, for our part, can clearly demonstrate the cogency of the teachings of the apostles and prophets. Every country under the sun is filled with their words. And the Hebrew has been translated, not only into Greek, but also into Latin, Egyptian, Persian, Indian, Armenian, Scythian, Sarmatian, in a word into all the languages which all peoples have continued to use"). John Chrysostom makes a similar point in his description of fifth-century missionary activity: "κἂν μυριάκις καταγελῶσιν Ἕλληνες τῆς τῶν ὀνομάτων ἀγροικίας, οὐδὲν ἧττον μετὰ πλείονος αὐτὰ τῆς παρρησίας ἐρῶ· ὅσῳ γὰρ ἂν τὸ ἔθνος αὐτοῖς βάρβαρον φαίνηται καὶ τῆς Ἑλληνικῆς ἀπέχον παιδεύσεως, τοσούτῳ λαμπρότερα τὰ ἡμέτερα φανεῖται. Ὅταν γὰρ ὁ βάρβαρος καὶ ἀμαθὴς τοιαῦτα φθέγγηται, ἃ μηδεὶς τῶν ἐπὶ γῆς ἀνθρώπων συνεῖδέ ποτε, καὶ μὴ φθέγγηται μόνον, ἀλλὰ καὶ πείθῃ· καίτοι εἰ καὶ τοῦτο μόνον ἦν, μέγα τὸ θαῦμα ἦν· νῦν δὲ πρὸς τούτῳ καὶ ἕτερον τούτου μεῖζον παρέχῃ τεκμήριον, τοῦ θεόπνευστα εἶναι τὰ λεγόμενα, τὸ τοὺς ἀκούοντας πείθειν ἅπαντας διὰ τοῦ χρόνου παντός, τίς οὐ θαυμάσεται τὴν ἐνοικοῦσαν αὐτῷ δύναμιν; Καὶ γὰρ καὶ τοῦτο μέγιστον, ὅπερ ἔφην, τεκμήριον τοῦ μηδὲν οἴκοθεν αὐτὸν νομοθετεῖν. Οὗτος δὴ οὖν ὁ βάρβαρος, τῇ μὲν τοῦ εὐαγγελίου γραφῇ τὴν οἰκουμένην κατέλαβεν ἅπασαν, τῷ δὲ σώματι μέσην κατέσχε τὴν Ἀσίαν, ἔνθα τὸ παλαιὸν ἐφιλοσόφουν οἱ τῆς Ἑλληνικῆς συμμορίας ἅπαντες, κἀκεῖθεν τοῖς δαίμοσίν ἐστι φοβερός, ἐν μέσῳ τῶν ἐχθρῶν διαλάμπων, καὶ τὸν ζόφον αὐτῶν σβεννὺς, καὶ τὴν ἀκρόπολιν τῶν δαιμόνων καταλύων· τῇ δὲ ψυχῇ πρὸς τὸν χῶρον ἀνεχώρησεν ἐκεῖνον, τὸν ἁρμόττοντα τῷ τὰ τοιαῦτα ἐργασαμένῳ. Καὶ τὰ μὲν Ἑλλήνων ἔσβεσται ἅπαντα καὶ ἠφάνισται, τὰ δὲ τούτου καθ' ἑκάστην λαμπρότερα γίνεται" ("[. . . though the Greeks mock ten thousand times at the rusticity of the names, I shall not the less speak them with the greater boldness.] For the more barbarous his nation seems to them, and the more he seems removed from Greek education, so much the brighter does what we have with us appear. For when a barbarian and an untaught person utters things which no man on earth ever knew, and does not only utter, [though if this were the only thing it were a great marvel], but besides this, affords another and a stronger proof that what he says is divinely inspired, namely, the convincing all his hearers through all time; who will not wonder at the power that dwells in him? Since this is, as I said, the strongest proof that he lays down no laws of his own. This barbarian then, with his writing of the Gospel, has occupied all the habitable world. With his body he has taken possession of the center of Asia, where of old philosophized all of the Grecian party, shining forth in the midst of his foes, dispersing their darkness, and breaking down the stronghold of devils: but in soul he has retired to that place which is fit for one who has done such things. And as for the writings of the Greeks, they are all put out and vanished, but this man's shine brighter day by day," *On John*, PG 59:31). For a survey of apologetic arguments on the success of Christianity, see Dorival 2001:37–56, 45–46 with references to Theodoret.

philosophy. This view hinges on his conviction of the unity of humankind,[56] in spite of linguistic differences.[57] In addition, it serves to prove the intrinsic value of the evangelical laws and to cut across one of the most rigid distinctions of Greco-Roman culture, that of Hellene-barbarian.[58] Seen in this light, Theodoret's claim of Christianity's universal appeal is cast into sharper relief, and it chimes tellingly with accounts of missionary zeal in the early fifth century AD.[59]

Conclusion

From the analysis above, we have seen the incentives for Theodoret's defense of Christianity as a universal practical virtue. His effort is focused—but not limited to—defending the ascetics and, therefore, addressing the tension from both pagans and Christians related to the acceptance of their role. On the one hand, he invests the ascetics with easily recognizable attributes that he expropriates from Greek philosophy. On the other, he discredits Greek philosophers for failing to live up to the standards of their beliefs and indulging instead in their passions.

---

[56] *Therapeutikê* 5.55: "'Ὡς ἂν δὲ μή τις ὑπολάβῃ ἄλλως μὲν Ἕλληνας φῦναι, ἄλλως δὲ Ῥωμαίους, καὶ Αἰγυπτίους ἑτέρως, καὶ Πέρσας καὶ Μασσαγέτας καὶ Σκύθας καὶ Σαυρομάτας ἄλλης οὐσίας μετηλειχέναι, ἐδίδαξεν ὁ τὴν κοσμογονίαν ξυγγράψας τὴν ἡμετέραν, ὡς ἄνδρα ἕνα ἀπὸ γῆς ὁ ποιητὴς διαπλάσας καὶ ἐκ τῆς τούτου πλευρᾶς τὴν γυναῖκα δημιουργήσας, ἐκ τῆς τούτοιν ὁμιλίας ἅπασαν τὴν οἰκουμένην ἀνθρώπων ἐπλήρωσε τῶν παίδων τῶν ἐκείνων καὶ τῶν ἐκγόνων κατὰ μέρος αὐξησάντων τὸ γένος" ("So that nobody would presume that the Greeks were made one way, the Romans another, the Egyptians another way still, and that the Persians, Massagetes, Scythians, and Sarmatians have all been endowed with different essences, the author of our cosmogony has taught that the Creator made from the earth only one man, and that from one of his ribs he made a woman, and that then from the union of this one couple he filled the whole earth with people, and their children and grandchildren for their part increased the race"). The argument is developed more fully in *Dialexis* V. On Human Nature.

[57] Summed up in the declaration: "All languages have the same meaning since human nature is one; that is a fact of experience," (*Therapeutikê* 5.71).

[58] Theodoret's attitude toward barbarians has attracted the attention of many scholars; see Lechner 1955, Sevçenko 1964:220-236, Podskalsky 1985:330-351, and Winkelmann 1989:221-235, who shows how the material in the *Therapeutikê* stands in tension with Theodoret's views on barbarians in the rest of his writings. However, an integrated study of Theodoret's attitude toward barbarians is very much needed in view of the piecemeal approach to his ideas on the part of previous scholarship and in light of current emphases that render previous scholarship due for revision.

[59] Missionary activity in Byzantium, along with its religious, social, political, and intellectual underpinnings, is a seriously understudied topic, especially covering the early fifth century. Despite the lack of a monographic treatment, some perspective can be gained from Engelhardt 1974. For evidence of keen interest in mission in the Antiochene environment, see Andres 1935, Auf der Maur 1959, and Yannoulatos 1969:208-226, which includes many references to Theodoret, mainly from the *Religious History*.

It is important to stress that, in Theodoret's view, practical virtue is not confined to ascetics—even if they are the embodiment of this virtue *par excellence*—but extends to the entire society of Christians who practice it. To further support his argument, he introduces an ethnographic dimension. The reason evangelical laws spread throughout the empire and well beyond it— among various ἔθνη—is because of their intrinsic value. This counters pagan criticisms found already in Celsus but more forcefully reiterated by emperor Julian, who sought to peripheralize the importance of Christianity and reduce it to a local phenomenon.

5

Theodoret's Rhetoric,
Style, and Argumentation:
Some Literary Considerations

THE THERAPEUTIKÊ'S LITERARY FEATURES are informed by a set of recognizable historical, religious, educational, and cultural concerns, which have yet to be integrated into a coherent account.[1] More specifically, a number of these features form an integral part of Theodoret's apologetic program. He makes this explicit in the preface to the Therapeutikê, where he summarizes his central claims succinctly:[2]

Πολλάκις μοι τῶν τῆς Ἑλληνικῆς μυθολογίας ἐξηρτημένων ξυντετυχηκότες τινές τήν τε πίστιν ἐκωμώδησαν τὴν ἡμετέραν, οὐδὲν ἄλλο λέγοντες ἡμᾶς τοῖς τὰ θεῖα παρ' ἡμῶν παιδευομένοις ἢ τὸ πιστεύειν παρεγγυᾶν, καὶ τῆς τῶν ἀποστόλων κατηγόρουν ἀπαιδευσίας, βαρβάρους ἀποκαλοῦντες, τὸ γλαφυρὸν τῆς εὐεπείας οὐκ ἔχοντας· ... Καὶ διεῖλον μὲν εἰς δυοκαίδεκα διαλέξεις τὴν πραγματείαν, τὸν ἀνειμένον δὲ χαρακτῆρα τοῖς λόγοις ἐντέθεικα· τῇ διδασκαλίᾳ γὰρ εἶναι τοῦτον ὑπείληφα πρόσφορον, ἄλλως τε καὶ ταῖς Πλάτωνος καὶ τῶν ἄλλων φιλοσόφων χρώμενον μαρτυρίαις ἔδει καὶ τοὺς λόγους μὴ παντάπασιν ἀπᾴδοντας ξυναρμόσαι, ἀλλ' ἔχοντάς τινα πρὸς ἐκείνας ἐμφέρειαν.

Therapeutikê, prologue 1–3

I have often encountered those devotees of Greek mythology who are convinced of its truth, and who make fun of our faith under the pretext

---

[1] For a circumspect discussion, see Prostmeier 2005:1–29.

[2] The preface structures and unifies the *Therapeutikê*, rendering explicit the main aims of the work. For its affinities with the rest of the prefaces in late antique literary culture, see Schissel 1930:18–22. On the importance of the preface in Syriac literary culture, see Riad 1988. We will return to the importance of the preface for Theodoret's project later.

that the only option we give to those who are being instructed in divine things is to believe. *They accuse the apostles of ignorance and regard them as barbarians because they lack the refinement of elegant diction* . . . I have divided my work into twelve chapters and have given a flowing quality to my style *because this method seems most suited to my didactic purposes,* especially since, in utilizing arguments from Plato and the other philosophers, it would be appropriate if my style should not be at complete variance with theirs, but should bear some resemblance to it.

Apaideusia (lack of *paideia*) and *barbarism*, as well as lack of *euepeia*, become focal points of Theodoret's defense of Christian *paideia*.[3] This leads him to make a point of both using elegant Greek[4] and referring to the literary form that he selected, *dialexis*, as will be explained below. Style, then, and literary form are not mere literary choices but ones closely tied to his apologetic project.

Imagery

Imagery plays an important role in Theodoret's rhetoric and is integral to his argumentation.[5] There is a repeated emphasis on the medical imagery that is used from the outset of *Dialexis* I. On Faith, which sets the tone for the rest of the work.[6] Alongside this, Theodoret's images are taken from many different realms.[7] Preference is given to similes over metaphors, and they range from two or three words to almost an entire page in length. Theodoret deploys the images that unfold before the reader with great skill, at times with an eye to

---

[3]   For a discussion of these accusations, see Speyer and Opelt 2001:811–895 and Ackermann 1997:145–157, with an emphasis on the criticisms of the literary style of the Old Testament. Ackermann draws attention to the fact that the poor literary quality of the Bible was also a problem for Christians with a taste for elegant Greek. See Norden 1898:516–531 for a discussion of early Christian views on style with attention to the New Testament and the pagan criticisms of its style.

[4]   On Theodoret's elegant Greek, see the introduction by Canivet 2000–2001(I):60–67. See also Spadavecchia 1976, Festa 1928:584–588, and Hult 1990 for studies of Theodoret's syntax. Theodoret's turns of phrase and flourishes of sententiousness earned him a place in the textbooks used by the Greeks under Ottoman rule; see Stoupakês 2000:561–562.

[5]   Artzer 1970:148. While Artzer acknowledges the importance of imagery when it comes to account for its abundant use, he resorts to such puzzling and intriguing statements as: "As *a true oriental* he speaks in figures not in grammatical statements alone, with the imagination rather than pure reason, with art rather than prosaic pronouncements" (148, emphasis mine).

[6]   See Chapter Three.

[7]   E.g. war, athletic games, family and the home, animals, the human body, agriculture, music, painting, sculpture, theater, birds, architecture, clothing, commerce, crafts, education, fire, water, religious mysteries, the sea, ships, tools, travel.

their pedigree or to a detail that illustrates his point.[8] On the function of these images, Artzer writes:

> In many cases the image carries the message as much as the prose text which forms the setting to support the image. Often it sheds more light on the subject than the longer verbal explanation. The images are embedded in the substance; they are not patterns embroidered on a plain base, not accessories pinned on, neither inlay nor overlay, not applique or veneer.[9]

Collectively, images give a more vivid rendering of a thought process, with the effect of bringing before the eyes of the reader the point that is being argued.[10] This goes hand in hand with Theodoret's inventiveness with imagery, as when Greek gods—compared to bats—are put to flight[11] or when he recalls the entire life of Christ in one sentence by abstracting it to concrete objects that are grouped together and placed paratactically.[12]

---

[8] See e.g. the following passage: "τῶν τὸν θαλάττιον βίον ἀσπαζομένων οἱ μὲν τὰς φορτίδας ἐρέττουσιν, οἱ ταύτας τοῖς οἴαξι διευθύνουσιν, καὶ μέντοι καὶ πᾶς ἁλιευτὴς ἐφ' ἁλιάδος ὀχούμενος χαλᾷ δίκτυον καὶ θηρεύει τοὺς τῶν ὑδάτων τροφίμους, καὶ ἄλλος ἐπὶ πέτρας ἱδρυμένος καθίησιν ὁρμιὰν καὶ δελεάζων περιπείρει τῷ ἀγκίστρῳ τῶν ἰχθύων τινάς· εἰσὶ δὲ οἳ καὶ ναυαγίᾳ χρῶνται καὶ ὑποβρύχιοι γίνονται, ἢ ἐξ ἀβουλίας παρὰ καιρὸν ἀναχθέντες ἢ διὰ θράσος τῆς ζάλης κατατολμήσαντες. Ταῦτα δὲ οὐ τηνάλλως ὑθλῶν διεξῆλθον, ἀλλὰ τῶν τῇ κτίσει προσπταιόντων καὶ τῶν ἐν ταύτῃ πρυτανευομένων ἀνέδην κατηγορούντων ἐπιδεῖξαι τὴν ἄνοιαν διά τινος εἰκόνος πειρώμενος" ("Of those engaged in seafaring activities, some act as rowers of merchantmen, others direct the ships with the helm; and indeed every fisherman borne out on the briny water lowers his net and fishes for the products of the sea, while another sits propped up on a rock, casts his line, and tries to lure the fish with bait. But there are those who suffer shipwreck and become submerged, either because in their folly they put out to sea when it is still not the season to sail, or because they rashly decide to confront the surge of the billows. *I make these observations, not just to indulge in idle cliches, but in an attempt to utilize an image to show up the folly of those who put themselves in opposition to creation and unrestrainedly criticize the providence governing it,*" *Therapeutikê* 6.1–2 [emphasis mine]).

[9] Artzer 1970:148.

[10] Newman 2002:1–23.

[11] *Therapeutikê* 12.97: "῎Απαντα γὰρ αὐτῶν τὸν ὁρμαθόν, οἷόν τινας νυκτερίδας, τῷ σκότῳ παρέπεμψεν ἀνατείλαν τὸ φῶς" (". . . because the Light has risen and banished the lot of them like bats to darkness").

[12] *Therapeutikê* 8.8: "ἀλλὰ σπήλαιον καὶ φάτνην καὶ παρθένον χερνῆτιν καὶ βρέφος εὐτελέσι σπαργάνοις ἐνειλημμένον καὶ ἐπὶ κενῆς ἐρριμμένον τῆς φάτνης καὶ χωρίον ἄδοξον καὶ σμικρόν, ἐν ᾧ ταῦτα ἐγένετο, καὶ αὖ πάλιν πενίᾳ αὐξηθέντος τοῦ βρέφους καὶ πεῖναν καὶ δίψος καὶ τὸν ἐξ ὁδοιπορίας πόνον καὶ μετὰ ταῦτα τὸ παρὰ πάντων ᾀδόμενον πάθος, τὰς ἐπὶ κόρρης πληγάς, τὰς κατὰ νώτου μάστιγας, τὸ ἱκρίον, τοὺς ἥλους, τὴν χολήν, τὸ ὄξος, τὸν θάνατον" ("No, all they had were a cave, a manger, a poor virgin, an infant wrapped in swaddling clothes and laid in a bare manger, and a small, undistinguished place in which these events took place. And it is the poverty of this Infant which increases, His hunger, thirst, fatigue from journeys, and His passion, which is celebrated by all; the blows on His forehead, the lashes on His back, the nails, the vinegar, the gall, and finally His death").

To the above we should add a pair of features found particularly in Christian rhetoric: the tendency to build on oppositions (passible/impassible, divided/undivided, truth/falsity, part/whole, light/darkness, universality/particularity, simplicity/complexity) and the taste for paradox[13] (poor and powerless king, i.e. Jesus, etc.).

Literary Form and Style

Theodoret's use of *dialexis* as a formal means of conveying his ideas deserves special attention.[14] The emphasis on his choice of literary form needs to be stressed in view of the fact that formal considerations have been little discussed in previous scholarship on the *Therapeutikê*.[15] However, form could account for a number of Theodoret's choices, giving a new dimension to the nature of his project.

Dialexis as a literary form is akin to diatribe, *lalia*, and *meletê*.[16] It recalls the setting of a philosophical school or a classroom and was used by a number of ancient authors (e.g. Teles, Bion, Epictetus, Julian) in order to expound philosophical topics. The informal, conversational style of the lecture form renders it a flexible means of getting across a number of ideas, often by using popular[17] literary and philosophical commonplaces and set-pieces. Another aspect important for our discussion is that the *dialexis* aims to dispel erroneous beliefs

---

13 Cameron 1991:162 suggests that "the early emphasis on mystery and paradox in Christian discourse resisted the impetus to assimilation with public rhetoric."

14 For detailed discussions of the literary form, see the introduction to Trapp 1997a, as well as Trapp 1997b:1945-1976, which is by far the most accomplished case study of the application of this literary form. See also Fuentes González 1998, which, while it is a thorough study of the literary fragments of Teles, features, esp. in pages 44-78, an excellent and nuanced discussion of the affinities between *dialexis* and *diatribe*. See also Wehner 2000:13-18, which contains a discussion of related literary features. For a condensed discussion of *diatribe* and *dialexis* with forays into Christian material, see Stowers 1988:71-83 and 1994:627-633.

15 Canivet 2000-2001(I):65 writes: "Théodoret possède la technique de l' écrivain, mais son œuvre apologétique n'entre dans aucune genre littéraire." In light of recent work on *dialexis* (Trapp 1997a and b, Fuentes Gonzalez 1998, Wehner 2000), I think this view is no longer tenable and is in need of revision.

16 See the introduction by Trapp 1997a:xl.

17 I use the word advisedly and without assuming a rigid dichotomy between "high" and "low" culture. Instead, it is to be understood in the same vein as Fuentes Gonzalez's discussion of "*popular philosophie*". In his careful discussion of the notion, Fuentes Gonzalez 1998:56 criticizes nineteenth-century German scholarship—which coins the term—for the assumption that it "peut porter à croire qu' il s' agit d' une philosophie créée par le peuple ou simplement suivie par le peuple, *ce qui serait faux*." He continues: ". . . il peut être utile de parler de 'philosophie populaire' pour désigner *les motifs qui représentent les exigences les plus répandues d' une époque fortement caractérisée par un esprit d' universalisation* comme c' était le cas de l' époque hellénistico-romaine" [emphasis mine].

and lead the interlocutor to a right belief, which usually entails converting the interlocutor to the speaker's point of view.[18] The dialogical element is bound up with this (ultimately Socratic) form,[19] and this enables the speaker to engage in a lively and personal way the beliefs of the reader (or listener)—to censure, exhort, or praise according to his aim.[20] To this end, abundant use of imagery and quotations from poets and philosophers lends authority and vividly illustrates the claims and arguments that are set forth.

As a result, the *dialexeis* appear as a unique formal means by which to address pagan criticisms but also to instruct through the rehearsal of popular philosophical set-pieces. Didacticism could also be used to convey Theodoret's practice of putting order into several knotty and contested issues, of clarifying and simplifying and reducing a mass of material into well articulated positions. But, more importantly, in each *dialexis* he makes sure to give a careful presentation of central Christian beliefs and to offer an account for the grounds of these beliefs, incorporating ample proofs from the Bible.[21]

Audience

Theodoret combines knowledgeable exposition with a lively engagement with readers (or listeners). We can get an idea of his intended audience by looking at the occasional comments and reactions of "readers" that he conjures up throughout the *Therapeutikê*. Allowance has to be made for the fact that the interlocutors are fictive;[22] nevertheless, it is important to give attention to assumptions that are made even in the form of a (fictive) audience, as they determine the kind of arguments that inform the *Therapeutikê*. We are allowed

---

[18] So Fuentes González 1958:57. Fuentes González makes the interesting point (while commenting on the eristic elements of philosophical *dialexeis*): "Mais il faut peut-être nuancer l'idée que la *dialexis* philosophique suit une méthode *éristique*, si bien que l'on parle souvent de l' interlocuteur fictif comme d'un 'adversaire'. En effet, *le but du moraliste n' est pas la polémique pure et simple mais la conversion de l'individu, la transformation de son caractère dans le sens de la vertu et de la verité.* Un telle conception rattache bien un moraliste comme Télès à la tradition socratique. *Si l' on veut, on peut dire qu'il se sert d' un 'adversaire' théorique ou méthodique"* [emphasis mine].

[19] Trapp 1997a:xl draws attention to the derivation of *dialexis* from the verb *dialegesthai* and notes its ultimately Socratic origin. Kerferd 1981:59 points to a later meaning of "διαλέγεσθαι" in its sophistic context as "to discuss by the method of question and answer."

[20] For the dialogical element, see Tsekourakis 1980:61–78. The most detailed study of the dialogic element is Wehner 2000. For the coexistence of ἐλεγκτικός, προτρεπτικός, διδασκαλικὸς χαρακτήρ in *dialexis*, see Schmidt 1962:14–28; Long 2002:52–64.

[21] On Theodoret's didacticism in his *Questions on the Octateuch* and his correspondence, see Petruccione (forthcoming).

[22] Fuentes-Gonzalez's *"adversaire methodique"* comes to mind. However, to treat this as a purely literary device and deny any relationship with—an otherwise admittedly difficult to ascertain— reality would be to deny too much.

occasional glimpses beginning with the preface. Theodoret continues to cure the *oiêsis* of those who "have had a share of the expressions of the poets and the rhetoricians, and who have had a taste of the elegant diction of Plato, despise the sacred Scriptures under the pretext that these are totally devoid of the ornaments of style, and are reluctant to learn about [the truth of being] from men who are mere fishermen." He adds further:

Μόνην δ' ἄρα τῆς ἀληθείας τὴν μάθησιν ἀπεριέργως λαβεῖν οὐκ ἐθέλουσιν, ἀλλ' ἀτιμίαν ὑπολαμβάνουσιν, εἰ βάρβαρος αὐτοὺς ταύτην τὴν γλῶτταν παιδεύοι· καὶ τοῦτον ἔχουσι τὸν τῦφον ἄνδρες οὐδ' εἰς ἄκρον τῆς Ἑλληνικῆς φιλοσοφίας ἐληλακότες, ἀλλ' ὀλίγων τινῶν, τὸ δὴ λεγόμενον, ἄκροις χείλεσι γεγευμένοι καὶ σμικρὰ ἄττα ἔνθεν κἀκεῖθεν ἠρανισμένοι

Therapeutikê 1.11

But when it comes to the teaching of the truth they are unwilling to receive it in all simplicity, *but are disturbed if they are educated by one who does not speak Greek well.* And you will find this conceitedness not among those who have attained the summit of Greek philosophy, but among those who have only tasted it, so to speak, with the tips of their tongues, and got a smattering of a few things here and there [ἀλλ' ὀλίγων τινῶν, τὸ δὴ λεγόμενον, ἄκροις χείλεσι γεγευμένοι καὶ σμικρὰ ἄττα ἔνθεν κἀκεῖθεν ἠρανισμένοι].

The polemical setting notwithstanding, these passages are important because they reflect (however obliquely) an audience attracted to rhetorical elegance (with a preference for Plato), who disdain the wisdom of fishermen.[23] Word choice is important here, as the term ἠρανισμένοι alludes to the habit of acquiring knowledge from handbooks and compendia, which—in combination with other comments—points to an audience of average education.[24]

Commenting on their admiration of elegant style, Theodoret apostrophizes his audience thus: "My friends, you long to hear well-embellished speeches and seek to be enchanted by them. And if, by chance, you do not get them, then

---

[23] The motif was very widespread across Greek and Latin authors. For an excellent survey, see Hagendahl 1959:184–193; Cameron 1991:185 touches briefly upon it. Christians tried to make a positive virtue of the fact that the Bible was not written in lofty Greek by praising the simplicity of the message.

[24] On the culture of excerpting and sharing texts, see Konstan 2011:9–22 and Johnson 2010:153–156. For an interesting case study of fifth-century encyclopedism, see Piccione 2002:169–197.

you jeer and mock, and stuff up your ears, and refuse to listen to what is said."[25] At issue is the eager—but wrongly expended—admiration of Greek language and rhetoric that is bound up in their cultural identity.[26] At times Theodoret approaches overstatement in his effort to temper the excessive admiration of his readers for Greek culture. For example, he writes:

Ῥωμαῖοι δὲ καὶ ποιητὰς ἔσχον καὶ ξυγγραφέας καὶ ῥήτορας· καί φασιν οἱ ταύτην γε κἀκείνην ἠσκημένοι τὴν γλῶτταν καὶ πυκνότερα τῶν Ἑλληνικῶν τὰ τούτων ἐνθυμήματα εἶναι καὶ ξυντομωτέρας τὰς γνώμας. Καὶ ταῦτα λέγω οὐ τὴν Ἑλλάδα σμικρύνων φωνήν, ἧς ἀμηγέπη μετέλαχον, οὐδὲ ἐναντία γε αὐτῇ ἐκτίνων τροφεῖα, ἀλλὰ τῶν ἐπὶ ταύτῃ μεγαλαυχουμένων ξυστέλλων τὴν γνάθον καὶ τὴν ὀφρὺν καταστέλλων καὶ διδάσκων μὴ κωμῳδεῖν γλῶτταν τῇ ἀληθείᾳ λαμπρυνομένην μηδέ γε βρενθύεσθαι ἐπὶ λόγοις κομμωτικῇ τέχνῃ πεποικιλμένοις, τῆς δὲ ἀληθείας γεγυμνωμένοις, ἀλλὰ θαυμάζειν τοὺς τῆς ἀληθείας ὑποφήτας, κομμοῦν μὲν δαιδάλλειν εὐεπείᾳ τοὺς λόγους οὐ διδαχθέντας, γυμνὸν δὲ δεικνύντας τῆς ἀληθείας τὸ κάλλος καὶ τῶν ἀλλοτρίων καὶ ἐπεισάκτων ἀνθέων ἥκιστα δεηθέντας.

Therapeutikê 5.75

The Romans, for their part, have had their poets, historians, and orators; those who are bilingual even say that the Romans are more profound than the Greeks in thought and more concise in expression. I do not say this to detract from the Greek language, in which I, in a manner of speaking, participate myself, or to be remiss in paying the price of my nurture for the culture I have got, but simply to close the mouths of those who brag about it, and to expose their superciliousness and teach them not to ridicule a tongue that is resplendent with truth or to bear themselves haughtily at discourses adorned with the

---

[25] *Therapeutikê* 9.1–2: "'Ὑμεῖς μέν, ὦ ἄνδρες, κεκαλλιεπημένων ποθεῖτε λόγων ἀκούειν καὶ τούτοις κατακηλεῖσθαι ζητεῖτε· οὗ δ' ἂν τούτους μὴ εὕροιτε, γελᾶτε καὶ κωμῳδεῖτε καὶ τὰς ἀκοὰς βύετε καὶ τῶν λεγομένων ἐπαΐειν οὐ βούλεσθε" ("My friends, you long to hear well-embellished speeches and seek to be enchanted by them. And if, by chance, you do not get them, then you jeer and mock and stop up your ears, and you refuse to listen to what is said"). Isidore of Peluse repeatedly conjures up similar reactions of the literati against the language of the Gospels in his letter to the sophist Asclepius: "λανθάνουσιν Ἑλλήνων παῖδες, δι' ὧν λέγουσιν, ἑαυτοὺς ἀνατρέποντες. Ἐξευτελίζουσι γὰρ τὴν θείαν Γραφήν, ὡς βαρβαρόφωνον, καὶ ὀνοματοποιίαις ξέναις συντεταγμένην, συνδέσμων δὲ ἀναγκαίων ἐλλείπουσαν, καὶ περιττῶν παρενθήκῃ τὸν νοῦν μανθανέτωσαν τῆς ἀληθείας τὴν ἰσχύν. Πῶς γὰρ ἔπεισεν ἡ ἀγροικιζομένη τὴν εὐγλωττίαν; Εἰπάτωσαν οἱ σοφοί, πῶς βαρβαρίζουσα κατακράτος καὶ σολοικίζουσα νενίκηκε τὴν ἀττικίζουσαν πλάνην· πῶς Πλάτων μὲν τῶν ἔξωθεν φιλοσόφων ὁ κορυφαῖος, οὐδενὸς περιεγένετο τυράννου· αὕτη δὲ γῆν τε καὶ θάλατταν ἐπηγάγετο;" (Ep. 29, PG 78:1081).

[26] On Greek language and identity, see Swain 1996:17–42.

art of embellishment but devoid of truth, but rather to marvel at those who expound the truth without any training in embellishing and pret-tifying their discourses with eloquence, but rather revealing the truth in all its naked grandeur without the least recourse to extraneous and imported flourishes.

Another salient feature that arises in the context of Theodoret's engagement with his audience is the pervasive concern for the "countless threads of uninter-rupted communal and personal polytheism, not lacking in nostalgia, but among those, from peasant to philosopher, who were anyway used to doing without the supporting hand of the state, not without conviction either."[27] Paganism, deprived of its civic face and role continued to linger among the educated and uneducated, whether in the city or in the countryside.

The reactions that Theodoret evokes point to an audience devoted too eagerly to eloquence and its corollary, Greek *paideia*.[28] It is worth noting that literary education had always been integral to any definition of Greekness. In other words, to be Greek meant to have a Greek *paideia* (more so than ancestry or birth). Insofar as *paideia* was the preserve of pagans, it was shot through and through with pagan religious elements. As Christianity made headway, Christian authors began a process of absorption and appropriation of Greek *paideia* that involved—among other things—the filtering out of its religious elements.[29] As a result, long before Theodoret, Greek *paideia* and access to it had become deeply

---

[27] Fowden 1998:538–560, esp. 538. A few examples should suffice. In *Therapeutikê* 8.22, referring to the cult of Asclepius, Theodoret says: "With libations and smoke of sacrifice, formerly quite openly, even today perhaps in some remote corner, you honor him and deem his statues worthy of divine worship." And again in *Therapeutikê* 8.33: "You are well aware that they offered libations to the dead, you who dare these things by night in transgression of the laws." On this remark, see Canivet 1987:280. Libanius had alluded to this phenomenon thus: "But if they tell you that others have been converted by these [coercive] acts and are now of the same religious opinion as themselves, do not let it elude you that they are speaking of *seeming converts*, and of factual ones. For they put off nothing of their [belief], but only *say* they have. This is not to say that they honor one set of cults instead of others, but that the [Christian authorities] have been fooled. For they go with the crowds through the other places where they go for the sake of appearances, but when they assume the mien of men praying, they either call upon no one or else the gods, it not being proper to call upon them from such a place, but they do it all the same" (Libanus *Orations* 30.28 [emphasis mine]). Libanius' comment seems to have had the same relevance for Theodoret's time. For further evidence, see Milewski 1995:167–177.

[28] For evidence of how classical authors and literature were intertwined with everyday life, see Uytterhoeven 2009:321–342.

[29] Inglebert 2001:557 calls it a biblical filter: "Pour expliquer les modalités de l' extension du concept de culture religieuse chrétienne du domaine théologique de la foi et de l' érudition biblique à celui d' une explication du monde qui intégrait la plus grande partie des savoirs clas-siques, on a utilisé le modèle du 'filtre biblique', susceptible de quatre variantes, l' acceptation, le rejet, la création, la synthèse." On the early Christian attitudes toward pagan *paideia*, see also Sandnes 2009.

contested issues between pagans and Christians. However, two circumstances lent the issue of Greek *paideia* a renewed urgency: Julian delivered a proclamation that sought to exclude Christians from classical education[30] and, with the increasing bureaucratization[31] of the empire, literary education was becoming a highly sought-after pursuit.[32]

In the changed historical circumstances wherein Christianity has become the religion of the empire, Theodoret (along with Cyril, Isidore of Peluse, and others) is faced as much with the difficult task of winning the hearts and minds of the Greek literati as with edifying and supporting those *Kulturchristen*, "Christians [who] did more than share with zest in the classical tradition that they held in common with pagans of the same class and sensibilities"[33] [or those who had recently converted]. This shared admiration for the classical tradition required an explanation for how the glorious cultural and literary past fit into the Christian present and affected the use of the past, to which we will now turn.

---

[30] Athanassiadi 2002:277–278 speaks of Julian's edict as an indication of "a new conception of intellectual protectionism" motivated by "Iamblichus' systematic sanctification of Greek letters." She continues: "Greek culture as defined by Iamblichus was sacred, . . . As presented by Iamblichus, the ingredients of the new paganism were a set number of texts, a given hermeneutic methodology, and a ritual framework. Its authorized language was Greek, . . . The need for a 'metropolitan' theology expressed only in Greek was firmly launched by Iamblichus and in the following centuries every effort was made to integrate all local gods, cults, and myths in a systematic thought-world which bore the formal name Ἑλληνισμός, in response and open challenge to the term Χριστιανισμός." There is an ongoing debate as to the exact form and import of Julian's measures. For a review of the *status questionis* (with a collection of the references to these measures in patristic texts of the fourth and fifth centuries), see Dal Covolo 1988:73–85 and Banchich 1993:5–14. Banchich stressed, at the time, the need for a detailed study of the reaction of Christian authors (John Chrysostom, Theodoret) to Julian's educational policy. Tedeschi 1996:17–36; Germino 1997; Fiedrowicz 2001:73–87; Saracino 2002:123–141. For the most recent assessment, see Goulet 2009:175–200. In our case it is important to note how Theodoret presented both the Julian's measures and his reasons for implementing them: "Countless other deeds were dared at that time by land and by sea, all over the world, by the wicked against the just, for now without disguise the enemy of God began to lay down laws against true religion. First of all he prohibited the sons of the Galileans, for so he tried to name the worshippers of the Saviour, from taking part in the study of poetry, rhetoric, and philosophy, *for said he, in the words of the proverb 'we are shot with shafts feathered from our own wing,' for from our own books they take arms and wage war against us*" (*Ecclesiastical History* 3.8.1–2 [emphasis mine]). In some sense Theodoret, writing almost a century later, seems to be doing precisely this in the *Therapeutikê* [viz. shooting the pagans with shafts feathered from their own wings].

[31] Cameron 1991:140 writes: "The fourth century with its enlarged bureaucracy saw an increased need for educated men, the vast majority of whom were produced by the standard rhetorical schools; . . . Since everything conspired to make of the fourth century a time when rhetoric did indeed convey power, Christians needed to make it their own." This could be extended to the fifth century and the intense literary activity that continued unabated. See Schlange-Schöningen 1995.

[32] For the importance of Greek *paideia* in late antiquity, see Brown 1992.

[33] Brown 2011:72 citing approvingly Cameron's claim that "Paganism lasted much longer for Christians than pagans" (2011).

The Past

To the extent that *paideia* was interwoven with the great past and had become a revered tradition, Theodoret's readers can be counted as representatives of "an age that preferred to live its imaginative life in the words and the world of a great but vanished past."[34] This requires that Theodoret engage with the Greek past (literary and otherwise) on a number of levels in order to address a number of distinct (but interrelated) concerns.[35]

Christianity, lacking the ancient credentials of either paganism or Judaism, would have appeared keen on having a past.[36] Julian's polemic serves as a painful reminder of the fact.[37] As a true *pepaideumenos* Theodoret appears as "the mediator between past and present."[38] His command of Greek culture qualifies him to make judgments about the value of the past, to help make the transition from past to present (by using the particularly Christian rhetoric of the "new"), and ultimately to show how the past grew into the present.

He does this partly by using the dependency theme[39] and partly by imposing on human history a linearity in which paganism represents a previous stage (characterized—with few but important exceptions—by error) of humanity that is replaced irrevocably by the advent of Christianity.[40] Once the pattern of this logic has been applied, the advent and rise of Christianity flows as a natural, literally predictable (anticipated and foreshadowed in the prophecies), and irreversible outcome. In this respect the *Therapeutikê* addresses the

---

[34] Trapp 1997b:1972.

[35] It should be noted that, although there is no systematic account by Theodoret on this particular issue, his sporadic engagement with its various aspects allows us to form an idea.

[36] For the widespread perception in the Greco-Roman world that antiquity meant superiority, see Pilhofer 1990. For a stress in the competitive aspect of this phenomenon, see Droge 1989.

[37] Such was the impact of Julian's efforts to exclude Christians from Hellenic *paideia* that as late as the twelfth century Byzantine authors in their rhetorical exercises included a defense of their right to read Hellenic books against Julian's measures: Asmus 1906:125–136; Widmann 1935–1936: 22–23, 275–280.

[38] Anderson 1989:80–208, at 142.

[39] Riding 1995:197–230 is devoted to Theodoret. Riding's study is thorough but narrow in its focus. Tracing a single motif and reading everything through the lens of the dependency theme does not bring out the complexity of Theodoret's attitude toward Hellenism, which—in the words of Goldhill 2001:8—is "veined with a complex dynamic of attraction and rupture, affiliation and dismissal."

[40] Trying to explain this religious change from paganism to Christianity to his correspondent Agathodaimon, Isidore of Peluse argues similarly: "ἔξεστί [σοι] συνιδεῖν, ἄριστε, ἐκ τῶν συμβάντων τὰ μείζονα. Ὁ γὰρ Ἑλληνισμὸς πολλοῖς καὶ χρόνοις καὶ πόνοις καὶ πόροις καὶ ὅπλοις καὶ λόγοις κρατυνθείς, ἠφανίσθη. Ἡ δὲ ἡμετέρα θρησκεία ἰδιώταις καὶ ἀγραμμάτοις καὶ πτωχοῖς καὶ εὐτελέσιν ἐγχειρισθεῖσα ἐν βραχεῖ καιρῷ, δίκην ἀστραπῆς διῆλθε πανταχοῦ, οὐ τὰς ὄψεις μόνον, ἀλλὰ καὶ τὰς γνώμας φωτίσασα· ὅτι ὁ μὲν ψευδέσι μύθοις συνέκειτο· ἡ δὲ δόγμασιν οὐρανίοις συνήρμοστο" (Ep. 270, PG 78:341–344).

same contemporary concerns that arise in questions 16,[41] 55,[42] 86,[43] and 136[44] of Ps.-Justin's *Quaestiones et responsiones ad orthodoxos*.

At the same time, Theodoret builds up a new vision that elides the very contemporary realities that were briefly alluded to elsewhere. In *Therapeutikê* 6.87 he writes:

[41] "εἰ τὴν ἀρχαίαν λατρείαν ἀνεῖλεν ὁ θεὸς ὡς αὐτῇ μὴ ἀρεσκόμενος, τὴν δὲ τῶν χριστιανῶν ὡς ἀρεστὴν αὐτῷ ἀντεισήγαγεν, οἱ δὲ ὀρθόδοξοι μόνοι θεῷ ἀρέσκοντες Ἑλλήνων τε καὶ Ἰουδαίων καὶ πάντων αἱρετικῶν κατὰ τὸν ἀριθμὸν ὑπάρχουσιν ἥσσονες, τίς ἡ ἀπόδειξις τοῦ μὴ κατὰ πτωχείαν δυνάμεως τοῦ ταύτην ἀντ' ἐκείνης ἑλομένου λατρείαν τὴν πλάνην μένειν ἀνεκρίζωτον, πῶς δὲ οὐκ ἀνωφελὴς ἡ ἐκείνης κατάλυσις, πλάνης ἑτέρας κατεχούσης τὸν κόσμον;" ("If God abolished the ancient worship, because He did not like it, and introduced that of the Christians because he liked it and (if) only orthodox Christians are liked how are they less in number than the Greeks, Jews and all the heretics? How is the fact that error is not uprooted not proof of the lack of power since He chose this worship over the other? How is the dissolution of this error not useless since a different error prevails in the world?").

[42] "εἰ τῶν μερῶν τῆς κτίσεως οἱ δαίμονες οὐκ ἐξουσιάζουσι, διατί παρακουσθέντων τῶν χρησμῶν τοῖς Ἕλλησι τιμωρίας ἐπήγαγον, καὶ θεραπευθέντων τῶν εἰδώλων ταύτας ἀνέσχον καὶ ἀγαθὰ αὐτοῖς ἀντὶ τούτων παρέσχον; πόθεν οὖν αὐτοῖς δύναμις εἰς τὴν ἑκατέρου ἐνέργειαν;" ("If demons govern parts of the created world, why, when the oracles were not heeded by the Greeks, did they [viz. demons] bring punishments upon them, whereas when the idols were reverenced they put an end to the punishments and they [viz. demons] provided goods instead? Whence did their power come for either act?").

[43] "εἰ διὰ τὸ νενικῆσθαι τὸν ἑλληνισμὸν ὑπὸ τοῦ χριστιανισμοῦ ἐλπίδα οὐκ ἔχει ὁ ἑλληνισμὸς ἀνακλήσεως, πῶς πάλαι ὑπὸ τοῦ ἑλληνισμοῦ νικηθεῖσα ἡ ἀληθὴς θεοσέβεια νυνὶ τὴν ἀνάκλησιν δέδεκται; ὅτι γὰρ πρὸ τῆς πλάνης ἐκράτει ἡ ἀλήθεια, μαρτυροῦσιν αἱ θεῖαι γραφαί, τὸν Ἀδὰμ καὶ πολλοὺς ἐφεξῆς μετ' αὐτὸν δηλοῦσαι οὐκ εἰδώλοις ἀλλὰ τῷ θεῷ λατρεύσαντας, κἄν τινες αὐτῶν ἐν ἀτόποις ἐξητάσθησαν πράξεσιν" ("If Hellenism has no hope of being reinstated because it has been vanquished by Christianity, how is it that vanquished by Hellenism the true piety/religion is now restored? That before error truth reigned is attested in the sacred scriptures, stating that Adam with many others was not worshipping idols but God, even if some of them were involved in absurd deeds").

[44] "εἰ τοὺς εὐσεβεῖς ἀμείβεται ὁ θεὸς τῇ κατὰ τόνδε τὸν βίον λαμπρότητι, ὡς τὸν Ἀβραὰμ καὶ Ἰσαὰκ καὶ Ἰακὼβ καὶ τοὺς ἐξ αὐτῶν, πλούτῳ καὶ εὐπαιδίᾳ καὶ καρπῶν εὐθηνίᾳ, πόθεν καὶ τὰ ὅμοια παρείποντο Ἕλλησιν, ἡνίκα τὰ εἴδωλα πανταχοῦ ἐθεράπευον; πῶς δὲ ὁ ἑλληνισμὸς οὐ δείκνυται ὁσιώτερος; ὅτι ἕως μὲν ἐκείνῃ κατεῖχε τῶν πόλεων, πᾶσαι αἱ πόλεις καὶ οἱ ἀγροὶ εὐπραγίαν καὶ εὐθηνίαν ἐκέκτηντο, καὶ ταῦτα οὐ συχνότερον πολεμούμεναι· ἀφ' οὗ δὲ αὐτὰς τὸ χριστιανικὸν κατέλαβε κήρυγμα, καὶ οἶκοι καὶ οἰκούντων καὶ τῆς λοιπῆς εὐθηνίας κατέστησαν ἔρημοι, καὶ μόλις τὰ λείψανα τῶν πάλαι ὑπὸ τῶν Ἑλλήνων γεγενημένων κτισμάτων κατέχουσαι τοῦ ποτὲ πόλεις γεγενῆσθαι δεικνύουσι, τῆς παλαιᾶς εὐθηνίας καὶ τῆς νέας ἐρημίας ἑκατέρας τὰς θρησκείας αἰτίας ἀμφοτέρων προσφέρουσαι" ("If God rewards the pious with eminence in this life, just as with Abraham and Isaac and Jacob and their people with wealth, children, and abundance of crops, how is Hellenism not proven more holy? When it was prevailing in the cities, all the cities and the countryside were prospering and flourishing (while they did not have to engage in war more often). But after the Christian teaching prevailed they [viz. cities] lost their houses and their tenants and the entire prosperity and only the remains of the buildings built by the Greeks demonstrate that these were cities; the former prosperity and the latter devastation are offering each one of them the reasons for the [practice] of these two religions").

Καὶ μαρτυρεῖ τῷ λόγῳ τὰ πράγματα, γῆ καὶ θάλαττα τῆς προτέρας ἀγνοίας ἀπηλλαγμέναι, πεπαυμένος τῶν εἰδώλων ὁ πλάνος, τῆς ἀγνοίας ὁ ζόφος ἐληλαμένος, τοῦ τῆς γνώσεως φωτὸς αἱ ἀκτῖνες τὴν οἰκουμένην ἐμπλήσασαι, Ἕλληνες καὶ Ῥωμαῖοι καὶ βάρβαροι τὸν ἐσταυρωμένον θεολογοῦντες καὶ τοῦ σταυροῦ τὸ σημεῖον γεραίροντες καὶ ἀντὶ τῶν πολλῶν καὶ ψευδωνύμων θεῶν τῇ Τριάδι λατρεύοντες, τὰ τῶν δαιμόνων τεμένη φροῦδα γεγενημένα, οἱ βωμοὶ τῶν εἰδώλων ἐκ βάθρων ἀνεσπασμένοι, ἐκκλησίαι περιφανεῖς πανταχῆ δεδομημέναι, ἐν πόλεσιν, ἐν κώμαις, ἐν ἀγροῖς, ἐν ἐσχατιαῖς σηκοὶ μαρτύρων εἰς κάλλος ἐξειργασμένοι, ἀσκητῶν καταγωγαὶ τὰς τῶν ὀρέων κορυφὰς ἁγιάζουσαι καὶ τὰς ἀοικήτους ἐρήμους οἰκίζουσαι.

Therapeutikê 6.87

Facts bear out my words. Earth and sea are freed from their ancient ignorance; the error of idols is no longer to be seen; the darkness of ignorance has been dispersed, and the light of knowledge fills with its rays the whole inhabited world. Greeks, Romans, and barbarians recognize the divinity of the crucified and venerate the sign of the cross. The Trinity is worshipped in place of a multitude of false gods. The temples of the demons have been leveled to the ground. The altars of idols have been wrenched from their bases. Splendid churches have grown up on all sides; in towns, cities, in the countryside, and in the remotest areas beautiful monuments to the martyrs have been erected. The abodes of the ascetics sanctify the mountain tops and populate deserts which had previously been uninhabited.

As a result of this attitude, we are faced with a paradox: while Christianity is defended, it is Greek culture (which is allowed to possess good qualities) that is assimilated to the natural, new Christian reality through selective appropriation of certain aspects, becoming thus a cultural component of limited historical significance.[45]

Method

In the *Therapeutikê* Theodoret most often works through a theme in terms of its relevance to the inquiry launched in each *dialexis*. Given the cultural admiration for classical authors, the reason why Theodoret prefaces each step of

---

[45] Albeit, in this highly selective and qualified version with which we are presented in the *Therapeutikê*.

his *elenchus* with appeals to authority becomes more clear. His method weaves in and out,[46] conferring a rich texture to his *dialexeis*. The doxographic units become denser depending on the subject matter (e.g. on matter and cosmos and on the nature man). The implied role of the physician lends Theodoret the authority to arrange, discuss, refute, or endorse the different *doxai*. By selecting and combining Greek authorities he creates an *exetastic* buildup, which is intensified by the accumulation of opinions leading to each climactic declaration.

The transitions from one theme to another can be abrupt, at times even based on unstated conceptual links. Claims from external texts (suggestively juxtaposed) are sometimes set forth in order to win an argument rather than to explore all of their implications.[47] Many scholars have studied the use of Theodoret's quotations from Greek authors and have commented on the sheer number of them.[48] G. Bardy, quoting Schulte, refers to 500[49] authors mentioned in the text (philosophers, poets, historians, etc.), from whom about 350 quotations are used as testimonies.[50]

Theodoret does not always acknowledge his sources.[51] It is a well-established fact that most of his materials are derived from known works by Clement and

---

[46] An image used by Theodoret in *On Providence* to describe the process of writing: "Φέρε τοίνυν, ἐξ αὐτῆς τῆς κατηγορίας τὴν ἀπολογίαν ὑφαίνωμεν" (PG 83:625).

[47] E.g. see Theodoret's use of Porphyry's judgment of theurgy (and by implication Greek religion) as magic in *Dialexis* III. On Angels, Gods, and Demons.

[48] Roos 1883; Raeder 1900; Canivet 1957:161–290; Schulte 1904:42–105; Halton 1963; Bardy 1946:299–325. On the use of Aëtius by Theodoret, see Mansfeld and Runia 1996:272–290 and the judicious review by Frede 1999:135–149. Frede in his detailed discussion of Theodoret's treatment by Runia and Mansfeld entertains the possibility of Theodoret's use of Aëtius.

[49] Bardy 1946:308.

[50] Despite estimates like these, it is hard to precisely quantify Theodoret's readings, as there are places where he reproduces the thoughts of an author without quoting him. This results in a fair amount of unattributed sources.

[51] But see for example *Therapeutikê* 5.16–17: "῍Α δέ γε ξὺν Θεῷ λέξω, ἐκ τῶν Πλουτάρχῳ καὶ Πορφυρίῳ καὶ μέντοι καὶ Ἀετίῳ ξυγγεγραμμένων ἐρῶ" ("All that I am going to say I will borrow, with God's help, from the writings of Plutarch, Porphyry, and Aetius"). Goulet 1997:152 writes convincingly about this phenomenon: "Un cas de Cyr très éclairant est offert par la Thérapeutique des maladies helléniques de Théodoret de Cyr. P. Canivet a montré que cet auteur empruntait la quasi-totalité de ses citations anciennes—environ 360—à Clément d' Alexandrie, à Eusèbe de Césarée ou à une troisième source non identifiée ("X"). Jamais ces emprunts ne sont reconnus. Eusèbe, la source principale, n'est cité qu' une fois, dans un passage où Théodoret ne dit d' ailleurs pas qu' ils ait emprunté quoi que ce soit à son devancier. Devant ce qui à nos yeux de modernes est un plagiat manifeste, on en vient à se demander comment un compilateur comme Théodoret voyait les choses. Si on leur avait dit: vous nous laissez croire que vous citez directement d' innombrables auteurs anciens dont, en vérité, vous copiez le texte dans un ouvrage intermédiaire dont vous taiser le titre, ils auraient peut-être répondu que *primo* ils n' avaient jamais dit que ces auteurs étaient pour eux des sources et que *secundo* la source immédiate intermédiaire ne leur avait servi qu' à repérer des textes qu' ils auraient pu trouver par eux-mêmes chez les auteurs cités. D'une telle pratique, on peut en effet conjecturer que ces références et ces citations n' étaient peut-être pas dans leur esprit des sources qu' ils avaient

Eusebius,[52] which has led scholars to deplore his lack of independence. Yet we have seen how exhaustively Theodoret seeks to document his claims by adducing often-famous philosophical set-pieces that enjoyed wide currency at the time across a number of authors, pagan and Christian alike. This makes the *Therapeutikê* one of the most important pieces of Christian doxography.

Despite Theodoret's reliance on such authors as Clement and Eusebius, it is the presentation of these materials—their embedding in the *dialexeis* and the recontextualization that allows them to serve different argumentative purposes—that shows Theodoret's independence. Closer attention to this presentation will help us form a more nuanced view.

Argumentation

Simulated dialogue with fictive interlocutors adds to the liveliness of the *dialexeis* of the *Therapeutikê*, but it also enables Theodoret to address a number of criticisms.[53] This is consonant with the stated aim of *elenchus*,[54] the examination of an opponent's beliefs and the refutation of accusations. Theodoret's therapeutic approach, discussed in the first chapter of this book, involves injecting *doxai* into the minds (or rather the souls) of his readers.[55] In this respect it is more akin to what has been called enthymematic argumentation[56] (derived from the false etymology ἐν θυμῷ).

---

matériellement et immédiatement recopiées dans leur propre ouvrage, mais des autorités qui authentifiaient par leur témoignage le bien-fondé des propos rapportés."

52 Ulrich 2009:113–130.

53 The rhetorical figure that is employed is known as ὑποφορά and ἀνθυποφορά (*subiectio* in Latin); see Cooper 1971:10–23. Pernot 1993:421–437 discusses related rhetorical figures and their corresponding literary forms. For its use in the context of Cynic diatribe and homily, see Fuentes González 1998:58.

54 Note the term: "διελέγξαι τῶν κατηγορημάτων τὸ μάταιον" (*Therapeutikê*, prologue).

55 A good example is *Therapeutikê* 8.34–35, where Theodoret cites Pindar: "Εἰ δὲ ἀναισθήτως αὐτοὺς ἔχειν τῶν γινομένων νομίζετε καὶ μὴ θείας τινὸς καὶ τρισολβίας ὄντως λήξεως ἀπολαῦσαι, Πίνδαρος ὁ λυρικὸς ταύτην ὑμῶν ἐκβαλέτω τὴν δόξαν, λέγων ὡδί·" ("And if you think that they are insensible to what happened to them and that they do not enjoy some divine and truly thrice-blest lot, let Pindar, the lyric poet, expel this false opinion of yours when he says . . .").

56 Thoroughly analyzed by Walker 2000:184, where he gives the following definition of an enthymeme: "An 'enthymeme' is, on one hand, a complex, quasi-syllogistic structure of inference and affect that constitutes the substance and persuasive force of an argument as perceived by an audience. On the other hand, an 'enthymême' will typically and perhaps most forcefully appear in discourse as an emphatic, structural/stylistic turn that caps an *exetasis*, gives the inferential/affective substance a particular realization with a particular salience within a particular discursive moment, and thereby shapes its audience's perception of (and responses to) just what 'the argument' is" [emphasis in original]. The bibliography for enthymêmes and their role in rhetoric is considerable. However, the contributions most relevant to our discussion are Johnstone 2001:247–250 and Conley 1984:168–187.

Enthymême is a term that denotes a condensed form of syllogism whose premises have been suppressed because they are assumed by the audience to whom the arguments are addressed. The term has a long and complex history, but what is important for our analysis is that *enthymême* in later antiquity had come to mean 'a loosely defined argument' that could include such forms as quotation from philosophers, poets, etc.[57] Another thing to bear in mind is that an *enthymême* always presupposes the audience's knowledge of the premises during the process of inference making. So when Theodoret—in his defense of the cult of the martyrs (*Dialexis* VIII)—juxtaposes a number of quotations primarily from Plato, but also from Empedocles and Pindar, to prove that the souls of the pious go to heaven, he relies on the presupposed premises of the audience to draw the conclusion that just as the souls of the doctors (etc.) go to heaven so do the souls of the Christian martyrs.

Theodoret constructs an argument either by making a claim and then adducing as many *doxai* (understood as *enthymêmes*) from Greek authors as possible or by using testimonia such as *martyriai* and *apodeikseis* as asserted premises. This can give the impression that he aims not only to adduce the most prominent authors but also to compile a large number of quotations.[58] The quotations are placed with an eye to their thematic appropriateness, a process of decontextualizion and recontextualization whereby the logic of each quotation is aligned with Theodoret's claim. In this way, the quotation is made to sustain a different goal than that of its initial context, which creates the momentum for shared inferencing. The prior knowledge of the audience becomes infused with biblical understanding and is then reconfigured in a new direction.[59]

Literary Persona: A Christian *pepaideumenos?*

Of crucial importance for the intended audience of the *Therapeutikê*—and the ultimate success of his enterprise—is the persona that Theodoret adopts in his

---

[57] Theodoret's use of syllogisms has been pointed out recently by Barnes 2002:399–417. For an early use of enthymemes by Christian authors, see Schoedel 1959:22–32.

[58] Lemerle 1971:46, who rightly views the *Therapeutikê* as a part of larger project on the part of Christian authors to address the issue of Greek *paideia* and its relationship with Christianity, refers to the *Therapeutikê* in these words: "elle [*sc.* the *Therapeutikê*] se présente comme une bizarre mosaïque."

[59] Thus, instead of a "bizarre mosaïque" in Lemerle's words (to the extent that the *Therapeutikê* is to be seen as such), it is a mosaic in which each text is painstakingly selected and positioned—like a tessera in a mosaic—in order to make the most out of its place in the larger pattern.

dialexeis. The role of the physician, even when implied, is used throughout in order to make the speaker more ethically viable.[60]

At the same time, Theodoret is compelled to demonstrate his command of Greek rhetoric and knowledge of Greek culture. He accomplishes this through his style, including skillful use of imagery, and his displays of immense erudition.[61] Theodoret's aim is to appear at home with Greek culture—a true *pepaideumenos*[62]—and therefore to arrive at a position from which he is entitled to pronounce with authority on the inquiries and assessments that he sets out to undertake.[63] His adoption of an "insider's" point of view[64] is particularly important for refuting pagan criticisms, which he does using Greek *paideia* (which "[makes] him immediately part of tradition") in the form of arguments drawn from Greek philosophy and the Bible alike. It is in this vein that he refers in the same context to his education and love of Greek (*Therapeutikê* 5.75).[65]

---

[60] E.g. *Therapeutikê* 1.9: "Πρῶτον δέ γε τῶν ἄλλων τὸ τῆς οἰήσεως ἰατρεύσωμεν πάθος" ("But, before anything else, let us pay careful attention to the malady of self-conceit"). Also *Therapeutikê*, prologue 17.1-3: "Ἐγὼ μὲν οὖν τῆς τε τῶν νοσούντων ἕνεκα θεραπείας καὶ τῆς τῶν ὑγιαινόντων προμηθούμενος ὠφελείας τοῦτον ἀνεδεξάμην τὸν πόνον" ("I, for my part, have undertaken this labor for the sake of curing the ill and doing a service to the healthy").

[61] See also Mansfeld and Runia 1996: "His work is not only an apologetic exercise. It also aims to demonstrate a command of style, i.e. beating the Greeks at their own game" (289).

[62] For a detailed study of the concept, see Anderson 1989:80–208.

[63] On some occasions Theodoret's display of "cultural fluency" becomes an open challenge, such as when he confronts the superficial knowledge of the Hellenizers, taunts them, and ridicules their tendency to adorn speeches with phrases taken from Greek religion: "παίδευσιν δὲ ἄκραν καὶ λαμπρότητα λόγων ὑπολαμβάνοντες, εἰ ὀμνύντες εἴποιεν "Μὰ τοὺς θεούς" καὶ "Μὰ τὸν ἥλιον," καὶ τοιούτους τινὰς τοῖς λόγοις ἐπιπλάττοιεν ὅρκους. Εἰ δὲ οὐκ ἀληθῆ λέγω, εἴπατε, ὦ ἄνδρες, τίνα Ξενοφάνης ὁ Κολοφώνιος ἔσχε διάδοχον τῆς αἰρέσεως; τίνα δὲ Παρμενίδης ὁ Ἐλεάτης; τίνα Πρωταγόρας καὶ Μέλισσος; τίνα Πυθαγόρας ἢ Ἀναξαγόρας; τίνα Σπεύσιππος ἢ Ξενοκράτης; τίνα Ἀρκεσίλαος ἢ Φιλόλαος; τίνες τῆς Στωϊκῆς αἱρέσεως προστατεύουσιν; τίνες τοῦ Σταγειρίτου τὴν διδασκαλίαν κρατύνουσιν; τίνες κατὰ τοὺς Πλάτωνος πολιτεύονται νόμους; τίνες τὴν ὑπ᾽ ἐκείνου ξυγγραφεῖσαν πολιτείαν ἠσπάσαντο; Ἀλλὰ τούτων μὲν τῶν δογμάτων οὐδένα διδάσκαλον ἡμῖν ἐπιδεῖξαι δυνήσεσθε, ἡμεῖς δὲ τῶν ἀποστολικῶν καὶ προφητικῶν δογμάτων τὸ κράτος ἐναργῶς ἐπιδείκνυμεν· πᾶσα γὰρ ἡ ὑφήλιος τῶνδε τῶν λόγων ἀνάπλεως" ("... and they think it is the height of culture and linguistic distinction if they say when swearing, 'Yes, by God' and 'No, by the sun,' plastering their conversation with such swearwords. If what I say is untrue, then tell me, my friends, who succeeded Xenophanes of Colophon as head of his school? Who succeeded Parmenides of Elea? Who Protagoras and Melissus? Who succeeded Pythagoras or Anaxagoras? Who Speussipus or Xenocrates? Who succeeded Anaximander or Anaximenes? Who Arcesilas or Philolaus? Who were the heads of the Stoic school? Who follow the teachings of the Stagirite? Who are those whose way of life is in accordance with the *Laws* of Plato? Who are those who have adopted the way of life described in the *Republic*? Now you will be unable to show us one devotee of these teachings whereas we, for our part, can clearly demonstrate the cogency of the teachings of the apostles and prophets. Every country under the sun is filled with their words," *Therapeutikê* 5.64–66).

[64] This refers to the literary and cultural level as opposed to the religious one, to be sure.

[65] Adjusting his arguments each time to the circumstances and the people that he addresses, he does not hesitate to express his admiration for Homer or recommend a student to a Sophist. See Ep. 28; Bartelink 1981:6–28.

If Theodoret comes across as educated or didactically inclined, he is none-theless capable of harsh and abrasive tones.[66] However, this is never allowed to dominate his work, but is tempered with the rich intermixing of exhortation,[67] qualified praise,[68] and irony.[69]

Alongside the apologetic project, Theodoret's engagement with Hellenism is an important indication of the state of Greek education in fifth-century Antioch. Being born to Christian parents and raised among Syrian ascetics, Theodoret's *paideia* is a testimony to the educational possibilities available to a Christian of the fifth century, just as it is indicative of the ability of Christian elites to absorb classical culture.[70]

---

[66] I.e. when attacking Porphyry. However, compared with such harsh tones as that of Chrysostom, who refers to Plato and his teachings thus: "καὶ Πλάτωνος οὐδὲν ἔστι θαυμάσαι, ἢ τοῦτο μόνον. Καὶ καθάπερ τῶν τάφων τοὺς ἔξωθεν κεκονιαμένους, ἂν ἀπαμφιάσης, ἰχῶρος, καὶ δυσωδίας, καὶ διεφθορότων ὄψει γέμοντας ἰστῶν· οὕτω καὶ τὰ τοῦ φιλοσόφου δόγματα, ἂν τῆς κατὰ τὴν λέξιν ἀπογυμνώσης ὥρας, πολλῆς ὄψει τῆς βδελυγμίας πεπληρωμένα, καὶ μάλιστα ὅταν περὶ ψυχῆς φιλοσοφῇ, ἀμέτρως τιμῶν τε αὐτὴν καὶ βλασφημῶν" ("And as, if you uncover those sepulchers which are whitened without you will find them full of corruption, and stench, and rotten bones; so too the doctrines of the philosopher, if you strip them of their flowery diction, you will see to be full of much abomination, especially when he philosophizes on the soul, which he both honors and speaks ill of without measure," *On John*, PG 59:33), Theodoret's literary urbanity and decorum stand out.

[67] *Therapeutikê* 11.83ff.: "Ταῦτα καὶ ἡμεῖς ὑμῖν, ὦ φίλοι ἄνδρες, παραινοῦντές φαμεν. Οὐ γὰρ δὴ ἄκοντας τὰς θείας λαβεῖν ἀναγκάζομεν δωρεάς, ἀλλὰ παρακαλοῦντες καὶ λιπαροῦντες καὶ τὸ μέγεθος τούτων ἐπιδεικνύντες. Διά τοι τοῦτο καὶ τὴν δεσποτικὴν ταύτην καὶ θαυμασίαν ἐπιλέγομεν ῥῆσιν· 'Ὁ ἔχων ὦτα ἀκούειν ἀκουέτω'" ("My good friends, I will use the same words in my exhortation to you. For of course we do not force you against your will to accept the divine gifts, but we exhort and beseech you, and show you the greatness of what He has promised. And so we conclude with this remarkable saying of the Lord: 'Let the one who has ears to hear heed this'").

[68] In the case of Plato and Socrates, see Fabricius 1988:179–187.

[69] I.e. when criticizing the cult of Heracles, he says: "τετραετηρικοῖς ἀγῶσιν ἐτίμησαν, καὶ ταῦτά γε ἄνδρα εἰδότες, καὶ ἄνδρα οὐ σώφρονα οὐδὲ φιλοσοφίαν ἠγαπηκότα, ἀλλ' ἀκολασίᾳ καὶ λαγνείᾳ ξυνεζηκότα. Ἵνα γὰρ τὴν ἄλλην αὐτοῦ πᾶσαν ἀκρασίαν παρῶ, φασὶν αὐτὸν ἐν μιᾷ νυκτὶ πεντήκοντα μιγῆναι παρθένοις, τὸν τρίτον καὶ δέκατον ἴσως ἀγωνισάμενον ἄθλον" ("And not satisfied with offering annual celebrations, they have special games every four years in his honor. They are aware that he was a mere man, one who had esteemed neither temperance nor philosophy, but who had spent his life in debauchery and dissolute conduct. And, to pass over his other heinous actions, they say that in one night he slept with fifty virgins. That perhaps was labor number thirteen!" *Therapeutikê* 8.15–16).

[70] Inglebert 2001:555 stresses the importance of the integration of the classical *paideia* into the *doctrina christiana* because "elle aida les élites païennes à se rallier à la nouvelle religion sans avoir l' impression de trahir la tradition culturelle classique, un des fondements de leur identité sociale, puisqu' elles la retrouvaient avec une nouvelle signification." On the powerful influence of classical *paideia* on Christian members of the elite, see Brown 1992 and Salzman 2002.

Manual, *Aide-mémoire*?

But is there a different possibility envisaged for the *Therapeutikê* by its author? We have seen the thoroughness with which Theodoret compiled the *Therapeutikê*, the sheer number of quotations making it difficult for even the most well versed readers to absorb all of his arguments. Furthermore, the thematic orientation and cross-referencing indicate that Theodoret wanted to make the *Therapeutikê* easy to consult. Perhaps most tellingly, the preface condenses a number of distinct but complementary aims, outlines the entire work, and guides the reader. This reveals a striking consciousness of both the literary aim of the work and its compilatory nature.[71]

In the preface Theodoret writes, "I, for my part, have provided them with all the counter-arguments necessary to dissipate their charges," and a little further, "I have divided my work into twelve chapters (*dialexeis*) and have given a flowing quality to my style because this method seems most suited to my didactic purposes . . ." There is an insistence on the didactic aspect when Theodoret says of the third *dialexis*, "The third teaches . . ."[72]

Having thus indexed the *Therapeutikê*, carefully going through the thematic contents and the aims of each *dialexis*, Theodoret states the title of the work. He then indicates the rationale for the title along with the reason for compiling the work, from which, by means of a *captatio benevolentiae*, the following comment follows: "As for those who happen upon the labors of others, I pray that if they find everything that is written acceptable they should glorify the Author of these things and requite with prayers the human authors [sc. Theodoret]. But if there are any shortcomings let them not condemn everything forthright but rather profit from whatever is well composed."

A precious glimpse into the logic of Theodoret's citing habits is afforded in the following passage:

Ἐγὼ δὲ πάσας ξυναγαγεῖν τὰς προρρήσεις πάρεργον ὑπείληφα· πολλῶν γὰρ ἂν ἐδεήθην βιβλίων, καὶ πάσας γράφων καὶ περὶ ἑκάστης δέ γε τὰ πρόσφορα λέγων. Ἀρκεῖ δὲ ὑμῖν, ἂν ἐθέλητε, καὶ τῶν ἄλλων, ἐξ ὧν ἀκηκόατε, τὴν ἀλήθειαν διαγνῶναι.

Therapeutikê 10.101

---

71 That Theodoret's method is consistent with that of compilator is easily recognizable when compared to the methods described in later periods by Minnis 1979:385–421. Additional support can be gained by Theodoret's literary output, a large part of which consists of compilations that serve as thematically organized compendia with a didactic orientation (i.e. *Eranistês*, *Compendium of Heretical Falsehoods*, etc). The idea of the *Therapeutikê* as manual is also reticently suggested by Festa 1928:584–588.

72 *Therapeutikê*, prologue 6.1. This is to recur in a number of places in the *Therapeutikê*. See also *Therapeutikê*, prologue 13.1: "the tenth discourse, on the one hand, teaches what . . ."

But I thought that it would be superfluous to assemble all their predictions because I would need many books to write them all and to say what is appropriate about each. It will be enough for you, if you please, to deduce the truth of the others from the ones which we have examined.

At other times, however, he refers the reader to other doxographies for more extensive documentation that corroborates his point:

Εἰ δέ τις οἴεται κἀμὲ συκοφαντῆσαι τοὺς ἄνδρας, τὴν παμπόλλην αὐτῶν διαφωνίαν ἐλέγξαντα, ἀναγνώτω μὲν Ἀετίου τὴν Περὶ ἀρεσκόντων ξυναγωγήν, ἀναγνώτω δὲ Πλουτάρχου τὴν Περὶ τῶν τοῖς φιλοσόφοις δοξάντων ἐπιτομήν· καὶ Πορφυρίου δὲ ἡ Φιλόσοφος ἱστορία πολλὰ τοιαῦτα διδάσκει.

Therapeutikê 4.31–32

And if one supposes that I calumniate these fine gentlemen when I denounce the extreme contradictions in their teachings, let him read the collection of the *Placita* of Aëtius, or the work of Plutarch, *On the Opinions of the Philosophers*. *The History of Philosophy* by Porphyry also provides many similar examples.

The anthologizing thrust is confirmed by the statement with which Theodoret ends his first *dialexis*, which becomes a reflection on the entire enterprise:

Καὶ μὲν δὴ καὶ ταῖς μελίτταις οὗτος ὁ νόμος ἐμπέφυκεν· οὐ γλυκέσι γὰρ μόνοις, ἀλλὰ καὶ πικροῖς ἄνθεσιν ἐφιζάνουσαι, τὴν μὲν γλυκεῖαν ἀνιμῶνται ποιότητα, τὴν δὲ πικρὰν ἀποστρέφονται καὶ ἐκ διαφόρων ποιοτήτων, πικρῶν τε καὶ στρυφνῶν καὶ αὐστηρῶν καὶ δριμέων, τὸ γλυκύτατον μέλι τοῖς ἀνθρώποις κατασκευάζουσιν· ταύτας δὴ καὶ ἡμεῖς μιμούμενοι, ἐκ τῶν πικρῶν ὑμῶν λειμώνων τὸ γλυκὺ τῆς ὠφελείας ὑμῖν κατασκευάζομεν μέλι. Καὶ ὥσπερ οἱ τὰ σώματα θεραπεύοντες ἐκ τῶν ἰοβόλων θηρίων ὀνησιφόρα κατασκευάζουσι φάρμακα, καὶ τῶν ἐχιδνῶν τὰ μὲν ἀποβάλλοντες, τὰ δὲ ἕψοντες, πολλὰς διὰ τούτων ἐξελαύνουσι νόσους, οὕτως καὶ ἡμεῖς, τὰ τῶν ὑμετέρων ποιητῶν καὶ ξυγγραφέων καὶ φιλοσόφων πονήματα μεταχειρισάμενοι, τὰ μὲν ὡς δηλητήρια καταλείπομεν, τὰ δὲ τῇ τῆς διδασκαλίας ἐπιστήμῃ διασκευάσαντες, ἀλεξιφάρμακον ὑμῖν θεραπείαν προσφέρομεν· καὶ οὓς ἀντιπάλους ἡμῶν ὑπειλήφατε, τούτους τῶν ἡμετέρων λόγων ἀποφαίνομεν ξυνηγόρους καὶ τῆς πίστεως δείκνυμεν διδασκάλους.

Therapeutikê 1.126–127

Clearly, that too is a law of nature for the bees. For they light on bitter flowers as well as on sweet ones. Then they extract the sweet substance and leave behind what is bitter and from different qualities—bitter and sour, piquant and harsh—and they prepare for humanity the sweetest honey. And we, imitating the bees, prepare from your bitter meadows the honey whose sweetness will benefit you. And just as physicians prepare effective remedies from poisonous beasts, even from vipers; they first throw away some parts and boil the rest, and with this they expel many maladies, we also, who have taken in hand the works of your poets, your historians, your philosophers, we first lay on one side what is injurious and manipulate the rest for the knowledge of teaching. We apply to you this remedy that acts as an antidote. And even those whom you regard as our enemies we show you that they champion our teachings and we make you see that even they teach you the faith.[73]

In a similar vein he concludes the *Therapeutikê*:

Ταύτης καὶ ὑμᾶς τῆς ἀκτῖνος μεταλαχεῖν ἀξιῶ. Τοῦδε γὰρ χάριν καὶ τὸν πόνον ἀνεδεξάμην, καὶ οἷόν τινας βοτάνας πανταχόθεν ξυλλέξας, τὸ ἀλεξίκακον ὑμῖν κατεσκεύασα φάρμακον.

Therapeutikê 12.98

It is my hope that you get a share of those rays. It was for this reason that I undertook this labor, and that I have prepared this cure for you from herbs which I have collected from far and wide.

On a broader level, the *Therapeutikê* should be viewed in the wider context of Theodoret's time, which was characterized by a tendency to classify, abridge, condense, and summarize different types of knowledge. This is reflected in the proliferation of handbooks and anthologies (e.g. Stobaeus)[74] that sought to make knowledge more accessible.[75] In fact, the ninth-century patriarch Photius, when discussing Stobaeus' anthology, neatly outlines the ways in which a reader can profit from such manuals:

---

[73] For the favorite Christian image of the bee and its classical antecedents, see Ronnenberg 2008:138–164.

[74] Reydams-Schils 2011.

[75] On the process of condensing knowledge, see Horster and Reitz 2010.

Χρήσιμον δὲ τὸ βιβλίον τοῖς μὲν ἀνεγνωκόσιν αὐτὰ τὰ συντάγματα τῶν ἀνδρῶν πρὸς ἀνάμνησιν, τοῖς δ' οὐκ εἰληφόσι πεῖραν ἐκείνων, ὅτι διὰ συνεχοῦς αὐτῶν μελέτης οὐκ ἐν πολλῷ χρόνῳ πολλῶν καὶ καλῶν καὶ ποικίλων νοημάτων, εἰ καὶ κεφαλαιώδη, μνήμην καρπώσονται. Κοινὸν δ' ἀμφοτέροις ἡ τῶν ζητουμένων, ὡς εἰκός, ἀταλαίπωρος καὶ σύντομος εὕρεσις, ἐπειδάν τις ἀπὸ τῶν κεφαλαίων εἰς αὐτὰ τὰ πλάτη ἀναδραμεῖν ἐθελήσειε. Καὶ πρὸς ἄλλα δὲ τοῖς ῥητορεύειν καὶ γράφειν σπουδάζουσιν οὐκ ἄχρηστον τὸ βιβλίον.

Photius Bibliotheca 2.159, ed. Henry

This book is useful to those who have read the actual compositions of the writers for recalling them to mind. It will be useful to those who have no acquaintance with the complete works because, by dint of continuous study of the selections, they will quickly acquire a summary [κεφαλαιώδη] acquaintance with many beautiful and varied concepts. Common to both will be the advantage of being able quickly to find what they seek, should they wish to proceed to the relevant section of the entire work. Moreover, the book is not without utility for those who endeavor to speak and write correctly.[76]

As Inglebert has recently shown, such projects held a special interest for Christians, who were faced with the difficult task of coming to terms with an overwhelming body of Greek learning.[77]

If the *Therapeutikê* was indeed intended as a manual, as the sheer bulk of its raw materials would seem to suggest, it is not one that presents the reader with merely the disparate components needed for an apology. Instead, Theodoret has also provided an authoritative assessment that guides the reader, judiciously summarizing all of the available information necessary for arriving at the absolute truth.

Conclusion

In this chapter I have attempted to show how literary considerations are closely allied with Theodoret's apologetics. The emphasis on instruction, the choice of literary form, the compilatory nature of the *Therapeutikê*, all situate the text at the heart of fifth-century literary activity, amidst all of the challenges the period posed for a Christian *pepaideumenos*. At the same time, this emphasis is

---

[76] Trans. Wortley 1997:175.
[77] Inglebert 2001:555–558.

a testimony to the persistence of Greek culture crystallized in language, which becomes a means for the display of cultural fluency *par excellence*. As a result, language and style become intimately connected with cultural identity. It is for this reason that Theodoret makes a point of using elegant style: it establishes his literary authority and allows him to consciously manipulate the cultural identity that inheres in language.

Conclusion

THIS BOOK HAS SOUGHT TO STUDY several aspects of Theodoret's apologetics. By showing the number of methods that Theodoret employs to engage the larger problems of his period, his dynamism and the urgency of his project have become apparent. Rather than a "stale exercise,"[1] a new assessment of Theodoret's apologetic program has emerged. This needs to be said in view of the fact that his is, in hindsight, the last apology, which has both led to its neglect and contributed to its perception as a "scholastic" exercise with no real recipients, especially given that the empire had already become Christian at the time of writing.

Insofar as Theodoret's apologetics are based on his vision of Christianity and its role in the Roman Empire, works such as the *Therapeutikê of the Greek Maladies*, the *Religious History*, and the *Ecclesiastical History* lay out an important religious, literary, and, by implication, cultural program. In exalting the role of Christianity, Theodoret frames its growth and expansion in opposition to polytheist criticisms and accusations, addressing as well its internal divisions and theological controversies. More than an eclectic compilation of ideas, however, Theodoret's arguments should be seen as part of an ongoing debate with paganism.

Theodoret's sustained engagement with apologetics confirms what recent scholarship has acknowledged about the status of Christianization in the early fifth century.[2] Far from its being a simply rural phenomenon, there remained a

---

[1] Runia 1997:106, referring to Theodoret's use of the dependency theme, writes: "It is only when we reach Theodoret that the whole theme becomes a rather stale exercise—even the brief reign of Julian was two generations ago—and the aggressive tone begins to grate."

[2] See, for instance, Trombley 1993–1994, Whitby 1991:111–131, Hoffmann 1987:57–83, Flusin 2010:293–306, and Caseau 2011:541–571, which show the persistence of paganism well beyond the fifth century. See also Brown 1998:632–664, who writes: "In the period from the death of Constantine in 337 to the accession of Valentinian III at Ravenna in 425, a considerable section of the population of the Roman empire, at all social levels, remained largely unaffected by the claims of the Christian church. They were impenitently polytheistic, in that the religious common sense of their age, as of all previous centuries, led them to assume a spiritual landscape rustling with invisible presences—with countless divine beings and their ethereal ministers. Exclusive loyalty to the One God of the Christians, the dismissal of all ancient gods as maleficent (if not ineffectual) demons, and a redrawing of the map of Roman society in such a way as to see

large number of Christians with wavering religious loyalties[3], just as there were pagan literati who had yet to be convinced.

The case of Theodoret's apologetic program allows us to gauge the challenges to Christianity that crystallized mostly—but not exclusively—in what appear to be objections and criticisms echoing the more well-known polemics of Porphyry and Julian, as well as some going all the way back to Celsus. It is a testimony to the *Nachleben* of these polemics that by Theodoret's time they had been sufficiently intermingled and had gained momentum, a fact that is also supported by the concern— across a number of fifth-century texts—with refuting them (Cyril of Alexandria comes to mind as one of the most prominent examples).

In this respect, Theodoret's declaration that paganism had become extinct goes a long way towards effecting a much needed closure, despite the more complex reality and the considerable ambiguity remaining for many crucial aspects of the Christianized world. Furthermore, Theodoret attempts to normalize a set of practices (i.e. the cult of the martyrs) and to (re)structure beliefs by shaping their inferential and interpretive possibilities for his readers.

It would be too narrow an approach, though, to regard the *Therapeutikê* solely as an attempt to refute accusations against Christianity. Theodoret's overriding dual concern, manifested across a number of his writings, is not only defending Christianity but also strengthening the beliefs of those already converted. In its ambition to encompass the totality of human knowledge, his writing (especially the *Therapeutikê*) reveals a didactic aim.

This connects Theodoret's texts with the larger issue of Christian education and Greek *paideia* in the Theodosian age. Partly as a reaction to Julian's polemic against the use of Greek literature by Christians and partly as an aspect of a larger literary phenomenon, Theodoret expropriates and reinterprets Greek knowledge so that it accords with Christianity. On account of the bulk of learning displayed in the *Therapeutikê*, as well as the accessibility that is enabled by its organizational structure, it forms part of a larger trend—among pagans and Christians in late antiquity—to reorganize knowledge, and, for Christians, to reinterpret it along Christian lines where possible.[4] For, as Chin insists,

---

the world in terms of a single, all-embracing dichotomy between Christians and non-Christians; these views were already asserted, at this time, by some Christians; they would enjoy a long future in Byzantium and the medieval west; but in the year 425, they were not yet the views of the 'cognitive majority' of the Roman world" (632).

[3] Soler 2010:281–291.

[4] Inglebert 2001: "La méthode du filtre a donc comme principale finalité de montrer comment les chrétiens procédèrent pour convertir la culture antique. Ils intégrèrent la culture classique dans une nouvelle intertextualité, celle de la Bible et des autorités chrétiennes, ce qui créait de nouvelles significations et donc une autre culture, plus par une modification de la perspective

"[C]hristianization is not the same as an accumulation of individual conversions, nor is it the same as the demise of paganism; it is the addition of a new narrative of identity to the field of narratives being produced in late antiquity."[5] To overlook this is to miss, not only an important aspect of Theodoret's apologetics, but also the literary genius he displays in a number of rigorously organized compendia.

If Theodoret stands at the end of an apologetic tradition, it is also true that he looks ahead to the beginning of a new era. The changed historical circumstances wherein Christianity had become an official state religion may inform Theodoret's awareness, but they do not lead him to overlook Christianity's continued (and spreading) persecution in Persia, which in turn leads him to assert that Christianity is not co-extensive with the Roman Empire. To be sure, this assertion is made in response to post-Constantinian criticisms that Christianity was established and thrived due to imperial support; however, it seems to reflect Theodoret's convictions more generally.

But there is one last factor to consider. Theodoret's literary persona and performance illustrate both the resources of the rhetorical and philosophical tradition available to fifth-century Christianity and the versatility with which philosophical and rhetorical schooling—so skillfully displayed by Theodoret— could be applied to a debate with the Greeks. In a sense, Theodoret performs an identity that he already possessed, that of a Christian *pepaideumenos*. Above all, Theodoret's *Therapeutikê* is an important testimony to how deftly classical Greek literature and culture became entwined in Christianity by a variety of creative re-readings and reinterpretations in late antiquity and the early Middle Ages.

In the end, then, Theodoret's apologetic project is as much or more about these broader themes of Christianity and Hellenism—of identity and the classical past, of a pagan past and a Christian future, of Greek and Christian *paideia*— as it is about the defense of Christianity or its normalization among intellectuals and educated Christians.

---

que par l' apport de nouveaux savoirs; ces derniers furent le plus souvent complémentaires que concurrents des savoirs classiques. Il y eut donc plus transformation que remplacement" (557).
5   Chin 2008:171.

Bibliography

Primary Sources

Ambjörn, L., trans. 2008. *Zacharias of Mytilene. The Life of Severus.* Piscataway, NJ.

Burguière, P., and P. Évieux, eds. 1985. *Cyril of Alexandria. Contra Iulianum.* Sources chrétiennes 322. Paris.

Canivet, P., ed. 2000–2001. *Theodoret of Cyrrhus. Thérapeutique des maladies helléniques.* 2 vols. Revised ed. Sources chrétiennes 57. Paris.

Canivet, P., and A. Leroy-Molinghen, eds. and trans. 1977–1979. *Theodoret of Cyrrhus. Histoire des moines de Syrie: Histoire Philothée.* 2 vols. Sources chrétiennes 234, 257. Paris.

Datema, C., ed. 1970. *Asterius of Amasea. Homilies I–XIV.* Leiden.

De Lagarde, P., ed. 1979. *Ioannes Mauropous. Iohannis Euchaitorum Metropolitae quae in Codice Vaticano Graeco 676 supersunt.* 2nd ed. Amsterdam.

Des Places, É., ed. 1989. *Iamblichus. Protreptique.* Paris.

———. 1989. *Iamblichus. Les Mystères d'Égypte.* 2nd ed. Paris.

Dillon, J., and J. Hershbell, trans. 1991. *Iamblichus. On the Pythagorean Way of Life.* Texts and Translations 29. Graeco-Roman Religion Series 11. Atlanta.

Ettlinger, G. H., ed. 1975. *Theodoret of Cyrrhus. Eranistes.* Oxford.

Evieux , P., ed. 1997. *Isidore of Peluse. Correspondance.* 2 vols. Sources chrétiennes 422, 454. Paris.

Glykas, M. 1836. *Annales.* Ed. I. Bekker. Bonn.

———. 1906, 1912. *Eis ta apora tes Theias Graphes/Kephalaia.* Ed. S. Eustratiades. 2 vols. Athens, Alexandria.

Goulet, R., ed. 2003. *Macarios Magnes. Le Monogénès.* 2 vols. Paris.

Halton, T., trans. 1988. *Theodoret of Cyrrhus. On Divine Providence.* New York.

Koehler, F. G., ed. 1974. *Hierocles of Alexandria. Hieroclis in aureum Pythagoreorum carmen commentarius.* Stutgart.

Kugener, M.-A., ed. and trans. 1907. Zacharias of Mytilene. *Vita Severi.* Patrologia Orientalis 2. Paris. Revised ed. 1971:207–264. Turnhout.

Leone, P. A. M., ed. 1968. *Ioannes Tzetzes. Historiae.* Naples.

Masaracchia, E., ed. and trans. 1990. *Julian. Contra Galilaeos.* Rome.

Migne, J. P., ed. 1857–1866. *Anastasius of Sinai. Quaestiones et responsiones.* Patrologiae Cursus Completus, Series Graeca 89. Paris.

———. 1857–1866. *John Chrysostom. Ad illuminandos catecheses.* Patrologiae Cursus Completus, Series Graeca 49. Paris.

———. 1857–1866. *John Chrysostom. Adversus oppugnatores vitae monasticae.* Patrologiae Cursus Completus, Series Graeca 47. Paris.

———. 1857–1866. *John Chrysostom. Homiliae in epistulam ad Romanos.* Patrologiae Cursus Completus, Series Graeca 60. Paris.

———. 1857–1866. *John Chrysostom. Homiliae in Joannem.* Patrologiae Cursus Completus, Series Graeca 59. Paris.

———. 1857–1866. *John Chrysostom. Homiliae in Martyres.* Patrologiae Cursus Completus, Series Graeca 50:664–665. Paris.

———. 1857–1866. *John Chrysostom. Homiliae in Matthaeum.* Patrologiae Cursus Completus, Series Graeca 57. Paris.

———. 1857–1866. *Nilus of Ancyra. Letters.* Patrologiae Cursus Completus, Series Graeca 79:9–582. Paris.

———. 1857–1866. *Theodoret of Cyrrhus. Interpretatio in xiv epistulas sancti Pauli.* Patrologiae Cursus Completus, Series Graeca 82. Paris.

———. 1857–1866. *Theodoret of Cyrrhus. Haereticarum Fabularum Compendium.* Patrologiae Cursus Completus, Series Graeca 83. Paris.

Muscolino, G., ed. 2009. *Porphyry. Contro i cristiani.* Rome.

Nock, A. D., ed. 1926. *Sallustius. Concerning the Gods and the Universe.* Cambridge.

O'Brien Wicker, K., ed. 1987. *Porphyry, the Philosopher, to Marcella.* Atlanta.

Papadopoulos-Kerameus, A., ed. 1976. Θεοδωρήτου ἐπισκόπου πόλεως Κύρρου πρὸς τὰς ἐπενεχθείσας αὐτῷ παρά τινος τῶν ἐξ Αἰγύπτου ἐπισκόπων ἀποκρίσεις. Reprint ed. Leipzig.

Parmentier, L., ed. 1998. *Theodoret of Cyrrhus. Kirchengeschichte.* Berlin.

Pellegrin, P., trans. 1997. *Sextus Empiricus. Esquisses pyrrhoniennes.* Paris.

Raeder, I., ed. 1969. *Theodoret of Cyrrhus. Graecarum affectionum curatio.* 2nd ed. Stuttgart.

Ramos Jurado, E. A., et al., eds. 2006. *Porphyry. Contra los Cristianos: Recopilación de Fragmentos, Traducción, Introducción y Notas.* Cádiz.

Richard, M. and J.A. Munitiz , eds. 2006. *Anastasius of Sinai. Quaestiones et responsiones.* Corpus Christianorum Series Graeca 59. Turnhout.

Riedinger, R., ed. 1989. *Pseudo-Kaisarios. Caesarii Dialogi quatuor. Die Erotapokriseis.* Berlin.

Saffrey, H. D., and A. P. Segonds, eds. 2001. *Marinus. Proclus, ou, Sur le bonheur.* Paris.

Schibli, H., ed. and trans. 2002. *Hierocles of Alexandria.* Oxford.

Sodano, A. R., ed. 1958. *Porphyry. Lettera ad Anebo.* Naples.

Wachsmuth, C., and O. Hense, eds. 1884–1912. *Stobaeos. Anthologion.* Berlin.

Wright, W. C., ed. and trans. 1921. *Philostratus. Lives of the Sophists. Eunapius. Lives of the Philosophers and Sophists.* Loeb Classical Library. Cambridge, MA.

———. 1923. *Julian.* 3 vols. Loeb Classical Library. Cambridge, MA.

English Translations

Crafer, T. W., trans. 1919. *The Apocriticus of Macarius Magnes.* New York.

Ettlinger, G. H., trans. 2003. *Theodoret of Cyrrhus. Eranistes.* Washington, DC.

Hill, R. C., trans. 2001. *Theodoret of Cyrrhus. Commentary on the Letters of St. Paul.* 2 vols. Brookline, MA.

Price, R. M., trans. 1985. *Theodoret of Cyrrhus. A History of the Monks of Syria.* Kalamazoo.

Secondary Sources

Ackermann, S. 1997. *Christliche Apologetik und heidnische Philosophie im Streit um das Alte Testament.* Stuttgart.

Adnès, A., and P. Canivet. 1967. "Guérisons miraculeuses et exorcismes dans l''histoire Philothée' de Théodoret de Cyr." *Revue de l'Histoire des Religions* 171:53–82; 172:149–179.

Adnès, P. 1983. "Orgeuil." *Dictionnaire de Spiritualité* 11:907–933.

Agosti, G. 2011. "Le brume di Omero. Sofronio dinanzi alla paideia classica." *Il calamo della memoria. Riuso di testi e mestiere letterario nella tarda antichità* IV (eds. L. Cristante and S. Ravalico) 33–50. Trieste.

Algra, K. 2011. "Stoics on Souls and Demons: Reconstructing Stoic Demonology." *Demons and the Devil in Ancient and Medieval Christianity* (eds. N. Vos and W. Otten) 71–96. Leiden.

Allen, P. 1987. "Some Aspects of Hellenism in the Early Greek Church Historians." *Traditio* 43:368–381.

Allen, P., and C. T. R. Hayward. 2004. *Severus of Antioch.* London.

———. 2006. "The Syrian Church through Bishops' Eyes: The Letters of Theodoret of Cyrrhus and Severus of Antioch." *Studia Patristica* 42:3–21.

Alt, K. 2005. "Man and Daimones: Do the Daimones Influence Man's Life?" *The Philosopher and Society in Late Antiquity: Essays in Honour of Peter Brown* (ed. A. Smith) 73–90. Swansea.

Amato, E., A. Roduit, and M. Steinrück, eds. 2006. *Approches de la Troisième Sophistique. Hommages à Jacques Schamp.* Brussels.

Anderson, G. 1989. "The *pepaideumenos* in Action: Sophists and their Outlook in the Early Empire." *Aufstieg und Niedergang der römischen Welt* II 33.1:80–208.

———. 1994. *Sage, Saint, and Sophist: Holy Men and their Associates in the Early Roman Empire*. London and New York.

Andres, F. 1913. *Die Engel- und Dämonenlehre der griechischen Apologeten des zweiten Jahrhunderts und ihr Verhältnis zur griechisch-römischen Dämonologie*. Breslau.

———. 1918. *Paulys Realencyclopäde der classischen Altertumswissenschaft*. Suppl. 3 (ed. G. Wissowa), s.v. "Daïmon," cols. 267–322. Stuttgart.

Andres, P. 1935. *Der Missionsgedanke in den Schriften des heil. Johannes Chrysostomus*. Hünfeld.

Andresen, C. 1955. *Logos und Nomos: die Polemik des Kelsos wider das Christentum*. Berlin.

Arnim, H. F. A. von. 1921. *Plutarch über Dämonen und Mantik*. Amsterdam.

Artzer, J. J. 1970. *The Imagery in the 'De Providentia' and the 'Graecarum Affectionum Curatio' of Theodoret of Cyr*. PhD diss., Catholic University of America.

Ashbrook, H. S. 1990. *Society in Crisis: John of Ephesus and the Lives of the Eastern Saints*. Berkeley.

Asmus, J. R. 1894. "Theodorets Therapeutik und ihr Verhältnis zum Julian." *Byzantinische Zeitschrift* 3:116–145.

———. 1906. "Die Ethopöie des Nikephoros Chrysoberges über Julians Rhetorenedict." *Byzantinische Zeitschrift* 15:125–136.

Athanassiadi, P. 1981. *Julian and Hellenism. An Intellectual Biography*. Oxford.

———. 1993. "Dreams, Theurgy, and Freelance Divination: The Testimony of Iamblichus." *Journal of Roman Studies* 83:115–130.

———. 1999. "The Chaldean Oracles: Theology and Theurgy." *Pagan Monotheism in Late Antiquity* (eds. P. Athanassiadi and M. Frede) 149–183. Oxford.

Athanassiadi, P., and M. Frede, eds. 1999. *Pagan Monotheism in Late Antiquity*. Oxford.

———. 2002. "The Creation of Orthodoxy in Neoplatonism." In Clark and Rajak 2002:271–291.

Aubenque, P. 1963. *La prudence chez Aristote*. Paris.

Auf der Maur, I. 1959. *Mönchtum und Glaubensverkündigung in den Schriften des hl. Johannes Chrysostomus*. Freiburg.

Azéma, Y. 1984. "La date de la mort de Théodoret de Cyr." *Pallas* 31:137–155.

Bagnall, R. 2008. "Models and Evidence in the Study of Religion in Late Roman Egypt." In Hahn, Emmel, and Gotter 2008:23–41.

Banchich, T. M. 1993. "Julian's School Laws: Cod. Theod. 13.5.5 and Ep. 42." *Ancient World* 24:5–14.

Bardy, G. 1946. "Théodoret." *Dictionnaire de Théologie Catholique* 15:299–325.

———. 1949. "'Philosophie' et 'philosophe' dans le vocabulaire chrétien des premiers siècles." *Revue d'ascétique et de mystique* 25:97–108.

Barnes, J. 2002a. "Ancient Philosophers." In Clark and Rajak 2002:293–306.

———. 2002b. "Galen, Christians, Logic." *Classics in Progress: Essays on Ancient Greece and Rome* (ed. T. P. Wiseman) 399–417. Oxford.

Bartelink, G. J. M. 1960. "'Philosophie' et 'philosophe' dans quelques œuvres de Jean Chrysostome." *Revue d' ascétique et de mystique* 36:486–492.

———. 1981. "Homère dans les œuvres de Théodoret de Cyr." *Orpheus* 2:6–28.

Bartsch, E. 1968. *Tapferkeit und Mannhaftigkeit im Griechischen von Homer bis zum Ende der klassischen Zeit.* Göttingen.

Baumeister, T. 1983. "'Anytos und Meletos können mich zwar töten, schaden jedoch können sie mir nicht.'Platon, Apologie des Sokrates 30 c/d bei Plutarch, Epiktet, Justin Martyr und Clemens Alexandrinus." *Platonismus und Christentum: Festschrift für Heinrich Dörrie.* (eds. H. D. Blume and F. Mann) 58–63. Münster.

———. 1988. "Heiligenverehrung I." *Reallexikon für Antike und Christentum* 14:96–150.

Berchman, R. 2005. *Porphyry against the Christians.* Leiden.

Bevegni, C. 2006. "Sui modelli del *De Sancto Cypriano* dell' imperatrice Eudocia." In Amato, Roduit, and Steinrück 2006:389–405.

Bitton-Ashkelony, B. 2005. *Encountering the Sacred: The Debate on Christian Pilgrimage in Late Antiquity.* Berkeley and London.

Boeft, J. 1977. *Calcidius on Demons (Commentarius Ch. 127-136).* Leiden.

Borelli, D. 2007. "La follia di Nabucodonosor nel *Commento a Daniele* di Teodoreto di Cirro." *La cultura scientifico-naturalistica nei Padri della Chiesa (I-V sec.): XXXV Incontro di studiosi dell'antichità cristiana, 4-6 maggio 2006,* 467–477. Studia ephemeridis Augustinianum 101. Rome.

Borgeaud, P. 2007. "Rites et émotions. Considérations sur les mystères." In Bonnet et al. 2007:189–222.

Bossina, L. 2006. "Preistoria di un' 'editio princeps'. Teodoreto dal concilio di Trento alla guerra dei trent' anni." *"Editiones principes" delle opere dei padri greci e latini: atti del Convegno di studi della Società internazionale per lo studio del Medioevo latino (SISMEL), Certosa del Galluzzo, Firenze, 24-25 ottobre 2003* (ed. M.Cortesi) 231–291. Florence.

Bouffartigue, J. 1992. *L'Empereur Julien et la culture de son temps.* Paris.

———. 2005. "La diversité des nations et la nature des hommes: L'empereur Julien et Cyrill d'Alexandrie dans une controverse incertaine." (ed. S. Crogiez-Pétrequin et al.) 113–126. Caen.

———. 2007. "Les ténèbres et la crasse. L'empereur Julien et sa jeunesse chrétienne." *La religion que j'ai quittée* (ed. D. Tollet) 25–38. Paris.

Boulnois, M.-O. 2006. "Le Dieu suprême peut-il entrer en contact avec le monde? Un débat entre païens et chrétiens sur la transcendance divine à partir du Contre Julien de Cyrille d'Alexandrie." *La transcendance dans la philosophie grecque tardive et dans la pensée chrétienne, Actes du VIe congrès de philosophie grecque, Athènes 22-26 sept 2004* (eds. E. Moutsopoulos and G. Lekkas) 177–196. Paris.

———. 2008. "Dieu peut-il être envieux ou jaloux? Un débat sur les attributs divins entre l'empereur Julien et Cyrille d'Alexandrie." *Culture classique et christianisme. Mélanges offerts à Jean Bouffartigue* (eds. D. Auger and E. Wolff) 13–25. Paris.

———. 2010. " 'Dieu jaloux': Embarras et controverses autour d'un nom divin dans la littérature patristique." *Studia Patristica* 44:297–313.

———. 2011. "La diversité des nations et l'élection d'Israël: Y-at-il une influence du Contre Celse d' Origène sur le Contre les Galiléens de Julien?" *Origeniana decima: Origen as Writer. Papers of the 10th International Origen Congress, University School of Philosophy and Education "Ignatianum", Kraków, Poland, 31 August - 4 September 2009* (eds. S. Kaczmarek, H. Pietras, and A. Dziadowiec) 803–830. Leuven.

Bowersock, G. W. 1978. *Julian the Apostate.* Cambridge, MA.

———. 1982. "The Imperial Cult: Perceptions and Persistence." *Jewish and Christian Self-Definition* III (eds. E. P. Sanders and B. F. Meyer) 171–182, with notes 238–241. Philadelphia.

———. 1990. *Hellenism in Late Antiquity.* Ann Arbor.

———. 1995. *Martyrdom and Rome.* Cambridge.

Bowersock, G. W., et al., eds. 1999. *Late Antiquity: A Guide to the Postclassical World.* Cambridge, MA and London.

Boyancé, P. 1935. "Les deux démons personnels dans l' Antiquité grecque et latine." *Revue de Philologie de littérature et d'histoire anciennes* 61:189–202.

———. 1937. *Le culte des muses chez les philosophes grecs, etudes d'histoire et de psychologie religieuses.* Paris.

Bozóky, E. 2006. *La politique des reliques de Constantin à Saint Louis: protection collective et légitimation du pouvoir.* Paris.

Breitenbach, A. 2003. *Das "wahrhaft goldene Athen": die Auseinandersetzung griechischer Kirchenväter mit der Metropole heidnisch-antiker Kultur.* Berlin.

Brenan, T. 1998. "The Old Stoic Theory of Emotions." *The Emotions in Hellenistic Philosophy* (eds. J. Sihvola and T. Engberg-Pedersen) 21–70. Dordrecht.

Brisson, L. 2004. *How Philosophers Saved Myths: Allegorical Interpretation and Classical Mythology.* Trans. C. Tihanyi. Chicago.

Brittain, C. 2001. *Philo of Larissa: the Last of the Academic Sceptics.* Oxford and New York.

Brunschwig, J., and M. C. Nussbaum, eds. 1993. *Passions and Perceptions: Studies in Hellenistic Philosophy of Mind; Proceedings of the Fifth Symposium Hellenisticum.* Cambridge.

Brown, P. R. 1981. *The Cult of the Saints: its Rise and Function in Latin Christianity.* Chicago.

———. 1988. *The Body and Society: Men, Women, and Sexual Renunciation in Early Christianity.* New York.

———. 1992. *Power and Persuasion in Late Antiquity: Towards a Christian Empire.* Madison, WI.

———. 1998. "Christianization and Religious Conflict." In Cameron and Garnsey 1998:632–664.

———. 2000a. "Asceticism: Pagan and Christian." In Cameron, Ward-Perkins, and Whitby 2000:601–634.

———. 2000b. "Holy Men." In Cameron, Ward-Perkins, and Whitby 2000:781–810.

———. 2000c. "Enjoying the Saints in Late Antiquity." *Early Medieval Europe* 9:1–24.

———. 2003. *The Rise of Western Christendom: Triumph and Diversity, AD 200-1000.* 2nd ed. Oxford.

———. 2004. "Conversion and Christianization in Late Antiquity: The Case of Augustine." *The Past Before Us: The Challenge of Historiographies of Late Antiquity. [From the conference* "The World of Late Antiquity: The Challenge of New Historiographies" *held at Smith College in 1999]* (eds. C. Straw and R. Lim) 103–117. Turnhout.

———. 2009. "Back to the Future: Pagans and Christians at the Warburg Institute in 1958." In Testa 2009:277–285.

———. 2011. "Paganism: What We Owe the Christians." Review of A. Cameron, *Last Pagans of Rome* (Oxford 2011). *New York Review of Books*, April 7:68–69, 72.

Brown, P., and R. Lizzi Testa, eds. 2011. *Pagans and Christians in the Roman Empire: The Breaking of a Dialogue (IVth-VIth Century A.D.).* Berlin and Münster.

Buffière, F. 1956. *Les mythes d'Homère et la pensée grecque.* Paris.

Busine, A. 2005. *Paroles d'Apollon: pratiques et traditions oraculaires dans l'Antiquité tardive (IIe-VIe siècle).* Leiden and Boston.

Bussières, M. P., ed. Forthcoming. *La littérature des questions et réponses dans l'Antiquité: de l'enseignement à l'exégèse* [Question and Answer Literature in Antiquity: From Teaching to Commenting]. Turnhout.

Bynum, C. W. 1995. *The Resurrection of the Body in Western Christianity, 200-1336.* New York.

Cameron, Alan. 1976. "The Authenticity of the Letters of St. Nilus of Ancyra." *Greek, Roman and Byzantine Studies* 17:181–196.

———. 1982. "The Empress and the Poet: Paganism and Politics at the Court of Theodosius II." *Yale Classical Studies* 27:217–289.

———. 2007. "Poets and Pagans in Byzantine Egypt." *Egypt in the Byzantine World, 300–700* (ed. R. Bagnall) 21–46. Cambridge.

———. 2011. *The Last Pagans of Rome.* New York.

Cameron, Averil. 1991. *Christianity and the Rhetoric of Empire: the Development of Christian Discourse.* Berkeley.

Cameron, Averil, and P. Garnsey, eds. 1998. *The Cambridge Ancient History.* Vol. 13, *The Late Empire: 337–425.* Cambridge.

———. 1998. "Education and Literary Culture." In Cameron and Garnsey 1998:665–707.

Cameron, A., B. Ward-Perkins, and M. Whitby, eds. 2000. *The Cambridge Ancient History.* Vol. 14, *Late Antiquity: Empire and Successors, A.D. 425–600.* Cambridge.

———. 2003. "How to Read Heresiology." *Journal of Medieval and Early Modern Studies* 33:471–492.

———. 2004. "Democratization Revisited: Culture and Late Antique and Early Byzantine Elites." *Elites Old and New in the Byzantine and Early Islamic Near East. Papers of the Sixth Workshop on Late Antiquity and Early Islam* (eds. J. Haldon and L. I. Conrad) 91–107. Princeton.

Caner, D. 2002. *Wandering, Begging Monks: Spiritual Authority and the Promotion of Monasticism in Late Antiquity.* Berkeley and London.

Canivet, P. 1957. *Histoire d'une entreprise apologétique au Ve siècle.* Paris.

———. 1977. *Le monachisme syrien selon Théodoret de Cyr.* Paris.

———. 1980. "Le Michaelion de Hûarte (Ve s.) et le culte syrien des anges." *Byzantion* 50:85–117.

———. 1987. *Hûarte: sanctuaire chrétien d'Apamène: IVe–VIe s.* Paris.

Caseau, B. 1999. "Sacred Landscapes." In Bowersock et al. 1999:21–59.

———. 2001. "POLEMEIN LIQOIS. La désacralisation des espaces et des objets religieux païens durant l' Antiquité tardive." *Le sacré et son inscription dans l'espace à Byzance et en Occident: études comparées* (ed. M. Kaplan) 61–123. Paris.

———. 2004. "The Fate of Rural Temples in Late Antiquity and the Christianisation of the Countryside." *Recent Research on the Late Antique Countryside* (eds. W. Bowden, L. Lavan, and C. Machado) 105–144. Leiden and Boston.

———. 2011a. "Le cryptopaganisme et les frontières du licite: un jeu des masques?" In Brown and Lizzi Testa 2011:541–571.

———. 2011b. "Late Antique Paganism: Adaptation under Duress." In Lavan and Mulryan 2011:111–134.

Castelli, G. 1983. "Lo Θεὸς ζηλωτής ebraico nel' 'Contra Galilaeos' di Giuliano." *Il* *"Giuliano l'Apostata" di Augusto Rostagni: atti dell'incontro di studio di Muzzano del 18 ottobre 1981* (ed. I. Lana) 85–91. Turin.

Cavallo, G. 2007. "Qualque riflessione sulla 'collezione filosofica'." *The Libraries of the Neoplatonists: Proceedings of the Meeting of the European Science Foundation Network "Late antiquity and Arabic Thought: Patterns in the Constitution of European Culture" held in Strasbourg, March 12-14, 2004* (ed. C. D'Ancona) 155–165. Leiden and Boston.

Chin, C. M. 2008. *Grammar and Christianity in the Late Roman World.* Philadelphia.

Chuvin, P. 1991. *Chronique des derniers païens: la disparition du paganisme dans l'Empire romain, du règne de Constantin à celui de Justinien.* 2nd ed. Paris.

———. 2004. "Christianisation et résistance des cultes traditionnels: approches actuelles et enjeux historiographiques." In Narcy and Rebillard 2004:15–31.

Clark, G., and T. Rajak, eds. 2002. *Philosophy and Power in the Graeco-Roman World.* Oxford.

Clarke, E. C. 2001. *Iamblichus' De mysteriis: a Manifesto of the Miraculous.* Burlington, VT.

Classen, C. J. 1979. "Der platonisch-stoische Kanon der Kardinaltugenden bei Philon, Clemens Alexandrinus und Origenes." *Kerygma und Logos: Beiträge zu den geistesgeschichtlichen Beziehungen zwischen Antike und Christentum: Festschrift für Carl Andresen zum 70. Geburtstag* (ed. A. M. Ritter) 68–88. Göttingen.

Clayton, P. B. 2007. *The Christology of Theodoret of Cyrus: Antiochene Christology From the Council of Ephesus (431) to the Council of Chalcedon (451).* Oxford.

Clerc, J. B. 1994. "Les 'athées' de Jamblique, Les mystères d'Egypte 3,31 (179,13 Parthey) sont chrétiens." *Nova et Vetera* 69:294–313.

———. 1996. "Theurgica legibus prohibita: À propos de l'interdiction de la théurgie (Augustin, La cite de dieu 10, 9 1.16, 2; Code Theodosien 9, 16, 4)." *Revue des Études Augustiniennes* 42:57–64.

Conley, T. M. 1984. "The Enthymeme in Perspective." *Quarterly Journal of Speech* 70:168–187.

Cook, J. G. 2000. *The Interpretation of the New Testament in Greco-Roman Paganism.* Tübingen.

———. 2004. *The Interpretation of the Old Testament in Greco-Roman Paganism.* Tübingen.

———. 2011. "Porphyry's Contra Christianos and the crimen nominis Christianorum." In Morlet 2011a:231–275.

Cooper, G. L. 1971. *Zur syntaktischen Theorie und Textkritik der attischen Autoren.* Zürich.

Cooper, J. M. 1999. *Reason and Emotion: Essays on Ancient Moral Psychology and Ethical Theory.* Princeton.

Cope, G. 1990. *An Analysis of the Heresiological Method of Theodoret of Cyrus in the "Haereticarum fabularum compendium."* PhD diss., Catholic University of America.

Cordes, P. 1994. *Iatros. Das Bild des Arztes in der griechischen Literatur von Homer bis Aristoteles.* Stuttgart.

Courcelle, P. 1975. "Le Typhus, maladie de l'âme d'après Philon et d'après saint Augustin." *Corona Gratiarum. Miscellanea patristica historica et liturgica Eligio Dekkers O.S.B XII lustra complenti oblata* I (ed. E. J. de Smedt) 245–288. Instrumenta patristica 10. Brugge-Gravenage.

Cox Miller, P. 2000. "Strategies of Representation in Collective Biography: Constructing the Subject as Holy." *Greek Biography and Panegyric in Late Antiquity* (eds. T. Hägg and P. Rousseau) 209–254. Berkeley.

Cracco Ruggini, L. 1965. "Sulla cristianizzazione della cultura pagana: il mito greco e latino di Alessandro dall'età antonina al Medio Evo." *Athenaeum* n.s. 43:3–80.

———. 1972. "Simboli di battaglia ideologica nel tardo ellenismo." *Studi Storici in onore Ottorini Bertolini* I, 177–300. Pisa.

Crego, P. 1996. "Theodoret of Kyros on the Relationship of the Body and the Soul Before Birth." *Greek Orthodox Theological Review* 41:19–37.

Cremer, F. W. 1969. *Die Chaldäischen Orakel und Jamblich De mysteriis.* Meisenheim am Glan.

Cribiore, R. 2007. *The School of Libanius in Late Antique Antioch.* Princeton.

Crouzel, H. 1995. "Celse et Origène à propos des 'démons'." *Frontières Terrestres, Frontières Célestes dans l' Antiquité* (ed. A. Rousselle) 331–355. Paris.

Cumont, F. 1915. "Les anges du paganisme." *Revue de l'Histoire des Religions* 72:159–182.

Curta, F. 2002. "Language, Ἔθνη, and National Gods: A Note on Julian's Concept of Hellenism." *Ancient World* 33:3–19.

Dagron, G. 1981. "Le saint, le savant, l'astrologue. Étude de themes hagiographiques à travers quelques recueils de 'Questions et réponses' des Ve-VIIe siècles." *Hagiographie, cultures et sociétés: IVe-XIIe siècles: actes du colloque organisé à Nanterre et à Paris, 2-5 mai 1979* (eds. P. Riché and E. Patlagean) 143–156. Paris.

———. 1992. "L'ombre d'un doute: L'hagiographie en question, VIe-XIe siècle." *Dumbarton Oaks Papers* 46:59–68.

Dal Covolo, E. 1988. "La paideia anticristiana dell' Imperatore Giuliano: A proposito dell' editto del 17 giugno 362." *Crescita dell'uomo nella catechesi dei padri (età postnicena)* (ed. S. Felici) 73–85. Rome.

Decleva Caizzi, F. 1980. "Τῦφος: contributo alla storia di un concetto." *Sandalion* 3:53–66.

Delatte, A. 1953. "Le sage-témoin dans la philosophie stoïco-cynique." *Académie royale de Belgique, Bulletin de la Classe des Lettres et des Sciences Morales et Politiques*, 5e Série, Tome 39:166–186.

Delehaye, H. 1927. *Sanctus: essai sur le culte des saints dans l'antiquité.* Brussels.

———. 1933. *Les origines du culte des martyrs.* Brussels.

Desanti, L. 1990. *Sileat omnibus perpetuo divinandi curiositas: indovini e sanzioni nel diritto romano.* Milan.

Des Places, É. 1955. "Le Platon de Théodoret. Les citations des Lois et de l'Épinomis." *Revue des Études Grecques* 68:171–184.

———. 1956. "Le Platon de Théodoret. Les citations du Phédron, de la République et du Timée." *Studi in onore di A. Calderini e R.Peribeni* I, 325–336. Milan.

———. 1957. "Les citations de Platon chez les Pères." *Studia Patristica* 2:340–341.

———. 1962. "La tradition indirecte des Lois de Platon (Livres VII-XII)." *Studia Patristica* 5:473–479.

———. 1981. "La tradition indirecte des Lois de Platon (Livres I-IV)." *Études platoniciennes 1929-1979.* Leiden. Originally printed in 1944 as *Mélanges J. Saunier* (eds. P. Gardette, P. Gallay, and J. Molager) 27–40. Lyon.

Detienne, M. 1959. "La 'démonologie' d' Empédocle." *Revue des Études Grecques* 72:1–17.

Dignas, B. 2007. *Rome and Persia in Late Antiquity: Neighbours and Rivals.* Cambridge.

Dihle, A. 1998. "Theodorets Verteidigung des Kults der Märtyrer." *Chartulae: Festschrift für Wolfgang Speyer* (eds. E. Dassmann, K. Thraede, and J. Engemann) 104–108. Münster.

Dillon, J. 1987. "Iamblichus of Chalcis (c. 240-325 A.D.)." *Aufstieg und Niedergang der römischen Welt* II 36.2:862–909.

———. 2001. "Iamblichus on the Personal Daemon." *Ancient World* 32:3–9.

———. 2007. "The Religion of the Last Hellenes." *Rites et croyances dans les religions du monde Romain: huit exposés suivis de discussions: Vandoevres-Genève, 21-25 Août 2006* (eds. C. Bonnet et al.) 119–138, with discussion 139–147. Geneva.

Di Paola, L. 2006. "Vescovi, notabili, e governatori nella corrispondenza di Teodoreto di Cirro." *Le trasformazioni delle élites in età tardoantica: atti del convegno internazionale, Perugia, 15-16 marzo 2004* (ed. R. Lizzi Testa) 155–176. Rome.

Dirlmeier, F. 1935. "ΘΕΟΦΙΛΙΑ-ΦΙΛΟΘΕΙΑ." *Philologus* 90:57–77 and 176–193.

Dixsaut, M. 1995. *Contre Platon. Le Platonisme renversé* II. Paris.

———. 2007. *Contre Platon. Le Platonisme dévoilé* I. Revised ed. Paris.

Döring, K. 1979. *Exemplum Socratis: Studien zur Sokratesnachwirkung in der kynisch-stoischen Popular-philosophie der frühen Kaiserzeit und im frühen Christentum.* Wiesbaden.

Dörnemann, M. 2003. *Krankheit und Heilung in der Theologie der frühen Christentum.* Tübingen.

Dörrie, H. 1956. "Leid und Erfahrung. Die Wort- und Sinnverbindung παθεῖν-μαθεῖν im griechischen Denken." *Abhandlungen der geistes-und sozialwissenschaftlichen Klasse* 5:3–42.

Dörries, H. 1966."Erotapokriseis." *Reallexikon für Antike und Christentum* 6:342–370.

Donini, P. 1995. "Pathos nello stoicismo romano." *Elenchos* 16:187–230.

———. 1995. "Struttura delle passioni e del vizio e loro cura in Crissipo." *Elenchos* 16:305–329.

Dorival, G. 2001. "L'argument de la réussite historique du christianisme." *Historiographie de l'Eglise des premiers siècles* (eds. B. Pouderon and Y.-M. Duval) 37–56. Paris.

Drake, H. A. 2005. "Models of Christian Expansion." *The Spread of Christianity in the First Four Centuries: Essays in Explanation* (ed. W. V. Harris) 1–14. Leiden and Boston.

Droge, A. 1989. *Homer or Moses? Early Christian Interpretations of the History of Culture.* Tübingen.

Droge, A., and J. Tabor. 1992. *A Noble Death: Suicide and Martyrdom among Christians and Jews in Antiquity.* San Francisco.

Dulière, W. L. 1970. "Protection permanente contre des animaux nuisibles assurée par Apollonius de Tyane dans Byzance et Antioche: Evolution de son mythe." *Byzantinische Zeitschrift* 63:247–77.

Dumeige, G. 1972. "Le Christ-médecin dans la littérature chrétienne des premiers siècles." *Rivista di Archeologia Cristiana* 48:115–141.

———. 1980. "Médecin (Le Christ)." *Dictionnaire de Spiritualité* 10:891–901.

Duprez, A. 1970. *Jesus et les dieux guérisseurs.* Paris.

Duval, Y. 1988. *Auprès des saints corps et âme: l'inhumation 'ad sanctos' dans la chrétienté d'Orient et d'Occident du IIIe au VIIe siècle.* Paris.

Dzielska, M. 1986. *Apollonius of Tyana in Legend and History.* Trans. P. Pienkowski. Rome.

Edwards, M. 2000. *Neoplatonic Saints: The Lives of Plotinus and Proclus by their Students.* Liverpool.

———. 2006. *Culture and Philosophy in the Age of Plotinus.* London.

———. 2007a. "Porphyry and the Christians." *Studies on Porphyry* (eds. G. Karamanolis and A. Sheppard) 111–126. London.

———. 2007b. "Socrates and the Early Church." *Socrates From Antiquity to the Enlightenment* (ed. M. Trapp) 127–142. Aldershot.

Edwards, M., M. Goodman, and S. Price, eds. 1999. *Apologetics in the Roman Empire: Pagans, Jews, and Christians*. Oxford.

Ekroth, G. 2002. *The Sacrificial Rituals of Greek Hero-Cults in the Archaic to the Early Hellenistic Periods*. Liège.

Elm, S. 2003. "Hellenism and Historiography: Gregory of Nazianzus and Julian in Dialogue." *Journal of Medieval and Early Modern Studies* 33:493–515.

Elsner J. 1998. *Imperial Rome and Christian Triumph: The Art of the Roman Empire AD 100–450*. Oxford and New York.

Elsner, J., and I. Rutherford, eds. 2005. *Pilgrimage in Graeco-Roman and Early Christian Antiquity: Seeing the Gods*. Oxford and New York.

Engelhardt, I. 1974. *Mission und Politik in Byzanz: ein Beitrag zur Strukturanalyse byzantinischer Mission zur Zeit Justins und Justinians*. Munich.

Erler, M. 2001. "Legitimation und Projektion: Die 'Weisheit der Alten' im Platonismus der Spätantike." *Die Gegenwart des Altertums: Formen und Funktionen des Altertumsbezugs in den Hochkulturen der Alten Welt* (eds. D. Kuhn and H. Stahl) 313–326. Heidelberg.

Esser, H. P. 1967. *Untersuchungen zu Gebet und Gottesverehrung der Neuplatoniker*. PhD diss., Universität zu Köln.

Evieux, P. 1995. *Isidore de Péluse*. Paris.

Fabricius, C. 1988. "Zu den Aussagen der griechischen Kirchenväter über Platon." *Vigiliae Christianae* 42:179–187.

Fairbairn, D. 2007. "The Puzzle of Theodoret's Christology: A Modest Suggestion." *Journal of Theological Studies* 58:100–133.

Farnell, L. R. 1921. *Greek Hero Cults and Ideas of Immortality*. Oxford.

Fears, R. J. 1988. "Herrscherkult." *Reallexikon für Antike und Christentum* 14:1047–1093.

Ferngren, G. B. 2009. *Medicine and Health Care in Early Christianity*. Baltimore.

Festa, N. 1928. "Lo stile di Teodoreto nella Terapia." *Rendiconti della Reale Accademia Nazionale dei Lincei. Classe di scienze morali, storiche e filologiche* 6th ser. 4:584–588.

Fichtner, G. 1982. "Christus als Arzt. Ursprünge und Wirkungen eines Motivs." *Frühmittelalterliche Studien* 16:1–18.

Fiedrowicz, M. 2001. "Früchristliche Alternativen zu paganen Bildungskonzepten." *Deus semper maior: vom Bleibenden in den Zeiten; eine Festschrift fur Georg Kardinal Sterzinsky* (ed. R. Kampling) 73–87. Berlin.

Finamore J. 2002. "'In Angelic Space': Chaldean Oracles fr. 138 and Iamblicus, 425." *Unione e amicizia. Omaggio a Francesco Romano* (eds. M. Barbanti, G. R. Giardina, and P. Manganaro) 425–433. Catania.

Fitschen, K. 1998. *Messalianismus und Antimessalianismus: Ein Beispiel ostkirchlicher Ketzergeschichte*. Göttingen.

Fives, D. C. 1937. *The Use of the Optative Mood in the Works of Theodoret, Bishop of Cyrus*. Washington, DC.

Flusin, B. 2010. "Christianiser, rechristianiser: Jean d'Éphèse et les missions." In Inglebert, Destephen, and Dumézil 2010:293–306.

Fortenbaugh, W. W. 1975. *Aristotle on Emotion: A Contribution to Philosophical Psychology, Rhetoric, Poetics, Politics, and Ethics*. New York.

Foss, R. 1997. *Griechische Jenseitsvorstellungen von Homer bis Plato: Mit einem Anhang über Vergils sechstes Buch der Aeneis*. Aachen.

Fowden, G. 1999. "Religious Communities." In Bowersock et al. 1999:82–106.

———. 1998. "Polytheist Religion and Philosophy." In Cameron and Garnsey 1998:538–560.

———. 2005. "Late Polytheism." *The Cambridge Ancient History*. Vol. 12, *The Crisis of Empire A.D. 193-337* (eds. A. K. Bowman, P. Garnsey, and A. Cameron) 521–572. 2nd ed. Cambridge.

Frank, S. 1964. Ἀγγελικὸς Βίος: *Begriffsanalytische und begriffsgeschichtliche Untersuchung zum "engelgleichen Leben" im frühen Mönchtum*. Münster.

Frede, M. 1986. "The Stoic Doctrine of the Affections of the Soul." In Schofield and Striker 1986:93–112.

———. 1999. Review of J. Mansfeld and D. T. Runia, *Aëtiana: The Method and Intellectual Context of a Doxographer* (Leiden 1996). *Phronesis* 44:135–149.

Frohnhofen, H. 1987. *Apatheia tou theou: über die Affektlosigkeit Gottes in der griechischen Antike und bei den griechischsprachigen Kirchenvätern bis zu Gregorios Thaumaturgos*. Frankfurt am Main.

Fuentes González, P. P. 1998. *Les diatribes de Télès: introduction, texte revu, traduction et commentaire des fragments*. Paris.

Funk, F. X. 1907. "Pseudo-Justin und Diodor von Tarsus." *Kirchengeschichtliche Abhandlungen und Untersuchungen* 3:323–350. Paderborn.

Gaddis, M. 2005. *There Is No Crime for Those who Have Christ: Religious Violence in the Christian Roman Empire*. Berkeley and London.

Gaşpar, C. N. 2000. "Theodoret of Cyrrhus and the Glory of the Syrian Ascetics: Epic Terminology in Hagiographic Contexts." *Archaeus: Etudes d'Histoire des Religions* 4.1–2:211–240; 4.4:151–178.

Gawlikowski, M. 2000. "Un nouveau Mithraeum récemment découvert à Huarté près d'Apamée." *Comptes rendus des séances—Académie des inscriptions et belles-lettres* 2000:161–171.

Gazê, E. 2004. *Ο δεύτερος βίος των Τριών Ιεραρχών: Μια γενεαλογία του 'Ελληνοχριστιανικού πολιτισμού'*. Athens.

Geffcken, J. 1908. "Kaiser Julianus und die Streitschriften seiner Gegner." *Neue Jahrbücher für das klassische Altertum, Geschichte und deutsche Literatur* 21:161–195.

———. 1992. *Der Ausgang des griechisch-römischen Heidentums.* 2nd revised ed. Darmstadt.

Gemeinhardt, P. 2008. "Staatsreligion, Volkskirche oder Gemeinschaft der Heiligen? Das Christentum in der Spätantike: Eine Standortbestimmung." *Zeitschrift für Antike Christentum* 12:453–476.

Gentile, S., ed. 1996. *Umanesimo e padri della Chiesa: manoscritti e incunaboli di testi patristici da Francesco Petrarca al primo Cinquecento.* Rome and Rose.

Germino, E. 1997. *La legislazione scolastica dell'imperatore Giuliano: C. Th. 13, 3, 5 ed Epistula 61C: tra misure anticristiane e riforma del munus docendi.* Naples.

Giannantoni, G. 1986. *Socrate: tutte le testimonianze: da Aristofane e Senofonte ai padri cristiani.* 2nd revised ed. Rome and Bari.

Giuffrida, C. 2003. "Il βασιλεύς nella Historia ecclesiastica di Teodoreto di Kyrrhos: apostolo, θεῖος ἀνήρ, principe dei demoni." *Mediterraneo Antico* 6:95–139.

Glubokovskii, N. 1890. *Blazhennîi Feodorit episkop Kirrskii.* 2 vols. Moscow.

Goldhill, S., ed. 2001. *Being Greek under Rome: Cultural Identity, the Second Sophistic and the Development of Empire.* Cambridge and New York.

Gotter, U. 2008. "Rechtgläubige—Pagane—Häretiker. Tempelzerstörungen in der Kirchengeschichtsschreibung und das Bild der christlichen Kaiser." In Hahn, Emmel, and Gotter 2008:43–89.

Goulet, R. 1981. "Les vies des philosophes dans l'antiquité tardive et leur portée mystérique." *Les Actes apocryphes des apôtres: christianisme et monde païen* (ed. F. Bovon) 161–208. Geneva.

———. 1997. "Les références chez Diogène Laërce: sources ou autorités?" *Titres et articulations du texte dans les oeuvres antiques. Actes du Colloque International de Chantilly 13-15 décembre 1994* (eds. J.-C. Fredouille et al.) 149–166. Paris.

———. 1998. "Histoire et mystère. Les vies de philosophes de l'antiquité tardive." *La biographie antique: huit exposés suivis de discussions* (ed. W. W. Ehlers) 217–254. Geneva.

———. 2004. "Hypothèses récentes sur le traité de Porphyre Contre les Chrétiens." In Narcy and Rebillard 2004:61–109.

———. 2009. "Réflexions sur la loi scolaire de l'empereur Julien." *L'enseignement supérieur dans les mondes antiques et médiévaux—Aspects institutionnels, juridiques et pédagogiques* (ed. H. Hugonnard-Roche) 175–200. Paris.

Goulet-Cazé, M.-O., and R. Goulet, eds. 1993. *Le Cynisme ancien et ses prolongements: actes du colloque international du CNRS, Paris, 22-25 juillet 1991.* Paris.

Graf, F. 2002. "Augustine and Magic." *The Metamorphosis of Magic From Late Antiquity to the Early Modern Period* (eds. J. N. Bremmer and J. R. Veenstra) 87–103. Leuven and Dudley, MA.

Grant, R. 2006. "Views of Mental Illness among Greeks, Romans, and Christians." *The New Testament and Early Christian Literature in Greco-Roman Context: Studies in Honor of David E. Aune* (ed. J. Fotopoulos) 369–404. Leiden.

Graver, M. 2007. *Stoicism and Emotion.* Chicago and London.

Greco, P. 1996. "Theodoret of Kyros on the Relationship of the Body and the Soul Before Birth." *Greek Orthodox Theological Review* 41:19–37.

Guerra Morisi, A. 1991. "Sulle orme di Savonarola. La riscoperta degli apologisti greci antipagani." *Rivista di Storia della Chiesa in Italia* 45:89–108.

Guinot, J. N. 1995. *L'exégèse de Théodoret de Cyr.* Paris.

———. 1995. "L'Homélie sur Babylas de Jean Chrysostome: la victoire du martyr sur l'hellénisme." *La Narrativa cristiana antica: Codici narrativi, strutture formali, schemi retorici (XXIII Incontro di studiosi dell' antichità cristiana, Roma, 5-7 maggio 1994)* 323–341. Rome.

———. 1997. "Les fondements scripturaires de la polémique entre Juifs et chrétiens dans les commentaires de Théodoret de Cyr." *Annali di Storia dell'Esegesi* 14:153–178.

———. 2001a. "Theodoret von Cyrus." *Theologische Realenzyklopädie* 23:250–254.

———. 2001b. "L'Expositio rectae fidei' et le traité 'Sur la Trinité et l'Incarnation' de Théodoret de Cyr. Deux types d'argumentation pour un même propos?" *Recherches augustiniennes* 32:39–74.

———. 2002. "Le recours à l' argument médical dans l'exégèse de Théodoret de Cyr." *Regards sur le monde antique: hommages à Guy Sabbah* (ed. M. Piot) 131–151. Lyon.

———. 2007. "Un nouveau fragment grec du Pentalogos de Théodoret de Cyr." *Warszawskie Studia Teolgiczne* 20:117–129.

———. Forthcoming. "Les Questions sur l'Octateuque et les Règnes de Théodoret de Cyr: œuvre originale ou simple compilation?" In Bussières forthcoming.

Hadot, P. 1987. "Théologie, exégèse, révélation, écriture, dans la philosophie grecque." *Les règles de l'interprétation* (ed. M. Tardieu) 13–34. Paris.

———. 1995. *Philosophy as a Way of Life: Spiritual Exercises from Socrates to Foucault.* Trans. M. Chase. Oxford and New York.

———. 2002. *What is Ancient Philosophy?* Trans. M. Chase. Cambridge, MA.

Haehling, R. von, ed. 2005. *Griechische Mythologie und frühes Christentum.* Darmstadt.

Hägg, T. 2004. "Apollonius of Tyana—Magician, Philosopher, Counter-Christ: The Metamorphoses of a Life 1999/2004." *Parthenope: Selected Studies in Ancient Greek Fiction (1969-2004)* (eds. L. B. Mortensen and T. Eide) 379–404. Copenhagen.

Hagen Hein, W. 1974. *Christus als Apotheker.* Frankfurt am Main.

Hagendahl, H. 1959. "Piscatorie et non aristotelice. Zu einem Schlagwort bei den Kirchenvätern." *Septentrionalia et Orientalia:studia Bernhardo Karlgren a. D. III Non. Oct. anno MCMLIX dedicate*, 184–193. Stockholm.

Hahn, J. 2004. *Gewalt und religiöser Konflikt: Studien zu den Auseinandersetzungen zwischen Christen, Heiden und Juden im Osten des römischen Reiches (von Konstantin bis Theodosius II)*. Berlin.

Hahn, J., S. Emmel, and U. Gotter, eds. 2008. *From Temple to Church: Destruction and Renewal of Local Cultic Topography in Late Antiquity*. Leiden.

Hall, L. J. 2004. *Roman Berytus: Beirut in Late Antiquity*. London and New York.

Halton, T. 1963. *Studies in De providentia of Theodoret of Cyrus*. PhD diss., Catholic University of America.

Hammerstaedt, J. 1996. "Die Vergöttlichung unwürdiger Menschen bei den Heiden als apologetische Argument in Schriften des Sokrates, Theodoret, Cyrill von Alexandrien und Johannes Chrysostom." *Jahrbuch für Antike und Christentum* 39:76–101.

Harnack, A. von. 1901. *Diodor von Tarsus. Vier pseudo-justinische Schriften als Eigentum Diodors nachgewiesen*. Texte und Untersuchungen zur Geschichte der altchristlichen Literatur 21.4. Leipzig.

Hartmann, A. 2010. *Zwischen Relikt und Reliquie: Objektbezogene Erinnerungspraktiken in antiken Gesellschaften*. Berlin.

Hauck, R. J. 1989. *The More Divine Proof: Prophecy and Inspiration in Celsus and Origen*. Atlanta.

Heid, S. 1996. "Die Tora als Staatsgesetz in der jüdisch-christlichen Apologetik." *Stimuli: Exegese und ihre Hermeneutik in Antike und Christentum; Festschrift für Ernst Dassmann* (eds. G. Schöllgen and C. Scholten) 49–65. Münster.

Hendriks, O. 1958. "L' activité apostolique des premiers moines syriens." *Proche-Orient Chrétien* 8:3–25.

Hengelbrock, J. 1971. "Affekt." *Historisches Wörterbuch der Philosophie* 1:89–93.

Herrin, J. 2008. "Book Burning as Purification." *Transformations of Late Antiquity: Essays for Peter Brown* (eds. M. Papoutsakis and P. Rousseau) 205–222. Aldershot.

Heyden, K. 2009. *Die "Erzählung des Aphroditian": Thema und Variationen einer Legende im Spannungsfeld von Christentum und Heidentum*. Tübingen.

Hoffmann, P. 1987. "Simplicius' Polemics." *Philoponus and the Rejection of Aristotelian Science* (ed. R. Sorabji) 57–83. London.

Honigmann, E. 1953. "Theodoret of Cyrrhus and Basil of Seleucia: the Time of Their Death." *Patristic Studies* 173:174-184.

Horn, C. 2007. "Children as Pilgrims and the Cult of the Holy Children in the Early Syriac Tradition: The Cases of Theodoret of Cyrrhus and the Child-Martyrs Behnam, Sarah, and Cyriacus." *ARAM* 19:439–462.

Horster, M., and C. Reitz, eds. 2010. *Condensing Texts, Condensed Texts.* Stuttgart.

Hult, K. 1990. *Syntactic Variation in Greek of the 5th Century A.D.* Göteborg.

Hunter, D. 1988. Introduction to *A Comparison between a King and a Monk; Against the Opponents of the Monastic Life: Two Treatises, by John Chrysostom.* Trans. D. Hunter. Lewiston, NY.

Hutter, M. 2002. "Die Auseinandersetzung Theodorets von Kyrrhos mit Zoroastrismus und Manichäismus." *Hairesis: Festschrift für Karl Hoheisel zum 65. Geburstag* (eds. M. Hutter, W. Klein, and U. Vollmer) 287–294. Münster.

Inglebert, H. 2001. *Interpretatio christiana: Les mutations des savoirs, cosmographie, géographie, ethnographie, histoire, dans l'antiquité chrétienne, 30–630 après J.-C.* Paris.

Inglebert, H., S. Destephen, B. Dumézil, eds. 2010. *Le problème de la christianisation du monde antique.* Paris.

———. 2010. Introduction to Inglebert, Destephen, Dumézil 2010:7–17.

Johnson, A. P. 2006. *Ethnicity and Argument in Eusebius' Praeparatio Evangelica.* Oxford.

———. 2011. "Porphyry's Hellenism." In Morlet 2011a:165–181.

Johnson, S. F. 2006a. *The Life and Miracles of Thekla: A Literary Study.* Cambridge, MA and London.

———, ed. 2006b. *Greek Literature in Late Antiquity: Dynamism, Didacticism, Classicism.* Aldershot.

Johnson, W. A. 2010. *Readers and Reading Culture in the High Roman Empire: A Study of Elite Communities.* Oxford.

Johnston, S. 1989. *Hekate Soteira: A Study of Hekate's Role in the Chaldean Oracles and Related Literature.* Atlanta.

Johnstone, C. L. 2001. "Enthymeme." *Encyclopedia of Rhetoric* (ed. T. O. Sloane) 247–250. Oxford and New York.

Jones, C. P. 2006. "Apollonius of Tyana in Late Antiquity." In Johnson 2006b:49–64.

———. 2010. *New Heroes in Antiquity: From Achilles to Antinoos.* Cambridge, MA and London.

Jüthner, J. 1923. *Hellenen und Barbaren aus der Geschichte des Nationalbewusstseins.* Leipzig.

Junod, E. 1988."Polémique chrétienne contre Apollonius de Tyane." *Revue de theologie et de philosophie* 120:475–482.

Kaegi, W. E. 1968. *Byzantium and the Decline of Rome.* Princeton.

Kallis, A. 1976. "Geister, (Griechische Väter)." *Reallexikon für Antike und Christentum* 9:700–715.

Kamtekar, R. 2002. "Distinction Without a Difference? Race and Genos in Plato." *Philosophers on Race: Critical Essays* (eds. J. K. Ward and T. L. Lott) 1–13. Oxford and Malden, MA.

Kaplan, M. 1999. "De la dépouille à la relique: formation du culte des saints à Byzance du Ve au XIIe siècle." *Les reliques: Objets, cultes, symboles* (eds. E. Bózoky and A.-M. Helvétius) 19–38. Turnhout.

Karpozêlos, A. 1982. Συμβολή στή μελέτη τοῦ βίου καὶ τοῦ ἔργου τοῦ Ἰωάννη Μαυρόποδος. Ioannina.

———. 1997–2002. Βυζαντινοί ιστορικοί και χρονογράφοι. 2 vols. Athens.

Kaster, R. 1999. "Education." In Bowersock et al. 1999:421–423.

Kerferd G. B. 1981. *The Sophistic Movement.* Cambridge and New York.

Kidd, I. 1995. "Some Philosophical Demons." *Bulletin of the Institute for Classical Studies* 40:217–240.

Kindstrand, J. F. 1981. *Anacharsis, the Legend and the Apophthegmata.* Stockholm.

Kinzig, W. 1998. "War der Neuplatoniker Porphyrios ursprünglich Christ?" *Mousopolos Stephanos: Festschrift für Herwig Görgemanns* (eds. M. Baumbach, H. Köhler, and A. M. Ritter) 320–332. Heidelberg.

Klauser, T. 1974. "Christlicher Märtyrerkult, heidnischer Heroenkult und spätjüdische Heiligenverehrung neue Einsichten und neue Probleme." *Klauser Theodor, Gesammelte Arbeiten zur Liturgiegeschichte, Kirchengeschichte und christlichen Archäologie* (ed. E. Dassmann) 221–229. Münster.

Klein, R. 1987–1988. "Zur Beurteilung Alexanders des Grossen in der patristischen Literatur." *Zu Alexander d. Gr.: Festschrift G. Wirth zum 60. Geburtstag am 9.12.86* (eds. W. Will and J. Heinrichs) 925–929. Amsterdam. Reprinted 1999 in *Roma versa per aevum: ausgewählte Schriften zur heidnischen und christlichen Spätantike* (eds. R. von Haehling and K. Scherberich) 460–517. Hildesheim and New York.

Knipp, D. 1998. *Christus "Medicus' in der frühchristlichen Sarkophagskulptur: Ikonographische Studien der Sepulkralkunst des späten vierten Jahrhunderts.* Leiden.

Kobusch, T. 2002. "Christliche Philosophie: Das Christentum als Vollendung der antiken Philosophie." *Metaphysik und Religion: Zur Signatur des Spätantiken Denkens. Akten des internationalen Kongresses vom 13.-17. März 2001 in Würzburg* (eds. T. Kobusch et al.) 239–259. Munich.

Konstan, D. 1996. "Problems in the History of Christian Friendship." *Journal of Early Christian Studies* 4:87–113.

———. 2006. *The Emotions of the Ancient Greeks: Studies in Aristotle and Classical Literature.* Toronto and Buffalo.

———. 2011. "Excerpting as Reading Practice." In G. Reydams-Schils 2011:9–22.

Konstan, D., and S. Saïd, eds. 2006. *Greeks on Greekness: Viewing the Greek Past under the Roman Empire.* Cambridge.

Koschorke, K. 1983. "Taufe und Kirchenzugehörigkeit in der Geschichte der Kirche—zwei Problemskizzen. Taufe und Kirchenzugehörigkeit im 4.

und frühen 5. Jahrhundert." *Taufe und Kirchenzugehörigkeit: Studien zur Bedeutung der Taufe für Verkündigung, Gestalt und Ordnung der Kirche* (ed. C. Lienemann-Perrin) 129–146. Munich.

Kötting, B. 1990. "Die Anfänge der christlichen Heiligenverehrung in der Auseinandersetzung mit Analogien außerhalb der Kirche." *Heiligenverehrung in Geschichte und Gegenwart* (eds. P. Dinzelbacher and D. R. Bauer) 67–80. Ostfildern.

Kornexl, E. 1970. *Begriff und Einschätzung der Gesundheit des Körpers in der griechischen Literatur von ihren Anfängen bis zum Hellenismus.* Innsbruck and Munich.

Krueger, D. 1993. "Diogenes the Cynic among the Fourth Century Fathers." *Vigiliae Christianae* 47:29–49.

Labriolle, P. de. 1934. *La réaction païenne; étude sur la polémique antichrétienne du Ier zu VIe siècle.* Paris.

Lacroix, L. 1989. "Quelques aspects du culte des reliques dans les traditions de la Grèce ancienne." *Bulletin de la Classe des lettres et des sciences morales et politiques (Academie Royale de Belgique)* 75:58–99.

Laín Entralgo, P. 1970. *The Therapy of the Word in Classical Antiquity.* New Haven.

La Matina, M. 1998. "Plutarco negli autori cristiani greci." *L'eredità culturale di Plutarco dall' antichità al Rinascimento. Atti del 7. Convegno plutarcheo, Milano-Gargnano, 28–30 maggio 1997* (ed. I. Gallo) 81–110. Naples.

Lavan, L. 2011. "The End of The Temples Towards a New Narrative?" In Lavan Muryan 2011:15–65.

Lavan, L., and M. Mulryan, eds. 2011. *The Archaeology of Late Antique 'Paganism.'* Late Antique Archaeology 7. Leiden.

Lechner, K. 1955. *Hellenen und Barbaren im Weltbild der Byzantiner. Die alten Bezeichnungen als Aus-druck eines neuen Kulturbewusstseins.* Munich.

———. 1955. "Byzanz und die Barbaren." *Saeculum* 6:292–306.

Leemans, J., et al., eds. 2003. *"Let us die that we may live": Greek Homilies on Christian Martyrs from Asia Minor, Palestine, and Syria (c. AD 350–AD 450).* London and New York.

Lemerle, P. 1971. *Le premier humanisme byzantin; notes et remarques sur enseignement et culture à Byzance des origines au Xe siècle.* Paris.

Léonas, A. 2005. *Recherches sur le langage de la Septante.* Fribourg and Göttingen.

Lepelley, C. 2002. "La diabolisation du paganisme et ses conséquences psychologiques: les angoisses de Publicola, correspondant de saint Augustin." *Impies et païens entre Antiquité et Moyen Age* (eds. M. Lionel and M. Sot) 81–96. Paris.

Leppin, H. 1996a. *Von Constantin dem Grossen zu Theodosius II: Das christliche Kaisertum bei den Kirchenhistoriken Socrates, Sozomenus und Theodoret.* Göttingen.

———. 1996b. "Zum kirchenpolitischen Kontext von Theodorets Mönchsgeschichte." *Klio* 78:212–230.

———. 2004. "Zum Wandel des spätantiken Heidentums." *Millennium* 1:59–81.

———. 2009. "Theodoret und Evagrius Scholasticus: Kirchenhistoriker aus Syrien zwischen regionaler und imperialer Tradition." *Jenseits der Grenzen: Beiträge zur spätantiken und frühmittelalterlichen Geschichtsschreibung* (eds. A. Goltz, H. Leppin, and H. Schlange-Schöningen) 153–168. Berlin and New York.

Leschhorn, I. E. 1985. *Der Gesundheits- und Krankheitsbegriff in der griechischen Antike von Homer bis Demokrit.* PhD diss., RWTH Aachen University.

Leven, K. H. 1987. *Medizinisches bei Eusebios von Kaisareia.* Düsseldorf.

———. 1988. "Zur Polemik des Zosimus." *Roma renascens: Beiträge zur Spätantike und Rezeptionsgeschichte; Ilona Opelt von ihren Freunden und Schülern zum 9.7.1988 in Verehrung gewidmet* (ed. M. Wissemann) 177–197. Frankfurt am Main.

Levieils, X. 2007. *Contra Christianos: la critique sociale et religieuse du christianisme des origines au concile de Nicée.* Berlin and New York.

Lewy, H. 1978. *Chaldean Oracles and Theurgy: Mysticism, Magic and Platonism in the Later Roman Empire.* Revised and expanded ed. Paris.

Liebeschuetz, J. H. W. G. 2001. *Decline and Fall of the Roman City.* Oxford.

———. 2009. "The View from Antioch: From Libanius via John Chrysostom to John Malalas and Beyond." In Lizzi Testa 2009:441–470.

Lizzi Testa, R., ed. 2009. *Le relazioni tra pagani e cristiani: Nuove prospettive su un antico tema.* Cristianesimo nella Storia 31.2. Bologna.

———. 2009. "Legislazione imperiale e reazione pagana: I limiti del conflitto." In Lizzi Testa 2009:385–409.

———. 2010. "L'eglise, les *domini*, les païens *rustici*: Quelques stratégies pour la christianisation de l'Occident (IVe-VIe siècle)." In Inglebert, Destephen, and Dumézil 2010:77–113.

Lucius, E. 1908. *Les origines du culte des saints dans l'Eglise chrétienne.* Paris.

Maas, M. 2003. " 'Delivered From Their Ancient Customs': Christianity and the Question of Cultural Change in Early Byzantine Ethnography." *Conversion in Late Antiquity and the Early Middle Ages: Seeing and Believing* (eds. K. Mills and A. Grafton) 152–188. Rochester.

MacMullen, R. 1997. *Christianity and Paganism in the Fourth to Eighth Centuries.* New Haven.

Maiburg, U. 1983. "Und bis an die Grenzen der Erde..." *Jahrbuch für Antike und Christentum* 26:38–53.

Maier, H. O. 1994. "Clement of Alexandria and the Care of the Self." *Journal of the American Academy of Religion* 62:719–745.

Majercik, R. 1989. *The Chaldean Oracles: Text, Translation, and Commentary.* Leiden and New York.

Malherbe, A. 1988. "Herakles." Trans. U. Maiburg. *Reallexikon für Antike und Christentum* 14:559–583.

Malingrey, A. M. 1961. *Philosophia; étude d'un groupe de mots dans la littérature grecque, des présocratiques au IVe siècle après J. C.* Paris.

Malone, E. E. 1950. *The Monk and the Martyr: The Monk as the Successor of the Martyr.* Washington, DC.

Mansfeld, J., and D. T. Runia. 1996. *Aëtiana: The Method and Intellectual Context of a Doxographer.* Leiden and New York.

Marasco, G. 2005. *Filostorgio: cultura, fede e politica in uno storico ecclesiastico del V secolo.* Rome.

Markus, R. A. 1990. *The End of Ancient Christianity.* Cambridge and New York.

Martin, A. 2005. "Rufin et Théodoret: deux mal aimés de l'historiographie." *Dieu(x) et hommes: histoire et iconographie des sociétés païennes et chrétiennes de l'antiquité à nos jours: mélanges en l'honneur de Françoise Thelamon* (eds. S. Crogiez-Pétrequin et al.) 135–147. Caen.

———. 2008. "Théodoret de Cyr et la tradition chrétienne contre l'empereur Julien." *Culture classique et christianisme: Mélanges offerts à Jean Bouffartigue* (eds. D. Auger and E. Wolff) 71–82. Paris.

Mates, B. 1996. *The Skeptic Way: Sextus Empiricus's Outlines of Pyrrhonism.* Oxford.

McCollough, T. C. 1984. *Theodore of Cyrus as Biblical Interpreter and the Presence of Judaism in Later Roman Syria.* PhD diss., University of Notre Dame.

———. 1989. "A Christianity for an Age of Crisis: Theodoret of Cyrus' Commentary on Daniel." *Religious Writings and Religious Systems: Systemic Analysis of Holy Books in Christianity, Islam, Buddhism, Greco-Roman Religions, Ancient Israel, and Judaism* II (eds. J. Neusner, E. S. Frerichs, and A. J. Levine) 157–174. Atlanta.

McLynn, N. 2009. "Pagans in a Christian Empire." *A Companion to Late Antiquity* (ed. P. Rousseau) 572–587. Chichester.

Mercati, G. 1901. "Un' apologia antiellenica sotto forma di Martirio." *Studi e Testi* 5:207–226.

Merki, H. 1952. Ὁμοίωσις Θεῷ. *Von der platonischen Angleichung an Gott zur Gottähnlichkeit bei Gregor von Nyssa.* Freiburg.

Michl, J. 1962. "Engel." *Reallexikon für Antike und Christentum* 5:53–200.

Milewski, I. 1995. "Die 'hellenischen' Sitten im täglichen Leben der Christen im Lichte der Schriften von Johannes Chrysostomus. Ein Beitrag zum Kampf der alten Kirche gegen das Heidentum im 4 Jh." *Eos* 83:167–177.

Millar, F. 2004. "Christian Emperors, Christian Church and the Jews of the Diaspora in the Greek East, CE 379–450." *Journal of Jewish Studies* 55:1–24.

———. 2006. *A Greek Roman Empire: Power and Belief Under Theodosius II (408–450)*. Berkeley.

———. 2007. "Theodoret of Cyrrhus: A Syrian in Greek Dress." *From Rome to Constantinople: Studies in Honour of Averil Cameron* (eds. H. Amirav and R. B. ter Haar Romeny) 105–125. Leuven.

Mills, K., and A. Grafton, eds. 2003. *Conversion in Late Antiquity and the Early Middle Ages: Seeing and Believing*. Rochester.

Minnis, A. J. 1979. "Late Medieval Discussions of *Compilatio* and the Role of the *Compilator*." *Beiträge zur Geschichte der deutschen Sprache und Literatur* 101:385–421.

Momigliano, A. 1963. *The Conflict between Paganism and Christianity in the Fourth Century: Essays*. Oxford.

Monaci Castagno, A. 1996. *Il diavolo e i suoi angeli: testi e tradizioni (secoli I–III)*. Fiesole.

———. 2010. "Origène et les anges des nations." *Les forces du bien et du mal dans les premiers siècles de l'Église: actes du colloque de Tours, septembre 2008* (eds. Y.-M. Blanchard, B. Pouderon, and M. Scopello) 319–333. Paris.

Morlet, S., ed. 2011a. *Le traité de Porphyre contre les chrétiens. Un siècle de recherches, nouvelles questions Actes du colloque international organisé les 8 et 9 septembre 2009 à l'Université de Paris IV-Sorbonne Collection des Études Augustiniennes: Antiquité (EAA 190)*. Paris.

———. 2011b. "Comment le problème du *Contra Christianos* peut-il se poser aujourd'hui?" In Morlet 2011a:11–49.

Moss, C. R. 2010. *The Other Christs: Imitating Jesus in Ancient Christian Ideologies of Martyrdom*. New York and Oxford.

Moss, G. C. 1967. "Mental Disorder in Antiquity." *Diseases in Antiquity: A Survey of the Diseases, Injuries, and Surgery of Early Populations* (eds. D. Brothwell and A. T. Sandison) 709–722. Springfield, IL.

Müller, C. W. 1965. "Die Heilung 'durch das Gleiche' in den hippokratischen Schriften *De morbo sacro* und *De locis in homine*." *Südhoffs Archiv für Geschichte der Medizin* 49:225–249.

Narcy, M., and E. Rebillard, eds. 2004. *Hellénisme et christianisme. Collection Mythes, Imaginaires, Religions*. Villeneuve-d'Ascq.

Nardi, C. 1991. "Una pagina 'umanistica' di Teodoreto di Ciro e un'interpretazione di Zanobi Acciaiuoli." *Atti e memorie dell' accademia Toscana di scienze e lettere La Colombaria* n.s. 56:9–63.

Nazzaro, A. V. 1998. "La parafrasi agiografica nella tarda antichità." *Scrivere di santi: atti del II Convegno di studio dell'Associazione italiana per lo studio della santità, dei culti e dell'agiografia, Napoli, 22-25 ottobre 1997* (ed. G. Luongo) 69–106. Rome.

Nesselrath, H. G. 2001. "Kaiserlicher Held und Christenfeind: Julian Apostata im Urteil des späten 4. und des 5. Jh. n. Chr." *Die Welt des Sokrates von Konstantinopel: Studien zu Politik und Kultur im späten 4. und frühen 5. Jh. n.Chr.; zu Ehren von Christoph Schäublin* (eds. B. Bäbler and H. G. Nesselrath) 15–43. Munich.

———. 2005/2006. "Das Evangelium nach Homer. Bemerkungen zu Sprache, Metrik und Lexik in einer Langfassung der christlichen griechischen Homer-Centonen." *Jahrbuch für Antike und Christentum* 48/49:43–53.

———. 2006. "Sophisten bei Sokrates von Konstantinopel." In Amato, Roduit, and Steinrück 2006:179–192.

Newman, S. 2002. "Aristotle's Notion of 'Bringing-Before-the-Eyes': Its Contributions to Aristotelian and Contemporary Conceptualizations of Metaphor, Style, and Audience." *Rhetorica* 20:1–23.

Nock, A. D. 1933. *Conversion: The Old and the New in Religion from Alexander the Great to Augustine of Hippo.* London.

———. 1944. "The Cult of Heroes." *Harvard Theological Review* 37:141–174. Reprinted 1972 in *Essays on Religion and the Ancient World* II, 575–602. Cambridge, MA.

———. 1957. "Deification and Julian." *Journal of Roman Studies* 47:115–123. Reprinted 1972 in *Essays on Religion and the Ancient World* II, 833–846. Cambridge, MA.

Norden, E. 1898. *Die antike Kunstprosa vom VI. Jahrhundert V. Chr. bis in die Zeit der Renaissance.* Leipzig.

North, H. 1966a. *Sophrosyne: Self-knowledge and Self-restraint in Greek Literature.* Ithaca, NY.

———. 1966b. "Canons and Hierarchies of the Cardinal Virtues in Greek and Latin Literature." *The Classical Tradition: Literary and Historical Studies in Honor of Harry Caplan* (ed. L. Wallach) 165–183. Ithaca, NY.

North, J. 2005. "Pagans, Polytheists and the Pendulum." *The Spread of Christianity in the First Four Centuries: Essays in Explanation* (ed. W. V. Harris) 125–143. Leiden.

Nussbaum, M. C. 1986. "Therapeutic Arguments: Epicurus and Aristotle." *The Norms of Nature: Studies in Hellenistic Ethics* (eds. M. Schofield and G. Striker) 31–74. Cambridge.

———. 1994. *The Therapy of Desire: Theory and Practice in Hellenistic Ethics.* Princeton.

Nyström, E. 2009. *Containing Multitudes: Codex Upsaliensis Graecus 8 in Perspective.* Uppsala.

Opelt, I. "Eunapios." *Reallexikon für Antike und Christentum* 6:928–936.

Oppenheim, P. 1931. *Das Mönchskleid im christlichen Altertum.* Freiburg im Breisgau.

Papadoyannakis, Y. 2006. "Instruction by Question and Answer: The Case of Late Antique and Byzantine Erotapokriseis." *Greek Literature in Late Antiquity: Dynamism, Didacticism, Classicism* (ed. S. Johnson) 91–105. Aldershot.

———. 2008. "Defining Orthodoxy in Pseudo-Justin's *Quaestiones et responsiones ad orthodoxos.*" *Heresy and Identity in Late Antiquity* (eds. E. Iricinschi and H.Zellentin) 115–127. Tübingen.

———. 2009. "Michael Glykas and the Afterlife in Twelfth-Century Byzantium." *The Church, the Afterlife and the Fate of the Soul* (eds. P. Clarke and T. Claydon) 130–142. Studies in Church History 45. Rochester and Woodbridge, UK.

Parker, R. 1996. *Miasma: Pollution and Purification in Early Greek Religion.* Oxford and New York.

Pasquato, O. 1981. "Religiosità popolare e culto ai martiri, in particolare a Costantinopoli nei secc. IV-V, tra paganesimo, eresia e ortodossia." *Augustinianum* 21:207–241.

Pasztori-Kupan, I. 2006. *Theodoret of Cyrus.* London.

Peers, G. 2001. *Subtle Bodies: Representing Angels in Byzantium.* Berkeley.

Pellegrino, M. 1955-1956. " 'Semen est sanguis Christianorum' (Tert., Apol. 50, 13)." *Atti dell' Accademia delle scienze di Torino* 90:371–442. Reprinted 1982 in *Ricerche Patristiche (1938-1980)* I, 453–524. Turin.

Penella, R. J. 1990. *Greek Philosophers and Sophists in the Fourth Century A.D.: Studies in Eunapius of Sardis.* Leeds.

———. 1993. "Julian the Persecutor in Fifth Century Church Historians." *Ancient World* 24:31–43.

Pernot, L. 1993. "Un rendez-vous manqué." *Rhetorica* 11:257–283. Reprinted 1993 in *Rhétoriques de la conversation. Actes de la table ronde de Paris, 4 juin 1993* (ed. L. Pernot) 421–437. Berkeley.

Peterson, E. 1923. "Der Gottesfreund: Beiträge zur Geschichte eines religiösen Terminus." *Zeitschrift für Kirchengeschichte* 42:161–202.

Petitmengin, P. 2002. "Éditions patristiques de la contre-réforme romaine." *I padri sotto il torchio: le edizioni dell'antichità cristiana nei secoli XV-XVI : atti del convegno di studi, Certosa del Galluzzo (Firenze), 25-26 giugno 1999* (ed. M. Cortesi) 3–31. Florence.

Petruccione, J. Forthcoming. "The Audience of Theodoret's Questions on the Octateuch." In Bussières (forthcoming).

Pfister, F. 1909-1912. *Der Reliquienkult im Altertum.* 2 vols. Giessen.

Piccione, R. M. 2002. "Encyclopédisme et *enkyklios paideia.* À propos de Jean Stobée et de l'Anthologion." *Philosophie Antique* 2:169–197.

Piepenbrink, K. 2005. *Christliche Identität und Assimilation in der Spätantike: Probleme des Christseins in der Reflexion der Zeitgenossen.* Frankfurt am Main.

Pigeaud, J. 1981. *La maladie de l'âme: étude sur la relation de l'âme et du corps dans la tradition médico-philosophique antique.* Paris.

———. 1987. *Folie et cures de la folie chez les médecins de l'antiquité gréco-romaine: la manie.* Paris.

Pilhofer, P. 1990. *Presbyteron Kreitton: Der Altersbeweis der jüdischen und christlichen Apologeten und seine Vorgeschichte.* Tübingen.

Pirenne-Delforge, V., and E. Suárez de la Torre, eds. 2000. *Héros et héroïnes dans les mythes et les cultes grecs: actes du Colloque organisé à l'Université de Valladolid du 26 au 29 mai 1999.* Liège.

Pizzolato, L. 1993. *L'idea di amicizia nel mondo antico classico e cristiano.* Turin.

Podskalsky, G. 1985. "Die Sicht der Barbarenvölker in der spätgriechischen Patristik (4.-8. Jahrh.)." *Orientalia Christiana Periodica* 51:330–351.

Poggi, V. 1986. "Severo di Antiochia alla Scuola di Beirut." *L'Eredità classica nelle lingue orientali* (eds. M. Pavan and U. Cozzoli) 57–71. Rome.

Potter, D. 1993. "Martyrdom and Spectacle." *Theater and Society in the Classical World* (ed. R. Scodel) 53–88. Ann Arbor.

Pohlenz, M. 1909. *Vom Zorne Gottes: eine Studie über den Einfluss der griechischen Philosophie auf das alte Christentum.* Göttingen.

Price, R. 2007. "The Three Chapters Controversy and Council of Chalcedon." *The Crisis of the Oikoumene: The Three Chapters and the Failed Quest for Unity in the Sixth-Century Mediterranean* (eds. C. Chazelle and C. Cubitt) 17–37. Turnhout.

Pricoco, S. 1980. "L'editto di Giuliano sui maestri (CTh XIII 3, 5)." *Orpheus* n.s. 1:348–370.

Prokopé, J., and A. Kehl. 1989. "Hochmut." *Reallexikon für Antike und Christentum* 15:795–858.

Raeder, J. 1900. *De Theodoreti Graecarum affectionum curatione quaestiones criticae scripsit.* PhD diss., Københavns Universitet.

Ramos Jurado, E. 2000. "L'integration de la classe des héros dans la pensée grecque de l'Antiquité tardive." In Pirenne-Delforge and Suárez de la Torre 2000:101–110.

Rapp, C. 2005. *Holy Bishops in Late Antiquity: The Nature of Christian Leadership in an Age of Transition*. Berkeley.

———. 2008. "Hellenic Identity, Romanitas and Christianity in Byzantium." *Hellenisms: Culture, Identity and Ethnicity From Antiquity to Modernity* (ed. K. Zacharia) 127–147. Aldershot.

Rapp, C., and M. Salzman, eds. 2000. *Elites in Late Antiquity*. Special issue, *Arethusa* 33, no. 3.

Remus, H. 1987. "Outside/Inside: Celsus on Jewish and Christian *Nomoi.*" *Religion, Literature, and Society in Ancient Israel, Formative Christianity and Judaism: Ancient Israel and Christianity* (eds. J. Neusner et al.) 133–150. Lanham, MD.

Renucci, P. 2000. *Les idées politiques et le gouvernement de l'empereur Julien*. Brussels.

Reydams-Schils, G., ed. 2011. *Thinking through Excerpts: Studies on Stobaeus*. Turnhout.

Riad, E. 1988. *Studies in the Syriac Preface*. Uppsala.

Richard, M. 1935. "L'activité littéraire de Théodoret avant le concile d'Éphèse." *Revue des sciences philosophiques et théologiques* 24:83–106.

Ridings, D. 1995. *The Attic Moses: The Dependency Theme in Some Early Christian Writers*. Göteborg.

Riedweg, C. 1998. "Iustinus Martyr II (Pseudo-justinische Schriften)." *Reallexikon für Antike und Christentum* 19:848–873.

———. 1999. "Mit Stoa und Platon gegen die Christen: Philosophische Argumentations-struktur in Julians Contra Galilaeos." *Zur Rezeption der hellenistischenPhilosophie in der Spätantike* (eds. T. Fuhrer and M. Erler) 55–81. Stuttgart.

———. 2005. "Porphyrios über Christus und die Christen: De philosophia ex oraculis haurienda und Contra Christianos im Vergleich." *L'apologétique chrétienne gréco-latine à l'époque prénicénienne: sept exposés suivis de discussions: Vandœuvres-Genève, 13-17 Septembre 2004* (eds. A. Wlosok et al.) 151–203. Geneva.

Rinaldi, G. 1989. *Biblia Gentium: primo contributo per un indice delle citazioni, dei riferimenti e delle allusioni alla bibbia negli autori pagani, greci e latini, di età imperiali* [A First Contribution towards an Index of Biblical Quotations, References and Allusions Made by Greek and Latin Heathen Writers of the Roman Imperial Times]. Rome.

———. 1994. "Obiezioni al monachesimo da parte dei pagani in area mediterranea." *Cristianesimo e specificità regionali nel Mediterraneo latino (sec. IV-VI): XXII incontro di studiosi dell'antichità cristiana, Roma, 6-8 maggio 1993*, 31-82. Studia ephemeridis "Augustinianum" 46. Rome.

———. 1998. *La Bibbia dei pagani*. 2 vols. Bologna.

Rizzerio, L. 1997. "Platon Apôtre des Grecs dans l' œuvre de Clément d' Alexandrie." *Images de Platon et lectures de ses oeuvres: les interprétations de Platon à travers les siècles* (eds. A. Neschke-Hentschke and A. Etienne) 53–78. Louvain-la-Neuve and Louvain.

Rodis-Lewis, G. 1970. *La Morale stoïcienne.* Paris.

Rodríguez Moreno, I. 1998. *Ángeles, démones y héroes en el neoplatonismo griego.* Amsterdam.

———. 2000. "Le héros comme μεταξύ l'homme et la divinité dans la pensée grecque." In Pirenne-Delforge and Suárez de la Torre 2000:91–100.

Rolke, K. H. 1975. *Die bildhaften Vergleiche in den Fragmenten der Stoiker von Zenon bis Panaetios.* Hildesheim.

Rompay, L. van. 1995. "Impetuous Martyrs? The Situation of the Persian Christians in the Last Years of Yazdgrad I (419–421)." *Martyrium in Multidisciplinary Perspective: Memorial Louis Reekmans* (eds. M. Lamberigts and P. van Deun) 363–375. Leuven.

Ronnenberg, K. C. 2008. "'Vade ad apem et disce.' Die Biene in der Bibel und das literarische Echo bei den Christen der ersten vier Jahrhunderte." *"Ille operum custos": Kulturgeschichtliche Beiträge zur antiken Bienensymbolik und ihrer Rezeption* (eds. D. Engels and C. Nicolaye) 138–164. Hildesheim and New York.

Roos, C. 1883. "*Theodoreto Clementis et Eusebii Compilatore.*" PhD diss., Martin-Luther-Universität Halle-Wittenberg.

Roselli, A. 1992. "Ὁ τεχνίτης θεός: la pratica terapeutica come paradigma dell' operare di Dio in Phil 27 e PA III 1." *Il Cuore indurito del Faraone: Origene e il problema del libero arbitrio* (ed. L. Perrone) 65–83. Genoa.

Rosen, R. M., and I. Sluiter, eds. 2003. *Andreia: Studies in Manliness and Courage in Classical Antiquity.* Leiden and Boston.

Rousseau, P. 1998. "Monasticism." In Cameron and Garnsey 1998:745–780.

———. 2004. "Moses, Monks, and Mountains in Theodoret's *Historia religiosa.*" *Il Monachesimo tra Eredità e Aperture* (eds. M. Bielawski and D. Hombergen) 323–346. Rome.

———. 2008. "Late Roman Christianities." *The Cambridge History of Christianity.* Vol. 3, *Early MedievalChristianities, c.600–c.1100* (eds. T. F. X. Noble and J. M. H. Smith) 21–45. Cambridge.

Ruess, H. 1957. *Gesundheit, Krankheit, Arzt bei Plato. Bedeutung und Funktion.* PhD diss., Eberhard Karls Universität Tübingen.

———. 1967. "Rechtskunde und Heilkunde in Platons Staat." *Melemata: Festschrift für Werner Leibbrand zum siebzigsten Geburtstag* (ed. J. Schuhmacher) 95–103. Mannheim.

Runia, D. T. 1997. Review of D. Ridings, *The Attic Moses: The Dependency Theme in Some Early Christian Writers* (Göteborg 1995). *Vigiliae Christianae* 51:100–107.

Ruttimann, R. J. 1987. *Asclepius and Jesus: The Form, Character and Status of the Asclepius Cult in the Second-Century CE and its Influence on Early Christianity."* PhD diss., Harvard University.

Saffrey, H. D. 1975. "Allusions anti-chrétiennes chez Proclus. Le diadoque Platonicien." *Revue des Sciences philosophiques et theologiques* 59:553–563.

———. 1984. "Quelques aspects de la spiritualité des philosophes néoplatoniciens de Jamblique à Proclus et Damascius." *Revue des Sciences philosophiques et theologiques* 68:169–182.

———. 1992a. "Accorder entre elles les traditions théologiques: une caractéristique du néoplatonisme athénien." *On Proclus and his Influence in Medieval Philosophy* (eds. E. P. Bos and P. A. Meijer) 35–50. Leiden and New York.

———. 1992b. "Le thème du malheur des temps chez les derniers philosophes néoplatoniciens." *Sophiēs maiētores = Chercheurs de sagesse: hommage à Jean Pépin* (eds. M.-O. Goulet-Cazé, G. Madec, and D. O'Brien) 421–431. Paris.

———. 2008. "Analyse de la Réponse de Jamblique à Porphyre, connue sous le titre: *De mysteriis."* *Revue des sciences philosophiques et théologiques* 84:489–511.

Salzman, M. R. 2002. *The Making of a Christian Aristocracy: Social and Religious Change in the Western Roman Empire.* Cambridge, MA.

Sandnes, K. O. 2009. *Challenge of Homer: School, Pagan Poets and Early Christianity.* London.

Sandwell, I. 2007. *Religious Identity in Late Antiquity: Greeks, Jews, and Christians in Antioch.* Cambridge.

———. 2010. "John Chrysostom's Audiences and His Accusations of Religious Laxity." *Religious Diversity in Late Antiquity* (eds. D. Gwynn, S. Bangert, and L. Lavan) 523–542. Leiden and Boston.

Saracino, S. 2002. "La politica culturale dell'imperatore Giuliano attraverso il cod. Th. XIII 3,5 el'ep. 61." *Aevum* 76:123–141.

Saradi, H. 2011. "Late Paganism and Christianisation in Greece." In Lavan and Mulryan 2011:263–309.

Sarefield, D. 2006. "Bookburning in the Christian Roman Empire: Transforming a Pagan Rite." *Violence in Late Antiquity: Perceptions and Practices* (eds. H. A. Drake et al.) 287–296. Aldershot.

Schadewaldt, H. 1965. "Die Apologie der Heilkunst bei den Kirchenvätern." *Veröffentlichungen der Internationalen Gesellschaft für Geschichte der Pharmazie* N.F. 26:115–130.

———. 1967. "Asclepius und Christus." *Die Medizinische Welt* 18:1755–1761.

Schäfer, C. 2008. *Kaiser Julian "Apostata" und die philosophische Reaktion gegen das Christentum.* Berlin and New York.

Schamp, J. 2004. "'Vendez vos biens' (Luc. 12, 33): Remarques sur le Julien de Photios." *Philomathestatos: Studies in Greek and Byzantine Texts Presented to Jacques Noret For His Sixty-Fifth Birthday* (eds. B. Janssens et al.) 535–554. Leuven and Dudley, MA.

Schlange-Schöningen, H. 1995. *Kaisertum und Bildungswesen im spätantiken Konstantinopel.* Stuttgart.

Schmidt, E. G. 1962. "Die drei Arten des Philosophierens. Zur Geschichte einer antiken Stil- und Methodenscheidung, Friedrich Zucker zum 80. Geburtstag." *Philologus* 106: 14–28.

Schoedel, W. R. 1959. "Philosophy and Rhetoric in the *Adversus Haereses* of Irenaeus." *Vigiliae Christianae* 12:22–32.

Schöllgen, G. 2004. "Pegasios Apostata: Zum Verständnis von 'Apostasie' in der 2. Hälfte des 4. Jahrhunderts." *Jahrbuch für Antike und Christentum* 47:58–80.

Schofield, M. 2002. "Academic Therapy: Philo of Larissa and Cicero's Project in the Tusculans." In Clark and Rajak 2002:91–109.

Schofield, M., and G. Striker, eds. 1986. *The Norms of Nature: Studies in Hellenistic Ethics.* Cambridge.

Schor, A. M. 2011. *Theodoret's People: Social Networks and Religious Conflict in Late Roman Syria.* Berkeley and London.

Schott, J. 2008a. *Christianity, Empire, and the Making of Religion in Late Antiquity.* Philadelphia.

———. 2008b. "'Living Like a Christian But Playing the Greek': Accounts of Apostasy and Conversion in Porphyry and Eusebius." *Journal of Late Antiquity* 1:258–277.

Schulte, K. J. 1904. *Theodoret von Cyrus als Apologet: Ein Beitrag zur Geschichte der Apologetik.* Vienna.

Scicolone, S. 1981. "I presupposti politici della polemica di Giuliano contro i cristiani." *Religione e politica nel mondo antico* (ed. M. Sordi) 223–236. Milan.

———. 1982. "Le accezioni dell' apellativo 'Galilei'." *Aevum* 56:71–80.

Scorza Barcellona, F. 1995. "Martiri e confessori dell' età di Giuliano l' Apostata: dalla storia alla legenda." *Pagani e cristiani da Giuliano l'Apostata al sacco di Roma: atti del Convegno internazionale di studi: Rende, 12-13 novembre 1993* (ed. F. Ela Consolino) 53–83. Soveria Mannelli.

Sevčenko, I. 1964. "Three Paradoxes of the Cyrillo-Methodian Mission." *Slavic Review* 23:220–236.

———. 1988/1989. "Religious Missions Seen from Byzantium." *Harvard Ukrainian Studies* 12/13: 7–27.

Sfameni Gasparro, G. 1997. "Fra astrologi, teurgi e manichei: itinerario Agostiniano in un mondo che si interroga su destino, male e salvezza." *Il mistero del male e la libertà possibile (IV): ripensare Agostino: atti dell'VIII. Seminario del Centro studi agostiniani di Perugia* (eds. L. Alici, R. Piccolomini, and A. Pieretti) 48–131. Studia ephemeridis "Augustinianum" 59. Rome.

Shepardson, C. 2009. "Rewriting Julian's Legacy: John Chrysostom's *On Babylas* and Libanius' *Oration* 24." *Journal of Late Antiquity* 2:99–115.

Sillett, H. 2000. "Orthodoxy and Heresy in Theodoret of Cyrus' *Compendium of Heresies*." *Orthodoxie, Christianisme, Histoire* [Orthodoxy, Christianity, History] (eds. S. Elm, É. Rebillard, and A. Romano) 261–273. Rome.

Siniossoglou, N. 2008. *Plato And Theodoret: The Christian Appropriation of Platonic Philosophy and the Hellenic Intellectual Resistance.* Cambridge.

Smith, A. 1974. *Porphyry's Place in the Neoplatonic Tradition: A Study in Post-Plotinian Neoplatonism.* The Hague.

———. 1997. "Porphyry and Pagan Religious Practice." *The Perennial Tradition of Neoplatonism* (ed. J. J. Cleary) 29–35. Leuven.

Smith, R. B. E. 1995. *Julian's Gods: Religion and Philosophy in the Thought and Action of Julian the Apostate.* London and New York.

Soler, E. 2006. *Le sacré et le salut à Antioche au IVe siècle ap. J.-C.: pratiques festives et comportements religieux dan le processus de christianisation de la cité.* Beirut.

———. 2010. "Les 'demi-chretiens' d'Antioche: la pédagogie de l'exclusivisme chrétien et ses resorts dans la prédication chrysostomienne." In Inglebert, Destephen, and Dumézil 2010:281–291.

Sorabji, R. 2000. *Emotion and Peace of Mind: From Stoic Agitation to Christian Temptation; The Gifford Lectures.* Oxford and New York.

Spadavecchia, C. 1976. *Studies in the Letters of St. Basil of Caesarea and of Theodoret of Cyrrhus with Special Reference to their Assimilation of Hellenic Culture.* PhD diss., University of Edinburgh.

Spanneut, M. 1960. "Épictète chrétien." *Dictionnaire de Spiritualité* 4:830–854.

Speyer, W. A. B., and I. C. Opelt. 2001. "Barbar." *Reallexikon für Antike und Christentum.* Suppl. no. 1:811–895.

———. 1988. "Heros." *Reallexikon für Antike und Christentum* 14:861–877.

———. 2005. "Porphyrios als religiöse Persönlichkeit und als religiöser Denker." *Griechische Mythologie und frühes Christentum* (ed. R. von Haehling) 65–84. Darmstadt.

Staab, G. 2002. *Pythagoras in der Spätantike: Studien zu De Vita Pythagorica des Iamblichos von Chalkis.* Munich.

Staden, H. von. 2002. "La lecture comme thérapie dans la médecine gréco-romaine." *Comptes-rendus des séances de l'Académie des Inscriptions et Belles-Lettres* 146:803–822.

Stoupakes, N. M. 2000. Γεώργιος Κορρέσιος (1570 ci.-1659/60). Η Ζωή, το έργο του και οι πνευματικοί αγώνες της εποχής του. Chios.

Stowers, S. K. 1988. "The Diatribe." *Greco-Roman Literature and the New Testament: Selected Forms and Genres* (ed. D. E. Aune) 71–83. Atlanta.

———. 1994. "Diatribe." *Historisches Wörterbuch der Rhetorik* 2:627–633.

Straub, J. 1962."Die Himmelfahrt des Iulianus Apostata." *Gymnasium* 69:310–326. Reprinted 1972 in *Regeneratio Imperii. Aufsätze über Roms Kaisertum und Reich im Spiegel der heidnischen und christlichen Publizistik*, 159–177. Darmstadt.

———. 1970. "Divus Alexander-Divus Christus." *Kyriakon: Festschrift Johannes Quasten* I (ed P. Granfield and J. A. Jungmann) 461–473. Münster. Reprinted 1972 in *Regeneratio Imperii. Aufsätze über Roms Kaisertum und Reich im Spiegel der heidnischen und christlichen Publizistik*, 178–194. Darmstadt.

Straw, C. 2002. "A *Very Special Death*: Christian Martyrdom in its Classical Context." *Sacrificing the Self: Perspectives on Martyrdom and Religion* (ed. M. Cormack) 39–57. Oxford and New York.

Swain, S. 1996. *Hellenism and Empire: Language, Classicism, and Power in the Greek World, AD 50-250*. Oxford.

Szabat, E. 2007. "Teachers in the Eastern Roman Empire (Fifth–Seventh Centuries): A Historical Study and Prosopography." *Alexandria: Auditoria of Kom el-Dikka and Late Antique Education* (eds. T. Derda, T. Markiewicz, and E. Wipszycka) 177–345. Warsaw.

Tanaseanu-Döbler, I. 2009. " 'Nur der Weise ist Priester': Rituale und Ritualkritik bei Porphyrios." *Religion und Kritik in der Antike* (eds. U. Berner and I. Tanaseanu-Döbler) 109–155. Münster.

Taormina, D. P. 1999. *Jamblique critique de Plotin et de Porphyre: quatre études*. Paris.

Tardieu, M. 1997–1998. "Le marcionisme syrien: problèmes de géographie et d'ecclésiologie: 1. Arabie, 2. Cyrrhestique." *Annuaire du Collège de France* 98:596–605.

Tedeschi, A. 1996. "Sul divieto di insegnamento per i maestri cristiani (Giuliano, ep. 61c Bidez)." *Annali della Facoltà di Lettere e Filosofia di Bari* 39:17–36.

Thome, J. 1995. *Psychotherapeutische Aspekte in der Philosophie Platons*. New York.

Thomson, F. J. Forthcoming. "Byzantine Erotapocritic Literature in Slavonic Translation withSpecial Attention to the Important Role Played by Anastasius Sinaita's *Interrogationes et Responsiones* in the Conversion of the Slavs." In Bussières (forthcoming).

Thümmel, H. G. 1992. *Die Frühgeschichte der ostkirchlichen Bilderlehre: Texte und Untersuchungen zur Zeit vor dem Bilderstreit*. Berlin.

Tompkins, I. G. 1993. *"The Relations between Theodoret of Cyrrhus and his City and its Territory, with particular Reference to the Letters and Historia Religiosa."* PhD diss., University of Oxford.

Trapp, M. B. 1997a. *Maximus of Tyre. The Philosophical Orations.* New York.

———. 1997b. "Philosophical Sermons: The 'Dialexeis' of Maximus of Tyre." *Aufstieg und Niedergang der römischen Welt* II 34.3:1945–1976.

Troianos, S. N. 1992. "Das Gesetz in der griechischen Patristik." *Das Gesetz in Spätantike und frühem Mittelalter.* Bd. 4, Symposion der Kommission *"Die Funktion des Gesetzes in Geschichte und Gegenwart"* (ed. W. Sellert) 47–62. Göttingen.

———. 1999. "The Embryo in Byzantine Canon Law." *Bioenvironment* 3:179–184.

Trombley, F. R. 1993–1994. *Hellenic Religion and Christianization, c. 370–529.* Leiden.

Trompf, G. W. 2000. *Early Christian Historiography: Narratives of Retribution.* London.

Tsekourakis, D. 1980. "Το στοιχείο του διαλόγου στην κυνικοστωϊκή διατριβή." *Hellenica* 32:61–78.

Tsouna, V. 2009. "Epicurean Therapeutic Strategies." *Cambridge Companion to Epicureanism* (ed. J. Warren) 249–265. Cambridge.

Ulrich, J. 2009. "The Reception of Greek Christian Apologetics in Theodoretus' *Graecarum affectionum curatio.*" *Continuity and Discontinuity in Early Christian Apologetics* (eds. J. Ulrich, A. C. Jacobsen, and M. Kahlos) 113–130. Frankfurt am Main and Oxford.

Ungefehr-Kortus, C. 1996. *Anacharsis, der Typus des edlen, weisen Barbaren: ein Beitrag zum Verständnis griechischer Fremdheitserfahrung.* Frankfurt am Main and New York.

Urbainczyk, T. 2002. *Theodoret of Cyrrhus: The Bishop and the Holy Man.* Ann Arbor.

Uytterhoeven, I. 2009. "Know Your Classics! Manifestations of 'Classical Culture' in Late Antique Elite Houses." *Faces of Hellenism: Studies in the History of the Eastern Mediterranean (4th Century B.C.–5th Century A.D.)* (ed. P. Van Nuffelen) 321–342. Studia Hellenistica 48. Leuven.

Van Liefferinge, C. 1999. *La théurgie des Oracles chaldaïques à Proclus.* Liège.

Van Nuffelen, P. 2004. *Un héritage de paix et de piété: étude sur les histoires ecclésiastiques de Socrate et de Sozomène.* Leuven and Dudley, MA.

———. 2011. "Eusebius of Caesarea and the Concept of Paganism." In Lavan and Mulryan 2011:89–109.

Van Uytfanghe, M. 1988. "Heiligenverehrung (hagiographie)." *Reallexikon für Antike und Christentum* 14:150–183.

———. 2001. "Biographie II." *Reallexikon für Antike und Christentum.* Suppl. no. 1:1088–1364.

Vicario, C. M. 2000. "Zanobi Acciaiuoli e i Padri della Chiesa: autografi e traduzioni." *Tradizioni patristiche nell'umanesimo: atti del Convegno, Istituto nazionale di studi sul Rinascimento, Biblioteca Medicea Laurenziana, Firenze, 6-8 febbraio 1997* (eds. M. Cortesi and C. Leonardi) 119–158. Florence.

Vidal, M. 1959. "La 'Theophilia' dans la pensée religieuse des Grecs." *Recherche de science religieuse* 47:161–184.

Voelke, A. J. 1993. *La philosophie comme thérapie de l'âme: études de philosophie hellénistique.* Paris.

Vögtle, A. 1950. "Affekt." *Reallexikon für Antike und Christentum* 1:160–173.

Volp, U. 2002. *Tod und Ritual in den christlichen Gemeinden der Antike.* Leiden and Boston.

Walker, J. 2000. *Rhetoric and Poetics in Antiquity.* Oxford and New York.

Ware, K. 1989. "The Meaning of 'Pathos' in Abba Isaias and Theodoret of Cyrus." *Studia Patristica* 20:315–322.

Watts, E. 2005. "Winning the Intra-Communal Dialogues: Zacharias Scholasticus' *Life of Severus." Journal of Early Christian Studies* 13:437–464.

———. 2006. *City and School in Late Antique Athens and Alexandria.* Berkeley.

———. 2010. *Riot in Alexandria: Tradition and Group Dynamics in Late Antique Pagan and Christian Communities.* Berkeley and London.

Webb, R. 1997. "Imagination and the Arousal of Emotions in Greco-Roman Rhetoric." *The Passions in Roman Thought and Literature* (eds. S. Morton-Braund and C. Gill) 112–127. Cambridge.

Wehner, B. 2000. *Die Funktion der Dialogstruktur in Epiktets Diatriben.* Stuttgart.

Wells, L. 1998. *The Greek Language of Healing from Homer to New Testament Times.* Berlin.

Westerink, L. G. 1990. "Das Rätsel der untergründigen Neuplatonismus." *Philophronēma: Festschrift für Martin Sicherl zum 75. Geburtstag: von Textkritik bis Humanismusforschung* (ed. D. Harlfinger) 105–123. Paderborn.

Wey, H. 1957. *Die Funktionen der bösen Geister bei den griechischen Apologeten des zweiten Jahrhunderts nach Christus.* Winterthur.

Whitby, Mary. 2007. "The Bible Hellenized: Nonnus' Paraphrase of St John's Gospel and 'Eudocia's' Homeric centos." *Texts and Culture in Late Antiquity: Inheritance, Authority, and Change* (ed. J. H. D. Scourfield) 195–231. Swansea.

Whitby, Michael. 1991. "John of Ephesus and the Pagans: Pagan Survivals in the Sixth Century." *Paganism in the Later Roman Empire and in Byzantium* (ed. M. Salamon) 111–131. Krakow.

Whitmarsh, T. 2001. "Greece is the World: Exile and Identity in the Second Sophistic." *Being Greek under Rome: Cultural Identity, the Second Sophistic and the Development of Empire* (ed. S. Goldhill) 269–305. Cambridge and New York.

Widmann, F. 1935-1936. "Die Progymnasmata des Nikephoros Chrysoberges." *Byzantinisch-neugriechische Jahrbücher* 12:12–41, 241–299.

Wilfried, F. 1978. *Analogiemodelle bei Aristoteles: Untersuchungen zu den Vergleichen zwischen den einzelnen Wissenschaften und Künsten.* Amsterdam.

Wilken, R. 1983. *John Chrysostom and the Jews: Rhetoric and Reality in the Late 4th Century.* Berkeley and London.

———. 1984. *The Christians as the Romans Saw Them.* New Haven.

———. 2000. "Cyril of Alexandria: Apologist, Biblical Interpreter, Theologian." *Adamantius* 6:70–84.

Winkelmann, F. 1989. "Die Bewertung der Barbaren in den Werken der oströmischen Kirchenhistoriker." *Das Reich und die Barbaren* (eds. E. K. Chrysos and A. Schwarcz) 221–235. Vienna.

———. 1998. "Heiden und Christen in den Werken der oströmischen Historiker des 5. Jahr-hunderts." *Heiden und Christen im 5. Jahrhundert* (eds. J. van der Oort and D. Wyrwa) 123–159. Leuven.

Wisse, J. 1992."Affektenlehre: Antike." *Historisches Wörterbuch der Rhetorik* 1:218–224.

Wortley, J. 1997. "The Model and Form of the Synagoge." *Work and Worship at the Theotokos Evergetis, 1050-1200: Papers of the fourth Belfast Byzantine International Colloquium, Portaferry, Co. Down, 14-17 September 1995* (eds. M. Mullett and A. Kirby) 166–177. Belfast.

Wyss, B. 1959. "Doxographie." *Reallexikon für Antike und Christentum* 4:197–210.

Yannoulatos, A. 1969. "Monks and Mission in the Eastern Church during the Fourth Century." *International Review of Missions* 58:208–226.

Young, F. M. 1983. *From Nicaea to Chalcedon: A Guide to the Literature and its Background.* London.

Young, R. D. 1990. "Zacharias: The Life of Severus." *Ascetic Behavior in Greco-Roman Antiquity* (ed. V. Wimbush) 312–328. Minneapolis.

Zambon, M. 2002. *Porphyre et le moyen-platonisme.* Paris.

Zanettti, U. 1994. "Fêtes des anges dans les calendriers et synaxaires orientaux." *Culto e insediamenti micaelici nell'Italia meridionale fra tarda antichità e medioevo: atti del Convegno internazionale, Monte Sant'Angelo, 18-21 novembre 1992* (eds. C. Carletti and G. Otranto) 323–349. Bari.

Zanker, P. 1995. *The Mask of Socrates: The Image of the Intellectual in Antiquity.* Trans. A. Shapiro. Berkeley.

Zografou, A. 2005. "Images et 'reliques' en Grèce ancienne. L'omoplate de Pélops." *Les objets de la mémoire: Pour une approche comparatiste des reliques et de leur culte* (eds. P. Borgeaud and Y. Volokhine) 123–145. Bern.

Zuccotti, F. 1992. *"Furor haereticorum": studi sul trattamento giuridico della follia e sulla persecuzione della eterodossia religiosa nella legislazione del tardo impero romano.* Milan.

Index of Selected Subjects

CPSIA information can be obtained at www.ICGtesting.com
Printed in the USA
BVOW05s0554100314

347078BV00006B/17/P